A CONTEMPORARY INTRODUCTION TO

Free Will

FUNDAMENTALS OF PHILOSOPHY SERIES

Series Editors
John Martin Fischer, University of California, Riverside
John Perry, Stanford University

Mind: A Brief Introduction
John R. Searle

Biomedical Ethics
Walter Glannon

A Contemporary Introduction to Free Will
Robert Kane

A CONTEMPORARY
INTRODUCTION TO

Free Will

ROBERT KANE

University of Texas at Austin

New York ◆ Oxford
OXFORD UNIVERSITY PRESS
2005

Oxford University Press

Oxford   New York
Auckland   Bangkok   Buenos Aires   Cape Town   Chennai
Dar es Salaam   Delhi   Hong Kong   Istanbul   Karachi   Kolkata
Kuala Lumpur   Madrid   Melbourne   Mexico City   Mumbai   Nairobi
São Paulo   Shanghai   Taipei   Tokyo   Toronto

Published by Oxford University Press, Inc.
198 Madison Avenue, New York, New York 10016
www.oup.com

Library of Congress Cataloging-in-Publication Data

Kane, Robert, 1938-
   A contemporary introduction to free will / by Robert Kane.
      p.   cm. -- (Fundamentals of philosophy series)
   Includes bibliographical references.
   ISBN-13: 978-0-19-514969-2 (alk. paper)—
   ISBN-13: 978-0-19-514970-8 (pbk.: alk. paper)

   1. Free will and determinism. I. Title.   II. Fundamentals of
philosophy (Oxford, England)
   BJ1461.K365   2005
   123'.5--dc22

                                                    2005000944

Printing number: 9 8 7 6 5 4 3

Printed in the United States of America
on acid-free paper

Contents

Acknowledgments

All the authors whose writings are cited or discussed in this work have had an impact on my thinking about free will and hence on this book. I would like to specifically thank those who offered helpful comments on earlier drafts of the manuscript, especially Robert Miller (the Oxford editor of this series), Michael McKenna, Carl Ginet, John Martin Fischer, Christopher Panza, Ulrike Heuer, and several anonymous reviewers for Oxford University Press. Finally, I would like to thank Claudette Kane, whose critical eye and careful editing are everywhere in evidence in this work.

A Contemporary Introduction to

Free Will

CHAPTER 1

The Free Will Problem

1. Introduction

"There is a disputation that will continue till mankind is raised from the dead, between the necessitarians and the partisans of free will."

These are the words of Jalalu'ddin Rumi, twelfth-century Persian poet and mystic. The problem of free will and necessity (or determinism), of which he speaks, is one of the most difficult and "perhaps the most voluminously debated of all philosophical problems," according to a recent history of philosophy. Debates about free will have affected and been affected by both religion and science.

In his classic poem *Paradise Lost,* John Milton describes the angels debating how some of them could have sinned of their own free wills given that God had made them intelligent and happy. Why would they have done it? And why were they responsible for their sins rather than God, since God had made them the way they were and had complete foreknowledge of what they would do? While puzzling over such questions even the angels, according to Milton, were "in Endless Mazes lost" (not a comforting thought for us humans).

On the scientific front, issues about free will lead us to ask about the nature of the physical universe and our place in it (Are we determined by physical laws and movements of the atoms?), about human psychology and the springs of action (Can our actions be predicted by those who know our psychology?), and about social conditioning (Are we determined to be the kinds of persons we are by heredity and environment, birth and upbringing?).

In philosophy, debates about free will lead to issues about crime and punishment, blameworthiness and responsibility, coercion and control, mind and body, necessity and possibility, time and chance, right and wrong, and much more. In consequence, the free will problem is not fitted easily into one area of philosophy. It touches ethics, social and political philosophy, philosophy of mind, metaphysics, theory of knowledge, philosophy of law, philosophy of science, and philosophy of religion.

To understand what this "problem of free will" is and why it has puzzled so many minds for centuries, the best way to begin is with two familiar notions we all understand—or think we understand—freedom and responsibility.

2. Freedom

Nothing could be more important than freedom to the modern age. All over the world, people clamor for freedom; and the trend (in spite of frequent violent resistance to it) is toward societies that are more free. But why do we want freedom? The simple, and not totally adequate, answer is that to be more free is to be able to satisfy more of our desires. In a free society, we can buy what we want and travel where we please. We can choose what movies to see, what books to read, whom to vote for.

But these freedoms are what you might call *surface* freedoms. What we mean by *free will* runs deeper than these ordinary freedoms. To see how, suppose we had maximal freedom to make choices of the kinds just noted to satisfy our desires, yet the choices we actually made were in fact manipulated by others, by the powers that be. In such a world we would have a great deal of everyday freedom to do whatever we wanted, yet our freedom of *will* would be severely limited. We would be free to *act* or to choose *what* we willed, but we would not have the ultimate power over what it is that we willed. Other persons would be pulling the strings, not by coercing or forcing us to do things against our wishes, but by manipulating us into having the wishes they wanted us to have.

Now it may occur to you that, to some extent, we do live in such a world, where we are free to make choices but may be manipulated into making many of them by advertising, television, spin doctors, salespersons, marketers, and sometimes even by friends, parents, relatives, rivals, or enemies. One sign of how important free will is to us is that people feel revulsion at such manipulation and feel demeaned by it when they find out it has been done to them. They realize that they may have thought they were their own persons because they were choosing in accord with their own desires and purposes, but all along their desires and purposes had been manipulated by others who wanted them to choose exactly as they did. Such manipulation is demeaning because, when subjected to it, we realize we were not our own persons; and having free will is about being your own person.

The problem is nicely illustrated by twentieth-century utopian novels, such as Aldous Huxley's *Brave New World* and B. F. Skinner's *Walden Two*. (You may be familiar with more recent films or science fiction works with similar themes.) In the futuristic societies described in these classic works, people can have and do what they will or choose, but only to the extent that they have been conditioned since birth by behavioral engineers or neurochemists to will or choose what they can have and do. In *Brave New World*, the lower-class workers are under the influence of powerful drugs, so that they do not think about things they cannot have. They are quite content to play miniature golf all weekend. They can do what they want, but their wants are limited and controlled by drugs.

The citizens in Skinner's *Walden Two* have it better than the workers in *Brave New World*. Yet the desires and purposes of those who live in Walden Two are also covertly controlled, in this case by behavioral engineers. Citizens of Walden Two live collectively in what can be described as a rural commune; and because they share duties of farming and raising children, they have plenty of leisure. They pursue arts, sciences, and crafts, engage in musical performances, and enjoy what appears to be a pleasant existence. Indeed, the leading figure of the novel, a fellow named Frazier, who founded Walden Two, forthrightly says that their pleasant existence is brought about by the fact that, in his community, persons can do whatever they want or choose because they have been behaviorally conditioned since childhood to want and choose only what they can have and do.

Frazier then adds provocatively that, in his view, Walden Two "is the freest place on earth," since people there can choose and do anything they want. And in a sense he is right. There is no need for *coercion* in Walden Two or for *punishment* (there are no prisons). No one has to be forced to do anything against his or her will. No one harasses the citizens, and no one has to harass them. Yet we might wonder whether Walden Two *is* the freest place on earth. Is all this *surface* freedom in Walden Two not brought about at the expense of a *deeper* freedom of the will? The citizens of Walden Two can indeed do anything they want or will to do, but they do not have the ultimate say about what it is that they want or will. Their wills are determined by factors they do not control. Such an objection is in fact made by one of Frazier's critics in the novel, a philosopher named Castle who visits Walden Two.

But Frazier is untroubled by Castle's criticism. He admits that this supposedly deeper freedom of the will does not exist in Walden Two but argues that it is no real loss. Echoing the novel's author, B. F. Skinner (who was a foremost defender of behaviorism in psychology), Frazier thinks this so-called freedom of the will—the freedom that Castle and other philosophers have trumpeted for centuries—is an illusion. We do not and cannot have such a freedom anyway, he says, inside *or* outside Walden Two. In our ordinary lives, we are just as much the products of upbringing and social conditioning as the citizens of Walden Two, though we may delude ourselves into thinking otherwise. We may think we are the creators or originators of our own wills only because we are unaware of most of the genetic, psychological, and social factors that influence us. Moreover, the idea that we could be ultimate or "original" creators of our own wills—that we could somehow be "causes of ourselves"—is an impossible ideal, according to Frazier. If we trace the psychological springs of actions back to their origins—back to childhood, say—we find that we were less free then, not more.

Thus the gauntlet is thrown down by Frazier—echoing Skinner and many other modern thinkers: the so-called deeper freedom of the will is an illusion dreamt up by philosophers and theologians before we understood more about the hidden causes of behavior. It is an outdated idea that has no place in modern scientific picture of the world or of human beings. (Note that the philosopher who defends this "outdated" notion in Walden Two is given the medieval-sounding name "Castle.") Why sacrifice the everyday freedoms that really matter to us—freedoms from coercion, punishment, constraint, oppression, and the like—for an illusory freedom of the will that we cannot have anyway?

3. Responsibility

Reflecting in this way on the idea of *freedom* is one path to the free will problem. Another path is accessed by reflecting on the notion of *responsibility*. Free will is also intimately related to notions of accountability, blameworthiness, and praiseworthiness for actions.

Suppose a young man is on trial for an assault and robbery in which the victim was beaten to death. Let us say we attend his trial and listen to the evidence in the courtroom. At first, our attitude toward the defendant is one of anger and resentment. What the young man did was horrible. But as we listen daily to how he came to have the mean character and perverse motives he did have—a sad story of parental neglect, child abuse, sexual abuse, and bad role models—some of our resentment against the defendant is shifted over to the parents and others who abused and mistreated him. We begin to feel angry with them as well as with him. (Note how natural this reaction is.) Yet we aren't quite ready to shift all the blame away from the young man himself. We wonder whether some residual responsibility may not belong to him. Our questions become: To what extent is *he* responsible for becoming the sort of person he now is? Was his behavior *all* a question of bad parenting, societal neglect, social conditioning, and the like, or did he have any role to play in choosing it?

These are crucial questions about free will, and they are questions about what may be called the young man's ultimate responsibility. We know that parenting and society, genetic makeup and upbringing, have an influence on what we become and what we are. But were these influences entirely *determining,* or did they "leave anything over" for us to be responsible for? That is what we want to know about the young man. The question of whether he is merely a victim of bad circumstances or has some residual responsibility for being what he is—the question, that is, of whether he became the person he is *of his own free will*—seems to depend on whether these other factors were or were not *entirely* determining.

4. Determinism and Necessity

The problem of free will arises in human history when, by reflections such as these, people are led to suspect that their actions might be determined or necessitated by factors unknown to them and beyond their control. This is why doctrines of *determinism* or *necessity* are so important in the history of debates about free will. Whenever determinist doctrines arise, their appearance signals that humans have reached a higher stage of self-consciousness in which they begin to wonder about the sources of their behavior and about their place as actors in the universe. Philosophy begins in *wonder,* said the ancient philosopher Aristotle, and no wondering affects our self-image more profoundly than this one about free will. We do not want to be pawns in some unknown chess game.

Doctrines of determinism have taken many historical forms. People have wondered at different times whether their choices and actions might be determined by fate or by God, by laws of physics or laws of logic, by heredity and environment, by unconscious motives or psychological or social conditioning, and so on. But there is a core idea running through all historical doctrines of determinism that reveals why they are a threat to free will—whether the doctrines be fatalistic, theological, logical, physical, psychological, or social. According to this core idea:

An event (such as a choice or action) is *determined* when there are conditions obtaining earlier (such as the decrees of fate or the foreordaining acts of God or antecedent causes plus laws of nature) whose occurrence is a sufficient condition for the occurrence of the event. In other words, it *must* be the case that, *if* these earlier determining conditions obtain, then the determined event will occur.

In more familiar terms, we say that a determined event is *inevitable* or *necessary* (it cannot but occur), given the determining conditions. If fate decreed or God foreordained (or the laws of nature and antecedent causes determined) that John would choose at a certain time to go to Samarra, then John *will* choose at that time to go to Samarra. Determinism is thus a kind of necessity, but it is a conditional necessity. A determined event does not have to occur, no matter what else happens (it need not be *absolutely* necessary). But it must occur when the determining conditions have occurred. If the decrees of fate had been different or the past had been different in some way, John may have been determined to go to Damascus rather than to Samarra. Historical doctrines of determinism refer to different determining conditions. But all doctrines of determinism imply that every event, or at least every human choice and action, is determined by some determining conditions in this sense.

5. Free Choices and Open Futures

To see where the conflict lies between determinism and free will, consider again what free will requires. We believe we have free will when we view ourselves as agents capable of influencing the world in various ways. Open alternatives, or alternative possibilities, seem to lie before us. We reason and deliberate among them and choose. We feel (1) it is "up to us" what we choose and how we act; and this means we could have chosen or acted otherwise. As Aristotle noted: when acting is "up to us," so is not acting. This "up-to-us-ness" also suggests that (2) the ultimate sources of our actions lie in us and not outside us in factors beyond our control.

If free will implies these conditions, one can see why determinism would be a threat to free will. If one or another form of determinism were true, it seems that it would *not* be (1) "up to us" what we chose from an array of alternative possibilities, since only one alternative would be possible. And it seems that the (2) sources or origins of our actions would not be "in us" but in something else (such as the decrees of fate, the foreordaining acts of God, or antecedent causes and laws of nature) outside us and beyond our control.

To illustrate these conflicts, suppose Molly has just graduated from law school and has a choice between joining a large law firm in Dallas or a smaller firm in Austin. If Molly believes her choice is a *free* choice (made

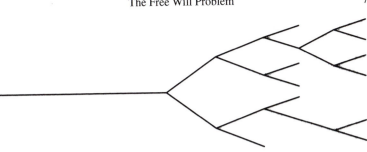

Figure 1.1   A Garden of Forking Paths

"of her own free will"), she must believe both options are "open" to her while she is deliberating. She could choose either one. (If she did not believe this, what would be the point of deliberating?) But that means she must believe there is more than one possible path into the future available to her and it is "up to her" which of these paths will be taken. Such a picture of an open future with forking paths—a "garden of forking paths," we might call it—is essential to our understanding of free will. Such a picture of different possible paths into the future is also essential, we might even say, to what it means to be a person and to live a human life.

But determinism threatens this picture, for it seems to imply that there really is only one possible path into the future, not many. And yet, first impressions are an unreliable guide on a subject as contentious and difficult as free will. We shall see that many philosophers and scientists, especially in modern times, have argued that, despite appearances to the contrary, determinism poses no real threat to free will, or at least to any kind of freedom or free will "worth wanting" (as Daniel Dennett has put it). The open future or garden of forking paths depicted in figure 1.1 looks convincing, they say, but it hides a multitude of puzzles and confusions.

So the question of whether determinism is true ("the Determinist Question") is not the only question that must concern us as we begin our inquiries into free will. We must also consider whether determinism really does conflict with free will. (This second question is often called "the Compatibility Question.") Let us look at these two questions in turn.

6. The Determinist Question and Modern Science

Many people wonder why worries about determinism persist today, when universal determinism is no longer accepted even in the physical sciences, which were once the strongholds of determinism. In the eighteenth century, a great physicist, the Marquis de Laplace, imagined that a super-intelligent being (often called Laplace's Demon), knowing all the physical facts about the universe at one moment and applying Newton's laws of motion, could know everything that is going to happen in the future, down to the minutest detail.

This Laplacian or Newtonian vision of universal physical determinism was taken for granted by many scientists and philosophers until the end of the nineteenth century, but it can no longer be taken for granted today. You are probably familiar with the claim that modern quantum physics has introduced indeterminism or chance into the physical world. Much of the behavior of elementary particles, it is said, from quantum jumps in atoms to radioactive decay, is not precisely predictable and can be explained only by statistical, not deterministic, laws. We are also told that the uncertainty and indeterminacy of this world of quantum physics, according to the standard view of it, is not due to our limitations as knowers, but to the unusual nature of elementary particles themselves, such as protons and electrons, which have both wavelike and particle-like properties. No superintelligence (not even God perhaps) could know the exact positions and momenta of all the particles of the universe at a given moment because the particles do not *have* exact positions and momenta at the same time (the Heisenberg uncertainty principle); hence their future behavior is not precisely predictable or determined.

One might think these indeterministic developments in modern physics would have disposed of philosophical worries about free will. Why be concerned that free will conflicts with determinism if determinism is not even true in the physical world? But the interesting fact is that despite these developments in physics, worries about free will did not go away in the twentieth century. Concerns about determinism of human behavior persist to this day, and debates about free will have become more heated than ever. Why is this so? There are four reasons why indeterministic developments in modern physics have not disposed of traditional concerns about free will and determinism.

First, the new quantum world of elementary particles is as mysterious as free will itself, and there is still much debate about how to interpret it. Standard views of quantum physics hold that the behavior of elementary particles involves chance and is undetermined. But these standard views have been challenged; and there exist alternative interpretations of quantum theory that are deterministic.[1] These alternative interpretations are the minority view among physicists at present, and they are controversial. But they cannot be ruled out. There is also the possibility that modern quantum physics will one day be superseded by a more comprehensive theory that is deterministic. So the question of determinism in the physical world is not finally settled. But it is true that modern physics does gives us more reason to believe that indeterminism and chance might have a more significant role to play in the physical universe than did the classical physics of Newton and Laplace. So there may be more room for free will in nature, though this is not guaranteed.

But there is a second problem. Suppose it were true that the behavior of elementary particles is not always determined? What would this have to do with *human behavior*? Contemporary determinists often point out that, while quantum indeterminacy may be significant for elementary particles, such as electrons and protons, its indeterministic effects are usually insignificant in large physical systems such as the human brain and body.[2] Complex physical systems involving many particles and higher energies tend to be regular and predictable in their behavior, according to quantum physics itself. Thus, modern determinists, such as Ted Honderich, argue that we can continue to regard human behavior as determined "for all practical purposes" or "near-determined," whatever the truth may be about electrons and protons. And this is all that matters in free will debates.

A third point complicates matters even further. Suppose for the sake of argument that quantum jumps or other undetermined events in the brain or body *do* sometimes have large-scale undetermined effects on human behavior. How would this help with free will? Suppose a choice was the result of a quantum jump or other undetermined event in a person's brain. Would this be a *free* or responsible choice? Such undetermined effects in the brain or body would happen by chance and would be unpredictable and uncontrollable, like the sudden occurrence of a thought or the jerking of an arm that one could not predict or control. Such an effect would be quite the opposite of what we take free and responsible actions to be.

A similar objection was made against the ancient Epicurean philosophers, who had argued that the atoms must "swerve" in chance ways if there was to be room in nature for free will. How, asked the critics, would chance swerves of the atoms help to give us free will? It seems that undetermined events happening in the brain or body would occur spontaneously and would be more of a nuisance, or a curse, like epilepsy, than an enhancement of our freedom. If free will is not compatible with *determinism,* it does not appear to be compatible with *indeterminism* either, since indeterminism would seem to be mere chance.

To these considerations, we can add a fourth and final reason why indeterministic developments in modern physics have not disposed of worries about free will and determinism. At the same time that determinism has been in retreat in the physical sciences in the past century, developments in sciences other than physics—in biology, biochemistry, and neuroscience, in psychiatry, psychology, and other social and behavioral sciences—have been moving in the opposite direction. These other sciences have convinced many persons that more of their behavior than previously believed is determined by causes unknown to them and beyond their control.

Developments in sciences other than physics that suggest determinism have been many, but they surely include a greater knowledge of the influence of genetics and heredity on human behavior. (Note the controversy caused by the recent mapping of the human genome, which naturally arouses fears of future control of behavior by genetic manipulation.) Other relevant scientific developments have raised more questions. We now have a greater awareness of biochemical influences on the brain: hormones, neurotransmitters, and the susceptibility of human moods and behavior to different drugs that radically affect the way we think and behave. The advent of psychoanalysis and other theories of unconscious motivation have proposed new ways of thinking about the human brain, no less than the development of computers and intelligent machines that can do many of the things we can do even though they are preprogrammed (like Deep Blue, the chess master computer). Comparative studies of animal and human behavior have further enriched our understanding, suggesting that much of our motivation and behavior is a product of our evolutionary history, and helping us to see the influences of psychological, social, and cultural conditioning upon upbringing and subsequent behavior.

It is difficult not to be influenced by these scientific developments, which we can read about in the newspapers every day. To be sure, these newly discovered influences on our behavior do not prove definitively that we lack free will. There may still be some leeway for us to exercise our free will in the midst of all the biological, psychological, and social influences upon us. But these new scientific developments in fields other than physics do show why worries about the determinism *of human behavior* persist in contemporary debates about free will, despite indeterministic developments in physics. And continuing worries about determinism of human behavior make the second pivotal question we are going to address (in the next chapter) all the more important, namely, the Compatibility Question: does determinism really conflict with free will, or are the two compatible? If there really is no conflict between free will and determinism, as many modern thinkers believe, then we do not have to worry about all these new scientific threats to our freedom. For we could still be free and responsible, even if determinism should turn out to be true.

Suggested Reading

Three collections of readings on free will that deal with many of the topics of this book are Gary Watson (ed.) *Free Will* (Oxford, 2003), Robert Kane (ed.) *Free Will* (Blackwell, 2002), and Laura Waddell Ekstrom (ed.) *Agency and Responsibility: Essays on the Metaphysics of Freedom* (Westview, 2000). More advanced discussion of most of the topics of the book can be found in *The Oxford Handbook of Free Will* (Kane, ed., Oxford, 2002).

CHAPTER 2

Compatibilism

1. Introduction

The view that there is really is no conflict between determinism and free will—that free will and determinism are compatible—is known as *compatibilism;* and it is the first view about free will we shall consider. Compatibilism has become an increasingly popular doctrine in modern philosophy because it provides what seems to be a neat, simple solution to the free will problem. If there really is no conflict between free will and determinism, as compatibilists say, then the age-old problem of free will is resolved in one fell swoop.

Compatibilism was held by some ancient philosophers, like the Stoics, and perhaps Aristotle too, according to some scholars. But it has become especially popular since the seventeenth century. Influential philosophers of the modern era, such as Thomas Hobbes, John Locke, David Hume, and John Stuart Mill, were compatibilists. They saw compatibilism as a way of reconciling ordinary experience of being free with scientific views about the universe and human beings. Compatibilism remains popular among philosophers and scientists today for similar reasons. If compatibilists are right, we can have both freedom and determinism, and need not worry that future science will somehow undermine our ordinary conviction that we are free and responsible agents.

This is a comforting thought. But is compatibilism believable? In my experience, most persons resist the idea that free will and determinism might be compatible when they first encounter it. The idea that determinism might be compatible with freedom and responsibility looks at first like a "quagmire of evasion," as William James called it, or a "wretched subterfuge" as Kant called the compatibilism of Hobbes and Hume. If compatibilism is to be taken seriously by ordinary persons, they have to be talked out of this natural belief in the incompatibility of free will and determinism by means of philosophical arguments; and supplying such arguments is what compatibilists try to do.

2. Freedom as the Absence of Constraints

The first step in the compatibilists' argument is to ask us to reflect on what we ordinarily mean by saying actions or choices are "free." What does it mean to say I am free to take the bus this morning? It does not mean I will actually take the bus, for I may choose not to take it. But I am free to take the bus, if I have the *power* or *ability* to take it, should I want or decide to do so. Freedom then is, first of all, a power or ability to do something, a power I may or may not choose to exercise.

Second, this power or ability, which is my freedom, entails that there are no *constraints* or *impediments* preventing me from doing what I want to do. I would not be free to take the bus if various things prevented me: such as being in jail or if some one had tied me up (physical restraint); or if someone were holding me at gunpoint, commanding me not to move (coercion); or if I were paralyzed (lack of ability); or if buses were not running today (lack of opportunity); or if fear of crowded buses compelled me to avoid them (compulsion), and so on.

Putting these thoughts together, compatibilists argue that to be free, as we ordinarily understand it, is (1) to have the *power* or *ability* to do what we want or desire to do, which in turn entails (2) an *absence of constraints* or impediments (such as physical restraints, coercion, and compulsion) preventing us from doing what we want. Let us call a view that defines freedom in terms of 1 and 2 "classical compatibilism." Most traditional compatibilists, such as Hobbes, Hume, and Mill, were classical compatibilists in this sense. Hobbes stated the view succinctly, saying a man is free when he finds "no stop in doing what he has the will, desire or inclination to do."[1] And Hobbes noted that if this is what freedom means, then freedom is compatible with determinism. For, as he put it, there may be no constraints or impediments preventing persons from doing what they "will or desire to do," even if it should turn out that what they will or desire was determined by their past.

But doesn't freedom also require alternative paths into the future, and hence the freedom *to do otherwise*? How do classical compatibilists account for the freedom to do otherwise? They begin by defining the freedom to do otherwise in terms of the same conditions 1 and 2. You are free to do otherwise than take the bus if (1) you have the power or ability to *avoid* taking it, which entails (2) that there are also no constraints preventing you from *not* taking the bus, if you wanted to (no one is holding a gun on you, for example, forcing you to get on the bus.)

Of course, an absence of constraints preventing you from doing otherwise does not mean you will actually do otherwise. But, for classical compatibilists, the freedom to do otherwise does mean that you *would* have done otherwise (nothing would have stopped you) *if* you had wanted or desired to do otherwise. And they argue that if the freedom to do otherwise has this *conditional* or *hypothetical* meaning (you *would* . . . , *if* you wanted to), then the freedom to do otherwise would also be compatible with determinism. For it may be that you *would* have done otherwise *if* you had wanted to, even though you did not in fact want to do otherwise, and even if what you wanted to do was determined.

3. Freedom of Will

Is this classical compatibilist account of freedom plausible? It does seem to capture the *surface freedoms* discussed in chapter 1. Surface freedoms, you may recall, were those everyday freedoms to buy what we want, walk where we please, take buses when we want to, without anything preventing us. These everyday freedoms do seem to amount to (1) the power or ability to do what we want (and the power to have done otherwise, *if* we had wanted to) and (2) doing so without any constraints or impediments getting in our way. But if the classical compatibilist analysis of freedom does capture these surface freedoms of *action* discussed in chapter 1, does it also capture the "deeper" freedom of the *will?*

Classical compatibilists respond to this question in two ways. First, they say:

> It all depends on what you mean by "freedom of will." In one sense, freedom of will has a perfectly ordinary meaning. For most of us, it means *freedom of choice* or *decision*. But freedom of choice or decision can be analyzed in the same way that we compatibilists analyze freedom of action generally. You are free to *choose* to lend money to a friend, for example, if (1) you have the power or ability to *choose* to lend the money in the sense that (2) no constraints would prevent you from making the choice, *if* you wanted to, and, in addition, nothing would have prevented you from *choosing otherwise* (choosing not to lend the money), if you had wanted to choose otherwise.

In short, compatibilists say that free choices or decisions can be treated like free actions of other kinds. For, choices or decisions can be subject to constraints just like other kinds of actions; and when choices or decisions are subject to constraints, they are also not free. For example, you might have been brainwashed or hypnotized, so that you could not have chosen otherwise (chosen not to lend money), even *if* you wanted to. Conditions such as brainwashing and hypnosis are two further constraints that can take away freedom; and they sometimes take away even the freedom to *choose* what we would otherwise have wanted to choose. When brainwashing or hypnosis do this they take away our freedom of *will*.

Here is another example of constraint on choices or decisions. If a man holds a gun to your head and says "Your money or your life," he is giving you a choice of sorts. You can choose to hand over your money or take a chance on losing your life. But in another sense, the man has not given you any *real* choice at all, if you believe he is serious. For the prospect of losing your life is so horrible this is no choice at all. Your choice to hand over the money is therefore not really free. It is *coerced;* and coercion is a constraint on your freedom of choice or freedom of will. The thief's actions have kept you from making the choice you really wanted to make, which was to keep both money *and* life.

So the first response of compatibilists regarding "freedom of will" is to say that if freedom of will means what we usually mean by it— *unconstrained freedom of choice or decision*—then freedom of will can also be given a compatibilist analysis. You have freedom of will when nothing would have prevented you from choosing *or* from choosing otherwise *if* you had wanted to; and if this is what freedom of will means, they argue, then freedom of will (as well as freedom of action) is consistent with determinism.

4. If the Past Had Been Different

But compatibilists are aware that many persons are not going to be satisfied with this account of free will as mere unconstrained choice or decision. So they have a second response.

If you are still not satisfied with the above account of freedom of will, then it is no doubt because you are thinking of free will in some further sense than simply the ability to choose or decide *as* you will without constraint. You must be thinking of freedom of will in something like the 'deeper' sense of free will of chapter 1—as a kind of *ultimate* control over what you will or want in the first place: A control incompatible with your will's being determined by any events in the past over which you did not have control. Now we compatibilists obviously can't capture *that* deeper sense of freedom of will, no matter what we do, because it is incompatible with determinism. But, as compatibilists, we believe that any so-called deeper freedom of the will—or any kind of free will that requires indeterminism—is incoherent anyway. No one *could* have a freedom of will of such a deeper kind.

Why do compatibilists believe that any kind of deeper freedom of will that requires indeterminism must be incoherent? Well, if determinism means (as it does): *same past, same future,* then, the denial of determinism—indeterminism—must mean: *same past, different possible futures.* (Think of the garden of forking paths of chapter 1.) But if that is what indeterminism means—same past, different possible futures—indeterminism has some odd consequences regarding free choices. Consider Molly again deliberating about whether to join the law firm in Dallas or the one in Austin. After much thought, let us say, Molly decided that the Dallas firm was a better one for her career plans and she chose it. Now if her choice was undetermined, she might have chosen differently (she might have chosen the Austin firm instead), *given the same past*—since that is what indeterminism requires: same past, different possible futures. But note what this requirement means in Molly's case: exactly the same prior deliberation, the same thought processes, the same beliefs, desires, and other motives (not a sliver of difference!) that led to Molly favoring and choosing the Dallas firm *might have issued in her choosing the Austin firm instead.*

That senario makes no sense, say compatibilists. It would be senseless and irrational for Molly to choose the Austin firm, given exactly the same motives and prior process of reasoning that *in fact* led her to believe the Dallas firm was the better one for her career. To say that Molly "could have chosen otherwise"in these circumstances must mean something else, say compatibilists—something like the following: *if* Molly had had *different* beliefs or desires, or had reasoned differently, or *if* other thoughts had entered her mind before she chose the Dallas firm, *then* she might have come to favor the Austin firm instead and chosen it. But this more sensible interpretation of "could have done otherwise," say compatibilists, means only that Molly would have done otherwise, if things had been different— if *the past had been different in some way.* And such a claim, they insist, does not conflict with determinism. In fact, this interpretation of "could have chosen otherwise" perfectly fits the classical compatibilists' *conditional* or *hypothetical* analysis—"Molly could have chosen otherwise" means "She *would* have chosen otherwise, *if* she had wanted to (if her mind-set had been different in some way). And such a hypothetical interpretation of "could have chosen otherwise" is, as we have seen, compatible with determinism.

One's first thought when encountering this argument is that there must be some way around the conclusion that if Molly's choice is undetermined, she must have been able to choose otherwise "given exactly the same past." But in fact there is no easy way around this conclusion. For indeterminism, which is the denial of determinism, *does* mean "different possible futures, given the same past." In the diagram of forking paths of chapter 1, the single line going back into the past is just that: a single line indicating "same past"; while the multiple lines going into the future represent "different possible futures." By contrast, determinism means only one line into the future. If Molly really is free to choose different options at any time during her deliberation, and her choice is not determined, then she must be able to choose *either* path (the Dallas firm or the Austin firm), given the *same* past up to the moment when she chooses.

You can't cheat here by suggesting that if the past had been a *tiny bit* different, then Molly might have chosen differently (chosen the Austin firm). *Determinists* and *compatibilists* can say this: for they insist that Molly might have sensibly and rationally chosen otherwise only if the past had been different in some way (however small the difference). But persons who believe free choices cannot be determined must say that Molly may have chosen different possible futures, given the same past at the time she did choose. And this does seem to make choosing otherwise in the same circumstances arbitrary and irrational.

To sum up: compatibilists have a twofold response to the objection that their view accounts only for freedom of action but not for freedom of will. On the one hand, they say, if "freedom of will" means what we ordinarily mean by free *choices* or *decisions* (those that are uncoerced and unconstrained), then freedom of will can also be given a compatibilist analysis and can thus be seen to be compatible with determinism. On the other hand, if "freedom of will" has a stronger meaning—if it refers to some kind of "deeper" freedom of the will that is not compatible with determinism—then that deeper freedom of will is incoherent and is not something we can have anyway.

5. Constraint, Control, Fatalism, and Mechanism

So far, the compatibilist argument has been that people believe determinism conflicts with free will because they have confused ideas about *freedom*. But compatibilist arguments about freedom of action and will are only half of the compatibilists' case. They also argue that people mistakenly believe determinism and free will conflict because they also have confused ideas about *determinism*. Determinism, compatibilists insist, is not the frightful thing we think it is. People believe determinism is a threat to freedom because they commonly confuse determinism with a host of other things that are a threat to freedom. But determinism does not imply these other threatening things, according to compatibilists. For example, they say:

1. "Don't confuse *determinism* with *constraint, coercion,* or *compulsion.*" Freedom *is* the opposite of constraint, coercion, and compulsion compatibilists insist; but it is not the opposite of determinism. Constraint, coercion, and compulsion act *against* our wills, preventing us from doing or choosing what we want. By contrast, determinism does *not* necessarily act against our wills; nor does it always prevent us from doing what we want. Causal determinism, to be sure, *does* mean that all events follow from earlier events in accordance with invariable laws of nature. But, say compatibilists, it is a mistake to think that laws of nature *constrain* us. According to A. J. Ayer (a noted twentieth-century compatibilist), many people think freedom is inconsistent with determinism because they have a mistaken image of natural causes or laws of nature "overmastering" us, forcing us against our wills. But, in fact, the existence of laws of nature indicates only that certain events follow others according to regular patterns. To be governed by laws of nature is not to be in chains.

2. "Don't confuse *causation* with *constraint.*" Compatibilists also insist that it is constraints, not mere *causes* of any kind, that undermine freedom. Constraints *are* causes, but they are causes of special kinds: impediments or hindrances to our doing what we want, such as being tied up or paralyzed. Not all causes are impediments to freedom in this sense. In fact, some causes, such as muscular strength or inner strength of will, actually *enable* us to do what we want. It is therefore a mistake to think that actions are unfree simply because they are caused. Whether actions are free or not depends on what *kinds* of causes they have: some causes enhance our freedom, while other causes (i.e., constraints) hinder our freedom.

It is a further mistake, say compatibilists, to think that, when we act or choose freely in accordance with our wills, our actions are entirely *uncaused.* To the contrary, our free actions are caused by our characters and motives; and this state of affairs is a good thing. For if actions were not caused by our characters and motives, we could not be held responsible for the actions. They would not be *our* actions. This point was made in a well-known passage by perhaps the most influential classical compatibilist, David Hume:

> Where [actions] proceed not from some *cause* in the character and disposition of the person who performed them, they can neither redound to his honour, if good; nor infamy, if evil. . . . The person is not answerable for them;

and as they proceeded from nothing in him that is durable and constant . . . it is impossible he can, upon their account, become the object of punishment or vengeance.[2]

Classical compatibilists follow Hume in saying that responsible actions cannot be uncaused; such actions must have the right kinds of causes— causes that come from inside our selves and express our characters and motives, rather than causes imposed upon us against our wills. It is a mistake to think that free will and determinism are not compatible because free actions should be uncaused. Free actions are *unconstrained,* not *uncaused.*

3. "Don't confuse *determinism* with *control* by other agents." Compatibilists can concede (and often do concede) that it *does* count against our freedom if we are controlled or manipulated by other *persons.* That is why sci-fi utopias, like *Brave New World* and *Walden Two,* where people are controlled by behavior engineers or neurochemists, seem to undermine human freedom. But compatibilists insist that determinism by itself does not necessarily imply that any other persons or agents are controlling our behavior or manipulating us.

Nature by itself "does not control us," says compatibilist Daniel Dennett, since nature is not an agent.[3] What is objectionable about control by other agents, Dennett argues—whether they be behavioral engineers or con men—is that other persons are using us as means to their ends, lording it over us and making us conform to their wishes. We resent this kind of interference. But merely being determined does not imply that any other *agents* are interfering with us or using us in this way. So compatibilists can reject Brave New World and Walden Two scenarios, says Dennett, without giving up their belief that determinism is consistent with freedom and responsibility.

4. "Don't confuse *determinism* with *fatalism.*" This is one of the most common confusions in free will debates. Fatalism is the view that whatever is going to happen, is going to happen, *no matter what we do.* Determinism alone does not imply such a consequence. What we decide and what we do would make a difference in how things turn out—often an enormous difference—even if determinism should be true. This important point was made by another influential classical compatibilist, John Stuart Mill:

> A fatalist believes . . . not only that whatever is about to happen will be the infallible result of causes that precede it [which is what determinists believe], but moreover that there is no use in struggling against it; that it will happen however we may strive to prevent it. . . . [Thus, fatalists believe that a man's]

character is formed *for* him, and not *by* him; therefore his wishing it was formed differently is of no use; he has no power to alter it. This is a grand error. He has, to a certain extent, a power to alter his character. Its not being, in the ultimate resort, formed for him, is not inconsistent with its being, in part, formed *by* him as one of the immediate agents. His character is formed by his circumstances . . . but his own desire to mold it in a particular way is one of those circumstances, and by no means the least influential.[4]

Determinism, Mill is saying, does not imply that we have no influence on how things turn out, including the molding of our characters. We obviously do have such an influence, and determinism alone does not rule it out. Believing in fatalism, by contrast, can have fatal consequences. A sick man may excuse himself for not seeing a doctor saying: "If your time is up, it doesn't matter what you do about it." Or a soldier may use a familiar line for not taking precautions: "There's a bullet out there with your name on it. When it comes, you will not be able to avoid it, no matter what you do." Mill is saying that such fatalist claims do not follow merely from determinism. To think they do is a "grand error."

The claims of the sick man and the soldier are in fact examples of what the ancient philosophers called the "lazy sophism" ("sophism" meaning a fallacy of reasoning). The proper answers to the sick man and the soldier would be, "*Whether* your time is now up may depend in great part on whether you see a doctor; and *whether* any bullet out there right now has your name on it may depend on what precautions you take. So instead of sitting around doing nothing, see a doctor and take precautions." This is the response that compatibilists, such as Mill, would give to the "lazy sophism." Believing that determinism is compatible with freedom, they would say, should not make you a fatalist. Indeed this belief should convince you that your life is to some extent in your own hands, since how you deliberate can still make a difference in your future, even if determinism should turn out to be true.

Sometimes our deliberations do not matter to our fate, but not always. For example, Dennett describes a despairing man who jumps off a bridge intending to commit suicide. Halfway down, the man deliberates again, and thinks of life from a different perspective, deciding that perhaps suicide isn't a good idea after all. Now *this* man's deliberation no longer does matter to his fate. But ordinarily when we deliberate we are not in such desperate straits. Indeed, conditions like this man's are rare. Most of the time, say compatibilists, our deliberations do affect our future, even if determinism should be true.

5. "Don't confuse *determinism* with *mechanism*." Another common confusion, according to compatibilists, is to think that if determinism were true, we would all be machines, running mechanically, like watches,

robots, or computers. Or, alternatively, we would be like amoebae or insects and other lower creatures responding automatically, and with a fixed set of responses, to the stimuli of our environment. But, compatibilists insist, none of these consequences follows from determinism either. Suppose it should turn out that the world is determined. There would still be an enormous difference between human beings, on the one hand, and amoebae and insects, or machines and robots, on the other. Unlike machines (even complex machines like computers) or robots, we humans have an inner conscious life of moods and feelings, and we react to the world accordingly. And unlike amoebae, insects, and other such creatures, we do not just react to the environment instinctually and in automatic ways. We reason and deliberate, question our motives, reflect on our values, make plans about the future, reform our characters, and make promises to others that we then feel obligated to keep.

Determinism does not rule out any of these capacities, say compatibilists, and they are the capacities that make us free and responsible beings, capable of moral action—as machines and insects are not. Determinism does not necessarily imply mechanical, inflexible, or automatic behavior either. Determinism is consistent with a whole spectrum of complexity and flexibility of behavior in living things, from the simplest amoeba all the way to human beings. The complexity and degrees of freedom of creatures in the world, from amoebae to humans, might differ incredibly, yet all these properties might be determined.

6. Assessing Classical Compatibilism

In summary, classical compatibilists say that our natural belief in the incompatibility of free will and determinism rests on confusions of two kinds—confusions about the nature of *freedom* and confusions about the nature of *determinism*. Once these confusions have been cleared up, they insist, we should see there is no necessary conflict between freedom and determinism. To assess the classical compatibilists' position, one must therefore ask whether their account of freedom really does capture what we mean by freedom of will and action; and one must ask whether the belief that determinism conflicts with free will does rest on confusions about determinism. Both these questions will be considered in the next chapter.

It is worth noting in conclusion, however, that classical compatibilists do seem to be right about certain things, whatever the final judgment may be about their view. They would appear to be right, for example, in saying determinism *in and of itself* does not imply *constraint, control by other agents, fatalism,* or *mechanism*. These *would* indeed rule out free will, but determinism does not necessarily imply them, and it would be a mistake to believe determinism to be incompatible with free will *merely* because determinism implied them. Many people probably have confused determinism with constraint or control or fatalism or mechanism, and so thought determinism to be incompatible with free will for the wrong reasons.

But if these are bad reasons for thinking free will and determinism are incompatible, there may nonetheless be some good reasons. We may still wonder whether determinism *itself* might not conflict with free will—not because it implies constraint, control, and so on, but *just because it is determinism.* For it seems that if determinism is true, there is only one possible future (hence no garden of many forking paths into the future); and this fact alone seems to rule out the possibility of free will and responsibility for actions.

To this objection, compatibilists issue a challenge of their own. "If there is an argument to show that determinism *must* be incompatible with free will, *just because* it is determinism, and *not* because it implies constraint or control by others or fatalism or mechanism, then provide us with such a direct argument for the incompatibility of free will and determinism! In short, "prove it." In the next chapter, we will consider how incompatibilists try to meet this challenge.

An Addendum on the Term Soft Determinism

In many writings on free will, compatibilists are often referred to as *soft determinists.* Soft determinists are compatibilists who also believe that determinism is true. Classical compatibilists, such as Hobbes, Hume, and Mill, were also soft determinists, since they believed that determinism was true in addition to believing that freedom and determinism were compatible.

Suggested Reading

A lively and readable defense of compatibilism is Daniel Dennett's *Elbow Room: The Varieties of Free Will Worth Wanting* (MIT, 1984). Defenses of classical compatibilism appear in essays by J.J.C. Smart (in Gary Watson, ed., *Free Will* [Oxford: Oxford University Press, 2nd ed., 2003]) and Kai Nielsen (in Robert Kane, ed., *Free Will*). Other selections from classical compatibilists are contained in Derk Pereboom, ed., *Free Will* (Hackett, 1997); and classical compatibilist positions are discussed in Ilham Dilman's historical introduction, *Free Will* (Routledge, 1999).

CHAPTER 3

Incompatibilism

1. The Consequence Argument

The popularity of compatibilism among modern philosophers and scientists means that *incompatibilists*—those who hold the traditional belief that free will and determinism are in conflict—must provide arguments to support their position. Incompatibilists cannot merely rely on their intuitions about forking paths into the future to make their case, as in chapter 1. They must back up their intuitions with arguments that show why free will and determinism must be incompatible. New arguments for incompatibilism have indeed been proposed in modern philosophy to meet this challenge. The most widely discussed of these new arguments for the incompatibility of free will and determinism is the subject of this chapter.

The argument is called the Consequence Argument, and it is stated informally as follows by one of its proponents, Peter van Inwagen:

> If determinism is true, then our acts are the consequences of the laws of nature and events in the remote past. But it is not up to us what went on before we were born; and neither is it up to us what the laws of nature are. Therefore the consequences of these things (including our own acts) are not up to us.[1]

To say it is not "up to us" what "went on before we were born," or "what the laws of nature are," is to say that there is nothing we can now do to change the past or alter the laws of nature (such things are beyond our control). This gives us two premises of the Consequence Argument.

(1) There is nothing we can now do to change the past.
(2) There is nothing we can now do to change the laws of nature.

Putting these two premises together, we get

(3) There is nothing we can now do to change the past and the laws of nature.

But if determinism is true, then

(4) Our present actions are the necessary consequences of the past and the laws of nature. (Or, equivalently, it is necessary that, given the past and the laws of nature, our present actions occur.)

So, if determinism is true, it seems that

(5) There is nothing we can now do to change the fact that our present actions are the necessary consequences of the past and the laws of nature.

But if there is nothing we can now do to change the past and the laws of nature (which is step 3) *and* nothing we can now do to change the fact that our present actions are the necessary consequences of the past and the laws of nature (step 5), it would seem to follow that, if determinism is true (step 4), then

(6) There is nothing we can now do to change the fact that our present actions occur.

In other words, we *cannot now do otherwise* than we actually do. Since this argument can be applied to any agents and actions at any times, we can infer from it that *if determinism is true, no one can ever do otherwise;* and if free will requires the power to do otherwise, then no one has free will.

2. Assessing the Argument

Van Inwagen thinks the first two premises of this Consequence Argument are undeniable. We cannot now change the past (1) or the laws of nature (2). Step 3 states what appears to be a simple consequence of premises 1 and 2: if you can't change the past or the laws, then you can't change the conjunction of both of them. Premise 4 simply states what is implied by the definition of determinism: if determinism is true, then our actions are the necessary consequences of the past and laws of nature in the sense that they *must* occur, *given* the past and the laws. By asserting premise 4, of course, the argument is assuming the truth of determinism. But it is doing so only hypothetically, in order to show that, *if* determinism is true (premise 4), *then* no one could have done otherwise (6). So the

Consequence Argument does not depend on determinism's actually being true; rather, it seeks to show what determinism would imply (no free will), *if* it were true.

We are left to assess steps 5 and 6. How are they arrived at? Step 5 ("There is nothing we can now do to change the fact that our present actions are the necessary consequences of the past and the laws of nature") follows from premise 4 by virtue of a rule that van Inwagen calls

> Rule Alpha. There is nothing anyone can do to change what *must* be the case (or what is necessarily so).

This rule gets us from premise 4 to step 5 in the following way. According to premise 4, it *must be that,* given laws of nature and the past, our present actions occur. But Rule Alpha says no one can now change *what must be.* So it follows that we cannot now change the fact that, given the laws of nature and the past, our present actions occur—which is what step 5 says.

Van Inwagen thinks this Rule Alpha is also undeniable. How, he asks, could anyone change what is necessarily so? If it is necessarily so that 2 + 2 = 4, then no one can change that; and if someone could change the fact that 2 + 2 = 4, then it would not be necessarily so.

This brings us to the conclusion of the argument, step (6): "There is nothing we can now do to change the fact that our present actions occur." This conclusion follows from earlier steps, as noted, by virtue of the following inference: if there is nothing we can now do to change the past and the laws of nature (step 3) and nothing we can now do to change the fact that our present actions are the necessary consequences of the past and the laws of nature (step 5), then there is nothing we can now do to change the fact that our present actions occur (6). This inference involves a second rule that van Inwagen calls

> Rule Beta. If there is nothing anyone can do to change X, and nothing anyone can do to change the fact that Y is a necessary consequence of X, then there is nothing anyone can do to change Y either.

Rule Beta has been called a "Transfer of Powerlessness Principle." For it says in effect that if we are "powerless" to change X, and if Y is necessarily going to occur if X does, and we are powerless to change that also, then we are also powerless to change Y. In other words, our powerlessness to change X "transfers" to anything that necessarily follows from X.

This Rule Beta also seems intuitively correct, according to van Inwagen. If we can't do anything to prevent X from occurring and Y is *necessarily* going to occur if X does, how could we do anything to prevent Y from occurring? Consider an example. Suppose the sun is going to explode in the year 2050 and there is nothing we can now do to change that fact. There is also nothing we can now do to change the fact that, if the sun explodes in 2050, all life on earth will end in 2050. If both these claims are true, it seems obvious that there is nothing anyone can now do to change the fact that all life on earth will end in 2050. Here is another example. If there is nothing anyone can now do to change the laws of nature, and nothing anyone can now do to change the fact that the laws of nature entail that nothing goes faster than the speed of light, then there is nothing anyone can now do to change the fact that nothing goes faster than the speed of light.

One could go on adding examples like these supporting Rule Beta. Suffice it to say that Rule Beta does *seem* to be as undeniable as Rule Alpha (which says that no one can change what is necessarily so); and if Rule Beta is also valid, since the other premises of the Consequence Argument seem undeniable, the argument would be both valid and sound, as van Inwagen and other incompatibilists claim. The Consequence Argument would show that determinism conflicts with anyone's power to do otherwise and thus conflicts with free will.

3. An Objection Concerning "Can" and "Power"

The Consequence Argument is a powerful argument for the incompatibility of free will and determinism, and it has swayed many persons. But it is also a controversial argument and has generated much debate. As you would expect, compatibilists and soft determinists reject the Consequence Argument. They must reject it or their views would be refuted in one fell swoop. But where do compatibilists and other critics of the Consequence Argument think it goes wrong, if it goes wrong at all? Most critics of the argument tend to focus on the crucial expression "There is nothing we can now do to change . . ." which appears in many steps of the version of the Consequence Argument presented in section 2. This expression contains the word "can"—one of the most difficult words in the language to interpret.

Talking about what persons "can" (and "cannot") do is talking about their *powers* or *abilities*. So how you interpret persons' powers and abilities has an obvious bearing on the Consequence Argument. For example, compatibilist critics of the Consequence Argument often argue that if you interpret terms like "can," "power," and "ability" in the *hypothetical* way proposed by classical compatibilists, the Consequence Argument will fail. As we saw in chapter 2, according to classical compatibilists, to say

"You *can* (or you have the *power* or the *ability*) to do something" means there are no *constraints* or *impediments* preventing you from doing it, so that

"You *would* do it, *if* you chose or wanted to do it."

Such an analysis of "can," "power," or "ability" is called "hypothetical" (or "conditional") because it has an "if" in it. But how does such an analysis refute the Consequence Argument? First, consider the initial two premises of the Consequence Argument: "There is nothing we can now do to change the past" and "There is nothing we can now do to change the laws of nature." On the hypothetical analysis of "can," to say we can change the past or the laws would mean that

"We *would* change the past or the laws of nature, *if* we *chose* or *wanted* to."

Now this claim is false. No persons would change the past or the laws of nature, *even if* they chose or wanted to, because no one has the power or ability to do it. So the initial *premises* of the Consequence Argument come out *true* on this compatibilist analysis. There is nothing anyone can now do to change the past and the laws of nature *even on the hypothetical analysis of "can"* favored by many compatibilists.

But the hypothetical analysis gives a different answer when we consider the *conclusion* of the Consequence Argument: "There is nothing any persons can do to change the fact that their present actions occur," or in other words, "No persons can do otherwise than they actually do." To show why this conclusion fails on the hypothetical analysis of "can," consider a simple everyday action, such as Molly's raising her hand. To say that Molly could have done otherwise than raise her hand (to say, for example, that she could have kept her hand by her side) means, on the hypothetical analysis, that

"She would have done otherwise than raise her hand, if she had chosen or wanted to do otherwise."

Now, as noted in chapter 2, this hypothetical claim can be true even if Molly's action was determined. For the hypothetical claim simply implies that Molly would have done otherwise, *if the past had been different in some way*—that is, if (contrary to fact) she had chosen or wanted differently.

Note that making this hypothetical claim does not imply that Molly could have *changed* the past or the laws of nature from what they actually were. The hypothetical claim merely means that no constraints or impediments would have prevented her from acting differently, *if she had chosen or wanted differently;* and this may well be true even though she did *not* in fact choose or want differently. In other words, with ordinary everyday actions, such as raising one's hand or getting on a bus, there may *sometimes* be constraints preventing us from doing them or doing otherwise (we may be tied up, paralyzed, or coerced). But often there may be no such constraints preventing us from doing these everyday things; and so we could have done them if we had wanted. By contrast, there are *always* constraints preventing us from changing the past and laws of nature.

As a result, the *premises* of the Consequence Argument come out *true* on the compatibilist hypothetical analysis of "can": Molly *cannot* change the past or the laws of nature, even if she wants to. But the *conclusion* of the Consequence Argument comes out *false:* Molly *can* nonetheless sometimes do otherwise than she actually does (e.g., do otherwise than raise her hand), in the hypothetical sense, because nothing *would* have prevented her, if she had wanted to. So, on the hypothetical analysis, the Consequence Argument would have true premises but a false conclusion, and it would be an invalid argument.

You might wonder at this point what *part* of the Consequence Argument goes wrong in this case—which premise or rule. The answer is Rule Beta. Even defenders of the Consequence Argument, such as van Inwagen, concede that Rule Beta is the hardest part of the argument to defend (though they themselves believe Rule Beta is valid). Rule Beta licenses the inference that gets one to the conclusion of the Consequence Argument (step 6), from steps 1 to 5: if there is nothing we can now do to change the past and the laws and nothing we can now do to change the fact that our present actions are the necessary consequences of the past and the laws, then we cannot now do otherwise than we actually do. On the compatibilist hypothetical analysis of "can," the premises of this inference are true, while its conclusion is false. For on the hypothetical analysis of "can" there *is* nothing we can now do to change the past and the laws of nature, but there is something we can now do to change ordinary actions, such as raising our hand. Rule Beta is therefore invalid (it has counterexamples); and the Consequence Argument fails.

4. Defenders of the Consequence Argument Respond

Now this objection to the Consequence Argument works, of course, only *if* the hypothetical analysis of "can," "power," or "ability" favored by classical compatibilists is correct. But why should we believe this hypothetical analysis of "can" and "power"? Defenders of the Consequence Argument, such as van Inwagen and Carl Ginet, see no good reason to believe in the compatibilists' analysis of these notions and so they typically respond to the above argument in the following way:

> So the hypothetical analyses of "can" (or "power" and "could have done
> otherwise") that you compatibilists favor would refute Rule Beta and the Con-
> sequence Argument. Should that make us incompatibilist defenders of the
> Consequence Argument doubt Rule Beta and the Consequence Argument?
> Not at all. It just gives us another reason for doubting your compatibilist hy-
> pothetical analysis of "can," which we never thought was very plausible in the
> first place. If your analysis allows you to say that Molly can do otherwise
> (than raise her hand), even though she can't change the past and the laws of
> nature and even though her action (of raising her hand) is a necessary conse-
> quence of the past and the laws of nature, *then something must be wrong
> with the hypothetical analysis* of "can" that you compatibilists favor. The
> premises and rules of the Consequence Argument, including Rule Beta, seem
> more intuitively true to us than any hypothetical analysis of "can." So, if we
> have to reject one or the other, we would reject your compatibilist analysis
> rather than the Consequence Argument. In fact, hypothetical analyses of
> "can" and "could have done otherwise" that many compatibilists favor are
> subject to serious objections anyway. So they should be rejected in any case
> and not just because one favors the Consequence Argument.[2]

What are the "serious objections" to hypothetical analyses of "can" and
"could have done otherwise" referred to in this passage? The objection
that many philosophers regard as the most serious goes like this: hypothetical analyses of "can" and "could have done otherwise" sometimes
(wrongly) tell us that agents can do otherwise, or could have done otherwise, in cases where it is clear that the agents could *not* have done otherwise. So the hypothetical analyses must be wrong. Here is an example of
Michael McKenna's illustrating this objection. Suppose that Danielle has
been scarred by a terrible childhood accident involving a blond Labrador
retriever. The accident rendered her

> psychologically incapable of wanting to touch a blond haired dog. Imagine
> that, on her sixteenth birthday, unaware of her condition, her father brings
> her two puppies to choose between, one being a blond haired Lab, the other
> a black haired Lab. He tells Danielle just to pick up whichever of the two
> she pleases and that he will return the other puppy to the pet store. Danielle
> happily, and unencumbered, does what she wants and picks up the black
> Lab.[3]

Was Danielle free to *do otherwise* (*could* she have done otherwise) than
pick up the black Lab? It seems not, McKenna says. Given her traumatic
childhood experience, she cannot even form a *want* to touch a blond-
haired Lab, hence she could not pick up one.

But notice that the compatibilist hypothetical analysis of "she could have done otherwise" would be true in this case: *If* Danielle *did* want to pick up the blond-haired Lab, then she would have done so. So the hypothetical analysis gives us the wrong answer in this case and in many other similar cases. It tells us Danielle could have done otherwise (because she would have, if she had wanted), when in fact she could *not* have done otherwise (because she could not have *wanted* to do otherwise).

The problem with the hypothetical analysis brought out by this example is the following: to truly capture the meaning of "She *could* have done otherwise," it is not good enough to simply say "She *would* have done otherwise, *if* she had wanted to"; one must add "*and* she *could also have wanted* to do otherwise." But then the hypothetical analysis merely pushes the question of whether the agent could have *done* otherwise back to another question of whether the agent could have *wanted* or *chosen* (or *willed*) to do otherwise. And answering this further question requires another "could" statement ("She could have wanted or chosen to do otherwise"), which in turn requires another hypothetical analysis: "She would have wanted or chosen to do otherwise, *if* she had *wanted or chosen to want or choose* otherwise." And the same question would arise about this further hypothetical analysis, requiring yet another "could" statement to be analyzed, and so on indefinitely.

The result is an infinite regress that would never allow one to eliminate the word "could" and would never allow one to definitively answer the original question of whether the agent could have done otherwise—which shows that something has gone wrong with the hypothetical analysis. For reasons such as this, defenders of the Consequence Argument think the hypothetical analysis of "could have done otherwise" favored by classical compatibilists is flawed. Such an analysis would undermine the Consequence Argument, if it were correct. But there are reasons to think it is not correct.

At this point, debates about the Consequence Argument tend to reach an impasse. Defenders of the Consequence Argument think its premises and rules are far more plausible than any compatibilist analysis of "could have done otherwise" (hypothetical or otherwise), while compatibilists obviously think the opposite. Many compatibilists today do concede that the *classical* compatibilist analysis of "could have done otherwise" may be flawed, for the reasons just given or for other reasons. But these same modern compatibilists insist that defenders of the Consequence Argument are begging the question when they assume that *no* compatibilist analysis of "could have done otherwise" could possibly be right, merely because the classical compatibilist analysis is flawed.

Perhaps this is so. But then the burden of proof lies with compatibilists to give a better account of "could have done otherwise" than classical compatibilists have offered—or to find some other way to refute the Consequence Argument. We shall see in later chapters that modern compatibilists have tried to do one or another of these two things. Some modern compatibilists have sought better compatibilist analyses of "could have done otherwise." Others have sought entirely new ways of refuting the Consequence Argument.

Suggested Reading

Van Inwagen's defense of the Consequence Argument is in his *An Essay on Free Will* (Oxford: Clarendon, 1983). The Consequence Argument is also defended by Carl Ginet in *On Action* (Cambridge, 1990). Other discussions for and against the Consequence Argument are included in the collections of readings cited in the suggested readings of chapter 1.

CHAPTER 4

Libertarianism, Indeterminism, and Chance

1. Libertarianism Defined

Even if some argument for incompatibilism, such as the Consequence Argument, should succeed, that success would not by itself show that we have free will. A successful argument for incompatibilism would show only that free will and determinism cannot both be true. If one is true, the other must be false. Thus, incompatibilists may go in either of two directions. They may affirm free will and deny determinism, or affirm determinism and deny free will. Incompatibilists who affirm free will and deny determinism are called *libertarians* in modern free will debates. It is this libertarian view that we are now going to consider. (The opposing view—affirming determinism and denying free will—is called hard determinism, and it will be considered in chapter 7.)

People who are libertarians about free will see themselves as defenders of the "deeper" freedom of the will of chapter 1, which they believe to be incompatible with determinism. This deeper freedom, as libertarians see it, is the "true" free will that most people have traditionally believed in before they began to worry about determinism. From the libertarian point of view, compatibilists give us only a pale image of this true freedom (a "wretched subterfuge," as Immanuel Kant said); libertarians claim to give us the real thing. But giving us the real thing (if libertarian free will really is the real thing) turns out to be more difficult than one may at first imagine, as we shall see in this chapter and the next.

Libertarianism will thus be defined from this point onward as the view that (1) free will and determinism are incompatible (incompatibilism),

(2) free will exists, and so (3) determinism is false. Libertarianism in this sense—libertarianism *about free will*—should not be confused with the political doctrine of libertarianism, the view that governments should be limited to protecting the liberties of individuals as long as the individuals do not interfere with the liberties of others. Libertarianism about free will and political libertarianism share a name—from the Latin *liber,* meaning "free"—and they share an interest in freedom. But libertarians about free will are not necessarily committed to all the views about limited government held by political libertarians. Libertarians about free will can in fact (and many do) hold different political views—conservative, liberal, libertarian, or whatever—so long as they share a commitment to the ideal of persons having responsibility for their actions and their lives in an ultimate sense that is incompatible with determinism.

2. The Libertarian Dilemma: Ascent and Descent Problems

To defend libertarianism about free will, one obviously has to do more than merely argue for the incompatibility of free will and determinism, as important as that may be. One must also show that we can actually have a free will that is incompatible with determinism. Many people believe that an incompatibilist free will of the kind that libertarians affirm is not even possible or intelligible and that it has no place in the modern scientific picture of the world. Critics of libertarianism note that libertarians have often invoked obscure and mysterious forms of agency or causation to defend their view.

To explain how free actions can escape the clutches of physical causes and laws of nature, libertarians have posited transempirical power centers, nonmaterial egos, noumenal selves outside space and time, unmoved movers, uncaused causes, and other unusual forms of agency or causation— thereby inviting charges of obscurity or mystery against their view. Even some of the greatest defenders of libertarianism, such as Immanuel Kant, have argued that we need to believe in libertarian freedom to make sense of morality and true responsibility, but we cannot completely understand such a freedom in theoretical and scientific terms.

The problem that provokes this widespread skepticism about libertarian free will has to do with the dilemma mentioned in chapter 1 and touched upon in chapter 2: if free will is not compatible with determinism, it does not seem to be compatible with *indeterminism* either. Let us call this the "Libertarian Dilemma."[1] Events that are undetermined, such as quantum

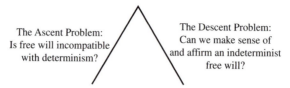

The Ascent Problem:
Is free will incompatible
with determinism?

The Descent Problem:
Can we make sense of
and affirm an indeterminist
free will?

Figure 4.1   Incompatibilist Mountain and the Libertarian
Dilemma

jumps in atoms, happen merely by chance. So if free actions must be
undetermined, as libertarians claim, it seems that they too would happen
by chance. But how can chance events be free and responsible actions? To
solve the Libertarian Dilemma, libertarians must not only show that free
will is *incompatible* with *determinism,* they must also show how free will
can be *compatible* with *indeterminism.*

Imagine that the task for libertarians in solving this dilemma is to
ascend to the top of a mountain and get down the other side. (Call the
mountain "Incompatibilist Mountain": figure 4.1). Getting to the top consists in showing that free will is incompatible with determinism. (Call it
the Ascent Problem.) Getting down the other side (call it the Descent
Problem) involves showing how one can make sense of a free will that
requires *indeterminism.*

Getting to the top of this mountain—demonstrating that free will and
determinism are incompatible—is a difficult enough task for libertarians, as
we have seen in chapter 3. But many critics of libertarianism believe the Descent Problem—making sense of a free will that requires indeterminism—
is even more difficult. Mountain climbers say that the descent from a mountain peak is often more difficult and dangerous than the ascent; and this may
be the case for libertarians. The air is thin and cold up there on Incompatibilist Mountain; and if you stay up for any length of time, say critics of
libertarianism, your mind gets foggy. You start having visions of fantastical
ideas, such as transempirical power centers, noumenal selves, and unmoved
movers, which libertarians have often invoked to explain their view.

3. Indeterminism the Bogeyman

Why is it so difficult to make sense of a free will that requires indeterminism (and hence to solve the Descent Problem) without slipping into mystery or obscurity? Some of the difficulties that indeterminism poses for
free will were suggested in earlier chapters. But let us see if we can get an
overview of them.

1. First, one often hears critics of libertarianism argue that events that are undetermined happen merely by chance and are not under the *control* of anything, hence are not under the control of the agent. It is not "up to" agents whether undetermined events occur or not. But if events are not under the control of an agent, they cannot be free and responsible actions.

2. A related argument was suggested in chapter 1. Suppose a choice was the result of a quantum jump or other undetermined event in a person's brain. Would this amount to a free and responsible choice? Such undetermined effects in the brain or body would be unpredictable and impulsive— like the sudden occurrence of a thought or the spasmodic jerking of an arm that one could not have predicted or influenced—quite the opposite of what we take free and responsible actions to be. It seems that undetermined events happening in the brain or the body would occur *spontaneously* and would be more likely to *undermine* our freedom rather than to *enhance* our freedom.

3. Nor would it help to suppose that the indeterminism or chance came *between* our choices and our actions. Imagine that you have chosen to make a delicate cut in a fine piece of cloth, but because of an undetermined twitching in your arm, you make the wrong cut. In this case, the undetermined twitching in your arm was no enhancement of your freedom, but a hindrance or obstacle to your carrying out your intended purposes. Critics of libertarian freedom often contend that this is what indeterminism would always be—a *hindrance* or *impediment* to freedom. It would get in the way, diminishing rather than enhancing *control* and *responsibility* for what happens. Note that the twitching of your arm is actually a *constraint* on your freedom in the classical compatibilist sense, since it *prevents* you from doing what you *want* to do, that is, make the delicate cut properly. So, far from giving us more freedom, it seems that indeterminism would turn out to be another kind of impediment limiting our freedom.

4. Even more absurd consequences follow if we suppose that indeterminism or chance is involved in the initiation of everyday actions. A nineteenth-century critic of undetermined free action, Arthur Schopenhauer, imagined the case of a man who suddenly found his legs start to move *by chance,* carrying him across the room against his wishes.[2] Is this what libertarians have in mind, Schopenhauer asked, when they insist that free actions must be undetermined? Such caricatures are popular among critics of indeterminist freedom for obvious reasons: undetermined or chance-initiated actions would represent the opposite of free and responsible actions.

5. Going a little deeper, critics of libertarian freedom also note that, if choices or actions are undetermined, they may occur otherwise, *given exactly the same past and laws of nature.* This follows, as we saw, from

indeterminism, which implies different possible futures, given the same past. But such a requirement has troubling consequences regarding free choices, as noted in chapter 2. Here is a further example illustrating the problem. Suppose Mike, who is deliberating about whether to vacation in Hawaii or Colorado, gradually comes to favor and choose Hawaii. If Mike's choice, when he finally makes it, was undetermined, as libertarians require, then he might have chosen otherwise (chosen to visit Colorado instead), given exactly the same deliberation up to the moment of choice that in fact led him to favor and choose Hawaii (the same thoughts, reasoning, beliefs, desires, and so on). As noted in our discussion of Molly's choosing a career, it is difficult to make sense of this. Mike's choosing Colorado in such circumstances (in which he had come to favor Hawaii) would seem irrational and inexplicable, capricious and arbitrary. If the choice of Hawaii came about by virtue of undetermined events in Mike's brain, this would not be an occasion for rejoicing in his freedom, but for consulting a neurologist about the waywardness of his neural processes.

4. Reasons, Randomness, and Luck

6. At this point, some defenders of indeterminist freedom appeal to the claim of the eighteenth-century philosopher Gottfried Leibniz, that prior reasons or motives need not determine choice or action, they may merely "incline without necessitating."[3] For example, Mike's reasons for wanting to vacation in Colorado (he likes skiing and wants to meet friends there) might "incline" him to choose Colorado over Hawaii. But these reasons do not "necessitate" or determine that he will choose Colorado. Similarly his reasons for favoring Hawaii (he also likes beaches and surfing) incline him toward Hawaii without determining that choice.

Leibniz's claim that reasons may "incline without necessitating" is an important one. But, unfortunately, it will not solve the problem about Mike's choice described in objection 5. For it is precisely *because* Mike's prior reasons and motives (his beliefs and desires about beaches and surfing) inclined him more strongly toward the choice of Hawaii that his choosing Colorado by chance at the end of the same deliberation would be arbitrary, irrational, and inexplicable. Similarly, if his reasons had inclined him more strongly toward Colorado, then choosing Hawaii by chance at the end of the same deliberation would have been irrational and inexplicable.

What if Mike's prior reasons and motives had not inclined him more strongly to *either* alternative? Then, if the choice were undetermined, matters would be even worse. For the choice would then be doubly arbitrary—arbitrary either way he might choose. Medieval philosophers, who discussed free will, had a name for the condition of an agent who has no better reasons for choosing one option rather than the other. They called it "liberty of indifference." You have probably heard the well-known illustration of the liberty of indifference involving Buridan's ass—the donkey that starved between two equidistant bales of hay because it had no reason to choose one over the other.

Jean Buridan was a medieval French philosopher to whom this famous example of the donkey is often wrongly attributed. The original example goes back to the medieval Arabic philosopher Al-Ghazzali, who imagined a camel starving between two groves of date trees. These examples of the liberty of indifference were often used later by philosophers, such as Hume and Schopenhauer, to ridicule libertarian or indeterminist free will. (Al-Ghazzali had used his example for a similar purpose.) Of course, a human, who was not an ass, would undoubtedly not starve to death in these conditions. It would be better to flip a coin and choose one option arbitrarily or by chance than to go without food altogether. But such a solution to the liberty of indifference—choosing by a coin flip—still amounts to choosing arbitrarily or by chance. Is that what indeterminist freedom amounts to?

7. Indeed, another frequently heard objection to indeterminist free will is precisely that undetermined free choices must *always* amount to mere *random* choices, like flipping a coin or spinning a wheel to select from among a set of alternatives. Perhaps there is a role for random choices in our lives—for sometimes settling choices by a coin flip or spinning a wheel—when we are indifferent to the outcomes. (Which movie should I see tonight when I like both available options?) But suppose that *all* our free and responsible choices—including momentous ones, like whether to act heroically or treacherously, to lie to a friend, or to marry one person rather than another—had to be settled by random selection in this way. Such a consequence, according to most philosophers, would be a reduction to absurdity of the view that free will and responsibility require indeterminism.

8. Finally, consider the following objection, which has been suggested by a number of critics of indeterminist free choice.[4] We may call it the "Luck Objection." Indeterminism, as noted earlier, implies different possible futures, given exactly the same past. Suppose then that two agents had exactly the same pasts up to a point at which they were faced with a choice between distorting the truth for selfish gain or telling the truth at great personal cost. One agent lies and the other tells the truth. Bruce Waller summarizes this objection as follows: if the pasts of these two agents "are really identical" in every way up to the moment of choice, "and the difference in their acts results from chance," would there "be any

grounds for distinguishing between [them], for saying that one person deserves censure for a selfish decision and the other deserves praise?"[5]

Another critic, Alfred Mele, poses the same problem in terms of a single agent in different possible worlds. Suppose that in the actual world, John fails to resist the temptation to do what he thinks he should not do, arrive on time at a meeting. If John could have done otherwise given the same past, then we could imagine that his counterpart, John*, in an alternative possible world (which is exactly the same as the actual world up to the moment of choice) resists the temptation and arrives on time. Mele then argues that "if there is nothing about the agents' powers, capacities, states of mind, moral character and the like that explains this difference in outcome, . . . the difference is just a matter of luck." It would seem that John* got lucky in his attempt to overcome temptation, while John did not. Would it be fair or just to reward the one and punish the other for what appears to be ultimately the luck of the draw?[6]

5. The Indeterminist Condition and Extra Factor Strategies

Objections such as the eight outlined in sections 3 and 4 lie behind the many charges often heard in the history of free will debates against libertarian free will—charges that undetermined actions would be "arbitrary," "capricious," "random," "uncontrolled," "irrational," "inexplicable," or "matters of luck or chance"—anything but free and responsible actions. The first task for libertarians, if they are to make sense of their view and solve the Descent Problem, is to address these familiar charges.

To understand how libertarians have gone about the task of trying to answer these charges, it helps to note that the problem lying behind all the objections just given is the problem of reconciling free actions with what we may call

The Indeterminist Condition: the agent should be able to act and act otherwise (choose different possible futures), *given the same past circumstances and laws of nature.*

It is this Indeterminist Condition that makes it seem irrational and inexplicable, capricious and arbitrary, for Mike to choose to vacation in Colorado given the same prior deliberation that in fact led him to favor and choose Hawaii. It is the same Indeterminist Condition that leads Mele to argue that if the circumstances of John and John* are exactly the same up to the moment of choice (if there is no difference in their "powers, capacities, states of mind, moral character and the like"), then "there is nothing about the agents that explains" why John failed to overcome the temptation and John* did not—except luck.

Reflecting on this Indeterminist Condition gives us some insight into the strategies libertarians have traditionally employed in their attempts to make sense of libertarian free will. Libertarians have typically reasoned in the following way. If agents may act or act otherwise, given the same past circumstances and laws of nature, then some *additional* factor *not included among the past circumstances or laws* must account for the difference in outcome—for an agent's acting or choosing in one way rather than the other. The agent's acting differently cannot be accounted for solely by the circumstances of the agent prior to action because, by hypothesis, there is no difference in these prior circumstances. So if the outcome is not to be merely random, arbitrary, and inexplicable, an extra factor must be involved over and above the past circumstances and laws to account for it.

Let us call any such strategy for making sense of libertarian free will an "extra-factor strategy." Throughout history, libertarians have regularly invoked some extra factor or other to explain how free will is possible in their sense. But the extra factors have varied. Libertarians have invoked immaterial minds or souls, noumenal selves outside space and time, special forms of agent causation that cannot be reduced to scientific modes of causation, "acts of will" or "volitions" that cannot by nature be determined by prior events, "reasons" or "purposes" or "final causes" that explain actions without being antecedent causes of actions, and so on. These extra factors are meant to explain why free choices or actions do not merely occur in an arbitrary, capricious, random, uncontrolled, or irrational way—even though the choices or actions are undetermined by prior causes and laws.

In the next chapter, we shall consider some of the most important traditional extra-factor strategies by which libertarians have attempted to make sense of the deeper kind of free will they believe in.

Suggested Reading

There are many critiques of the libertarian position on free will. Three readable critiques are Richard Double, *The Non-reality of Free Will* (Oxford, 1991), Bruce Waller, *Freedom Without Responsibility* (Temple, 1990), and Ted Honderich, *How Free Are You?* (Oxford, 1993). A useful collection of readings for and against libertarian views of freedom is *Agents, Causes, and Events: Essays on Free Will and Indeterminism,* edited by Timothy O'Connor (Oxford, 1995).

CHAPTER 5

Minds, Selves, and Agent Causes

1. Mind–Body Dualism

The most obvious extra-factor strategy that comes to mind when people think about how to make sense of libertarian free will involves a *dualism* of mind and body (such as that of René Descartes.) If the "mind" or "soul" were distinct from the body, it would be outside the physical world and its activity would not be governed by laws of nature that govern physical events. If, in addition, a disembodied mind or soul could interact with the physical world by influencing the brain, as Descartes imagined, then the mind or soul would be the "extra factor" libertarians need to explain free choice. Whatever could not be fully explained by the activity of brain or body might be explained by the activity of the mind or soul.

For such a dualist solution to the free will problem to work, the physical world would have to cooperate, allowing some indeterminism in nature, perhaps in the brain. It may be true that quantum jumps or other undetermined events in the brain would not by themselves amount to free choices. But undetermined events in the brain might provide the "leeway" or "causal gaps" in nature through which an extra factor, such as an immaterial mind or soul, might intervene in the physical world to influence physical events.

Those who take this dualist approach to free will could thus accept the Indeterminist Condition in a qualified form: they could say that free agents are able to choose or choose otherwise, all past *physical* circumstances remaining the same (because physical circumstances are the kind that are governed by laws of nature). But the activity of the agent's mind or soul would not be among the physical circumstances and would not be governed by laws of nature; and the activity of an immaterial mind or soul could account for why one choice was made rather than another. Thus free choices would not be arbitrary, random, or inexplicable after all; nor would they occur merely by chance or luck, even though it might look that way, if one just described the physical world.

This dualist solution to the free will problem has been tempting through the ages and still is. Many people naturally tend to think mind–body dualism is the obvious and perhaps the only way to solve the free will problem. So it is important to understand why many philosophers believe that affirming a dualism of mind and body will not by itself solve the problems about libertarian free will discussed in chapter 4. Let us put aside for the moment the usual philosophical concerns people have about an "interactionist" mind–body dualism of the kind posited by Descartes: How does an immaterial mind act on a physical body? Where does the mind act on the body? Are the laws of nature violated by the intervention of the mind, and if so, how? Whatever problems of these kinds a dualism of mind and body may have, the point of interest for us is that an appeal to mind–body dualism will not of itself solve the problems about free will posed by indeterminism that we have been considering.

To see why, ask the following question: if a free choice (such as Molly's choice to join the law firm in Dallas or Mike's to vacation in Hawaii or John's to arrive late) is not determined by the prior *physical* activity of the agent's brain, is the choice determined by the prior *mental* activity of the agent's mind or soul? Dualists who are libertarians about free will must answer that free choices in a libertarian sense cannot be determined by the prior activity of a disembodied mind or soul any more than free choices can be determined by prior physical activity of the body. For, determinism either way would rule out the possibility of doing otherwise, hence would rule out libertarian free will. If God had so made us that the activities and effects of our *minds* were also determined, we would be no better off *regarding free will* just because our minds were separate from our bodies.

But if determinism by the mind is no more acceptable than determinism by the body, then dualists who want to defend libertarian free will cannot merely say that Molly (or Mike or John) could have chosen or chosen otherwise, given all the same past *physical* circumstances. Dualists must also say that free agents could have chosen or chosen otherwise, given all the same past physical *and mental* circumstances. If dualists do *not* say this, they will not really have avoided determinism. But if dualists *do* say this, all the original problems about the Indeterminist Condition will come back to haunt them. If Molly might have chosen the law firm in Austin, given all the same prior thoughts, reasoning, and other mental (as well as physical) circumstances that in fact led her to favor the Dallas firm, then her choice to join the Austin firm would have been just as irrational, inexplicable, and arbitrary if it issued from a disembodied mind or soul as it would if it had issued from an embodied person. If John and John* might have chosen differently, given exactly the same mental (and physical) histories up to the moment when they did choose, then Mele's question comes back to haunt us: "What can account for the difference in their choices—why John failed to overcome the temptation and John* did not—except luck?"

For reasons such as these, placing the agent's thoughts and deliberations in a disembodied mind or soul does not solve the problems about an undetermined free will. Dualism simply transfers these problems to another level, from the physical sphere to the mental. That is why a critic of libertarianism, such as Simon Blackburn, can say: "The dualist approach to free will makes a fundamental philosophical mistake. It sees a problem and tries to solve it by throwing another kind of 'thing' into the arena [the controlling soul]. But it forgets to ask how the new 'thing' escapes the problems that beset ordinary things. . . . If we cannot understand how human beings are free [in a libertarian sense], we cannot understand how [a disembodied mind] can be free" either.[1] Of course, Blackburn's comment does not mean that dualism is necessarily false. But it does mean that appealing to a mind or soul separate from the body will not by itself solve the problem of free will, as some people have believed.

Dualists might appeal to mystery at this point. "We don't know very much about disembodied minds or soul-substances or how they operate," they may say. "How can we be sure an immaterial mind could not make undetermined choices that are not merely random, arbitrary, capricious, and inexplicable?" True enough. We do not know. But if dualists rely on this response and do nothing more, they merely confirm the most common criticism made of libertarian theories of free will—that one cannot make sense of libertarian free will without ultimately appealing to mystery of some kind or other. A great twentieth-century physicist, Erwin Schrödinger, once said something relevant to this point: "At the price of mystery," he said, "you can have anything"—though, we might add, in the words of Bertrand Russell, that you get it too easily, acquiring it by theft rather than honest toil.

2. Kant and Noumenal Selves

Some libertarians concede that libertarian free will is, and must always remain, mysterious. As noted earlier, Immanuel Kant thought libertarian freedom was necessary to make sense of morality and true responsibility.

But Kant also held that a libertarian freedom could not be understood in theoretical or scientific terms.[2] Science and reason, said Kant, can tell us only the way things *appear* to us in space and time—the world of *phenomena*. But science and reason cannot tell us about the way things are in themselves—the *noumena*. Thus, when scientists try to explain why an agent makes one free choice rather than another, if they are biochemists or neurologists, they will appeal to prior states and processes of agent's brain and body, which appear to us in space and time. If the scientists are psychologists, they will appeal to prior states and processes of the agent's mind which, according to Kant, appear to us in time, but not space. But, in either case, the scientists will fail to explain why one free choice occurs rather than another. For, if the choices are undetermined, it seems that the occurrence of one free choice rather than another cannot be adequately explained by prior states and processes of any kinds, physical or mental.

Now Kant in fact believed that all events occurring in space and time were determined. Writing in the eighteenth century, Kant was convinced that the mechanistic physics of Newton provided the true explanation of the physical world and that this physics was deterministic. But we do not have to assume that science is deterministic, as Kant did, to arrive at a conclusion like his—that free choices cannot be explained by science. For *viewed from science's perspective within space and time,* if free choices were *not* determined, then they would appear to be merely random events, such as quantum jumps in atoms. Either way—determined or random—they would not be free choices. So, had Kant known modern physics, he might have responded in this way: "Free choices can no more be explained by an indeterministic (quantum) physics than they can be explained by a deterministic (Newtonian) physics. I may have been wrong about the truth of Newton's physics. But I was not wrong in concluding that free choices are beyond scientific explanation."

Yet, we also know Kant thought we had to believe in libertarian free will even if science could not explain it. Such a free will was presupposed by our *practical* reason, and, in particular, by our moral life.[3] When we deliberate in practical life about whether to keep a promise to a friend, Kant reasoned, we must presuppose we can keep the promise *or* break it and that it is "up to us" what we do. If we did not believe this, deliberating would make no sense. But if we can keep the promise or break it, then the law governing our behavior is a moral law ("You ought to keep your promises") that we can choose to follow *or* to violate.

Kant believed that being governed by such a moral "law" is quite different from being governed by scientific "laws" of nature. Laws of nature are imposed upon us from outside and we cannot choose whether or not to obey them. By contrast, to act in accordance with a moral law is to be, in Kant's terms, *self-legislating* or *autonomous* (from the Greek *auto* [self] and *nomos* [law]). It is to be governed by a law we give to ourselves, a law we can choose to obey or not obey. Kant held that in our practical moral lives, we must suppose ourselves to be self-legislating or autonomous beings. Such *autonomy*—which amounted to *free will* for him—is not compatible with being governed by scientific laws of nature.

As a result, there is a difference (and a tension) in Kant's view between our *practical* or moral reasoning, which requires that we believe in libertarian free will, and our *theoretical* or scientific reasoning, which cannot explain this freedom. Kant tried to lessen this tension by claiming that science and reason describe the self only as it appears to us in space and time (the phenomenal self), not the self or person as it is "in itself" (the noumenal self). Our real or noumenal selves can be free, he argues, because they are not subject to the constraints of space and time or the laws of nature.

But when science and reason try to explain *how* the noumenal self can be free, they inevitably look for physical, psychological, or social causes of our behavior; and then the scientists are describing only the self as it appears to us, the phenomenal self, not the noumenal or real self. Indeed, anything we might say *about* this noumenal self—about its states or activities—would be describing its physical, psychological, or social circumstances, hence would be describing the phenomenal, not the real, self. The noumenal self is thus the "extra factor" in Kant's theory that is supposed to account for free will. But we cannot say *how* it does so. If free will were the product of a noumenal self in Kant's sense, it would indeed be a mystery.

3. Agent-causation

You can see from the preceding discussion why many modern philosophers who would like to believe in libertarian free will are not satisfied with either mind–body dualist or Kantian solutions to the free will problem. Both dualist and Kantian views require strong and controversial metaphysical assumptions without at the same time solving the problems about indeterminism and chance that make most people reject libertarian free will in the first place. The third traditional libertarian strategy we are going to consider has been more popular among contemporary philosophers. Sometimes this third strategy is combined with other libertarian strategies, such a dualism; but more often it is defended on its own.

This third libertarian strategy is often called an *agent–causal* strategy—or a theory of *agent-causation*—because it focuses on the notion of causation by agents. Free agents are capable of causing their own free acts in a special way, according to agent-causal views, a way that is not reducible to causation by circumstances, events, or states of affairs. Here is how Roderick Chisholm, a well-known defender of this kind of view, puts the matter:

> If we consider only inanimate natural objects, we may say that causation, if it occurs, is a relation between *events* or *states of affairs*. The dam's breaking was an event that was caused by a set of other events—the dam being weak, the flood being strong, and so on. But if a man is responsible for a particular deed, then . . . there is some event [his deed or action] . . . that is caused, *not* by other events or states of affairs, but by the agent, whatever he may be.[4]

Chisholm is suggesting a way out of the Libertarian Dilemma: libertarian free actions cannot be completely *caused* by prior circumstances, events, or states of affairs; and neither can they be *uncaused* or happen merely by chance. But there is a third possibility: we can say that free actions are indeed caused, but not by prior circumstances, events, or states of affairs. Free actions are caused by the *agent* or *self,* which is not a circumstance, event, or state of affairs at all, but a *thing* or *substance* with a continuing existence. We do not have to choose between determinism by prior causes or indeterminism or chance. We can say that free actions are *self*-determined or *agent*-caused even though they are undetermined by events.

Thus the "extra factor" that explains free will for agent-causalists is the agent. Or, to be more precise, the extra factor is a special or unique kind of causal *relation* between an agent and an action that is not reducible to, and cannot be fully explained in terms of, the usual kinds of causation by events, occurrences, and states of affairs, either physical *or* mental. The Indeterminist Condition can thus be true in a general sense on the agent-causal view: the agent may act or act otherwise, given all the same past physical *and* mental circumstances and laws of nature because the factor that makes the difference is causation by something (the agent) that is not a *circumstance* at all in the sense of an event or occurrence or state of affairs, whether physical or mental.

Agent-causation of such a *non-event* or *non-occurrent* kind is unusual, as even its defenders, such as Chisholm, acknowledge. (To indicate its special nature, the expression "agent-causation" is often hyphenated in writings on free will, a practice I am following.) We do in fact regularly speak of *things* or *substances* causing events or occurrences: "The stone broke the window." "The cat caused the lamp to fall." But causation by things or substances can usually be interpreted in everyday life as the causation of events or occurrences by other events or occurrences. It is the stone's *moving* and *striking* the window that caused it to break; and it is the cat's *leaping* onto the table and *hitting* the lamp that caused it to fall. These are *events* involving the stone and the cat, respectively.

But no such paraphrasing in terms of events or occurrences is possible in the case of agent-causation of the non-event or non-occurrent kind that is supposed to explain free will. Agents *non-occurrently* cause things to happen, not by virtue of doing something else or as a result of being in certain states or undergoing changes. In order to account for free actions that are undetermined by prior circumstances, agent-causalists argue that we must recognize another kind of causation alongside the usual causation of events or occurrences by other events or occurrences recognized by the sciences. We must recognize the possibility of direct causation of an event or occurrence by an agent or substance that is a primitive relation, not further analyzable into causation by events or occurrences.

Chisholm illustrates this idea of direct agent-causation by reference to a quotation from Aristotle's *Physics:* "A staff moves a stone, which is moved by a hand, which is moved by a man."[5] The staff's moving the stone is an instance of ordinary causation of an event by another event, which Chisholm calls *transeunt causation:* it is the staff's *moving* that moves the stone. Similarly, the hand's *moving* causes the staff to *move,* so the hand's moving the staff is another instance of transeunt or event causation. But what are we to say of the movement of the hand *by* the agent? Chisholm answers as follows:

> We *may* say that the hand was moved by the man, but we may *also* say that the motion of the hand was caused by the motion of certain muscles; and we may say that the motion of the muscles was caused by certain events that took place within the brain. But some event, and presumably one of those that took place within the brain, was caused by the agent and not by any other events.[6]

In other words, if we are going to say finally that the *agent* did anything for which the agent was responsible, then sooner or later we must say that the agent *directly* caused some event or other in this chain of events (say an event in the brain or a choice to move the stone), not *by* doing something else and *not* by being caused to do it by any other events. As another agent-cause theorist, Richard Taylor, has put it, "some . . . causal chains . . . have beginnings, and they begin with the agents themselves."[7]

Chisholm calls this direct causation by an agent *immanent causation,* to distinguish it from transeunt causation. He adds:

> If what I have been trying to say [about immanent causation] is true, then we have a prerogative which some would attribute only to God: each of us when

we act is a prime mover unmoved. In doing what we do, we cause certain events to happen, and nothing—or no one—causes us to cause those events to happen.[8]

On what grounds does Chisholm say that the agent's immanently causing an event is not caused by other events? The answer, according to Chisholm and other agent-causalists, is that agents are not themselves events or occurrences; so they are not the *kinds* of things that by their nature can be transeuntly caused by other events. If the agent's immanently causing an action could be explained in terms of other events involving the agent (such as states and processes of the agent's brain or mind), then we could ask what caused those other events, and the causal chain would not begin with the agent. But the distinguishing feature of non-event or non-occurrent agent-causation is that it *cannot* be explained in terms of events or occurrences involving the agent. The agent immanently causes an action or event directly and not *by* doing anything else. So there is no other occurrence or event about which to ask: what caused *it?* The causal chain begins with the agent, who is a "prime mover unmoved."

4. Assessing the Agent-causal View: Reid and Causal Power

What are we to say of this agent-causal view? It is not surprising that many critics of libertarian theories of free will find the notion of immanent causation as mysterious as Kantian noumenal selves or Cartesian immaterial minds. To say, as Chisholm does, that we are "prime movers unmoved" or "uncaused causes," like God, does not help, according to these critics, since it merely attempts to explain the obscure by the more obscure. What do we know of how God moves without being moved? And are we humans really like God in this respect, since we *are* clearly moved, at least in part, by many physical, psychological, and social factors, some of which are beyond our awareness?

Even some defenders of agent-causation admit that the notion is mysterious. Richard Taylor, mentioned earlier, says: "One can hardly affirm such a theory of agency with complete comfort . . . and wholly without embarrassment, for the conception of men and their powers which is involved in it, is strange indeed, if not positively mysterious."[9] Yet Taylor thinks such a notion of agent-causation is the only one consistent with libertarian free agency. "If I believe that something not identical to myself was the cause of my behavior —some event wholly external to myself, for instance, or even one internal to myself, such as a nerve impulse, volition, or whatnot—then I cannot regard the behavior as being an act of mine, unless I further believed that I was the cause of that external or internal event."[10]

Chisholm tries to lessen the air of mystery surrounding immanent causation by appealing to eighteenth-century Scottish philosopher Thomas Reid, who is generally regarded as the father of modern agent-cause theories. Reid argued that the notion of agent-causation, far from being derivable from, or reducible to, causation in terms of events, is more fundamental than event-causation. Only by understanding our own causal efficacy as agents can we grasp the notion a *cause* at all: the notion of cause, he says, "may very plausibly be derived from the experience we have . . . of our own power to produce certain effects."[11] We then extend this power from ourselves to other things in the world. But our understanding of causal power comes first from our own experience as agents. So agent-causation may be difficult to understand, according to Reid. But we must believe in it nevertheless because we have direct experience of it in our daily lives; and the concept of event-causation is derived from that of agent-causation, not the other way around. As Chisholm says, taking his cue from Reid, "if we did not understand the concept of immanent causation, we would not understand that of transeunt causation."[12]

Reid and Chisholm may be right that we get our first ideas of causal power from our own experience of agency. Some psychological studies support this idea. But this fact alone does not eliminate the problems surrounding their agent-causal view. The first problem is this: how can we know from the immediate experience of our own agency alone that our actions are not determined by events (some of which may be hidden from us)? We may feel this is not so. We may feel, as Taylor says, that *we,* as agents, are the only determiners of our actions. But how can we be sure? For agent-causalists to say that choices or actions that are immanently caused by agents cannot *by their very nature* be caused by prior events seems to answer this problem by stipulation. In saying such a thing, agent-causalists would seem to be defining immanent causation so that it cannot in principle be caused by other events. If so, they would be getting the result they want for free rather than by honest toil.

5. Agent-causation, Regresses, and Randomness

But for the sake of argument, suppose we grant their stipulation: the immanent causing of an action or event cannot by its nature be determined or caused by other events. Then a second problem arises: if agent-causal events are not determined or caused, are they random? Does the agent-causal theory really eliminate the problem of *randomness* or *arbitrariness* about undetermined free choices? Recall how that problem was posed: if Mike may have chosen to vacation in Hawaii or Colorado, given all the same prior mental and physical circumstances leading to his choice, including exactly the same prior thought processes, why wouldn't his choice of one or the other, Hawaii or Colorado, have been random or arbitrary? Agent-causalists respond that the choice would not have occurred merely randomly or arbitrarily, "out of the blue," so to speak (even though it was undetermined by prior circumstances) because Mike, the *agent,* would have immanently caused whichever choice was made in a way that could not be fully explained by, or reduced to, causation by prior circumstances.

But does this really solve the problem of randomness or arbitrariness? If it would have been irrational, inexplicable, random, or arbitrary for Mike to choose to vacation in Colorado, given the same mental circumstances and at the end of the same deliberation that led him to favor and choose Hawaii, why would it not have been equally irrational, random, arbitrary and so on, for Mike to *agent- (or immanently) cause* the choice to vacation in Colorado (in these same mental circumstances and at the end of the same deliberation that led him to favor and choose Hawaii)? The problem of randomness or arbitrariness, rather than being solved, seems to be merely transferred from the randomness and arbitrariness of the *choices* to the randomness and arbitrariness of *agents'- (immanently)-causing-the-choices.*

Similar questions arise when we consider problems about luck and chance. John succumbed to temptation and chose to arrive at his meeting late. In exactly the same circumstances, John* overcame temptation and chose to arrive on time. According to the Luck Objection, if there is nothing about John's and John*'s powers, capacities, states of mind, moral character, and the like leading up to their choices that explains why John chose one way and John* another, then the difference is just a matter of luck. John got lucky in his attempt to overcome temptation, while John* did not.

Agent-causalists respond that merely because the choices of John and John* were not caused by prior events does not mean they merely occurred out of the blue, uncaused by *anything.* The choices were caused, not by prior events, but by the agents. John agent-caused his choice to arrive late (in a direct or immanent way that could not be explained in terms of causation by prior events) and John* agent-caused his choice to arrive on time in a similarly direct manner. So it was up to them which choice occurred.

But is the Luck Objection really answered by this argument? If it is a matter of luck or chance that John* chose to overcome temptation and John did not, why is it not equally a matter of luck or chance that John* (immanently) *agent-caused*-the-choice to overcome temptation while John did not? Since the immanent agent-causing of one choice rather than another is also undetermined by prior circumstances, then there is nothing about John's and John*'s powers, capacities, states of mind, and other prior circumstances that explains why they immanently *agent-caused* different choices. It seems that problems about luck or chance, like problems about randomness and arbitrariness, are merely transferred from the *choices* to the *agent-causing-of-the-choices* without being solved.

Chisholm is aware of these difficulties. He argues that to be consistent with their general strategy, agent-causalists should respond that the *agent-causing-of-the-choices* is not caused by prior events, but neither does it occur by luck or chance. There is a third option: the agent-causing of the choices is itself immanently caused by the agent. Chisholm realizes that this response unfortunately seems to give rise to an infinite regress: if John (or John*) is the agent-cause of his choice, he is also the agent-cause of his being the agent-cause of his choice and also the agent-cause of his being the agent-cause of his being the agent-cause of his choice, and so on indefinitely. This is an unhappy consequence to say the least: it seems that an infinite series of agent-causings would be needed for each free choice. But Chisholm bites the bullet and accepts this consequence anyway because he thinks that if the regress stopped at any point, it would not be clear that the first immanent causing was "up to the agent" rather than occurring merely randomly or by chance. To make this infinite series of immanent causings seem less a violation of common sense, Chisholm adds that the agents need not be *aware* of all these agent-causings, for the doctrine of agent-causation does not require that agents be aware of all the events they agent-cause.

Nonetheless, most philosophers, and most agent-causalists themselves, are not comfortable with postulating an infinite series of agent-causings, as Chisholm does. Fortunately, there is another alternative open to them that most agent-causalists have preferred. "Chisholm's mistake," many of them say,

> is assuming that agent-causation is an event like any other event that must either be caused or occur randomly. The agent-causal relation is unique and cannot be treated like any other event or occurrence. To ask the question 'if the agent-causal relation is not caused, why doesn't it occur merely randomly or by chance?' is to show you do not really understand what the agent-causal relation is. Immanent agent-causation is not the sort of thing that *can* in principle occur randomly or by

chance, any more than it can in principle be caused. For the agent-causal relation just *is* the agent's exercising conscious control over an event; and an agent's exercising conscious control over an event is not the sort of thing that happens out of the blue, by chance or accident. For by its nature it is up to the agent. We do not need a further agent-causing to explain it.

This response avoids Chisholm's regress, to be sure. But if agent-causalists respond in this way, it seems they are once again solving the problems about libertarian free will by stipulation. In response to the objection that for all we know immanent agent-causation might be determined by hidden causes, they insist that immanent agent-causation is not the sort of thing that could in principle be caused or determined by prior events or circumstances. Now, in response to the randomness and luck objections, they add that the agent-causal relation is not the sort of thing that could in principle occur randomly or by chance either, since it is the agent's consciously controlling something.

To many critics of libertarianism, this solution looks like solving the Libertarian Dilemma—either determinism or mere chance—by a *double* stipulation, by introducing a special agent-causal relation defined in such a way that it (1) cannot by its nature be determined, but (2) cannot by its nature be random either. One can see why many critics of libertarianism think that agent-cause theories either lead to infinite regresses or solve the problems about libertarian free will by defining them out of existence (for "free" rather than by honest toil). Gary Watson states this criticism in the following words:

> All we know of this [agent-causal] relation is that it holds between an agent and an event when the agent is the responsible agent of that event, and the event is uncaused by other events. . . . Agent-causation meets [these] conditions . . . by stipulation. But the challenge is to say what this [agent-causal] relation amounts to in such a way as to give some reason for thinking it is empirically possible. 'Agent-causation' simply labels, not illuminates, what the libertarian needs.[13]

Watson's point is that if agent-causalists are to do more than merely label what libertarians need, they must say more about the nature of agent-causation and do more to show how such a thing is empirically possible. Failing to do that, agent-causalist solutions to the free will problem will remain as mysterious as Kantian and dualist solutions. In the next chapter, we will consider what other strategies are available to libertarians, agent-causalists, and others to make sense of the "deeper" freedom of the will they believe in.

Suggested Reading

Dualist views of free will are defended by John Eccles and Karl Popper, *The Self and Its Brain* (Springer-Verlag, 1977); Richard Swinburne, *The Evolution of the Soul* (Oxford: Clarendon, 1986); John Foster, *The Immaterial Self* (Routledge, 1991); and J. P. Moreland and Scott Rae, *Body and Soul* (InterVarsity, 2000). Kant's view of free will presented in this chapter appears in his *Critique of Pure Reason* and *Foundations of the Metaphysics of Morals*. Chisholm's agent-causal view as expressed in "Human Freedom and the Self" (appears in several edited volumes: Gary Watson, *Free Will,* 2nd ed. (Oxford, 2003); Robert Kane, *Free Will* (Blackwell, 2002); and Laura Waddell Ekstrom, *Agency and Responsibility; Essays on the Metaphysics of Freedom* (Westview, 2000). Thomas Reid's agent-causal view is sympathetically examined in William Rowe's *Thomas Reid on Freedom and Morality* (Cornell, 1991).

CHAPTER 6

Actions, Reasons, and Causes

1. Simple Indeterminism

Some modern libertarians argue that libertarian free will can be explained without the need to appeal to "extra factors" of the kinds discussed in the preceding chapter, such as minds outside space and time or non-event agent-causation. One theory that takes this line is called *simple indeterminism*. The key to understanding free will, according to simple indeterminists, is a distinction between two ways of *explaining* events— explanations in terms of *causes* and explanations in terms of *reasons* or *purposes*. Free actions are *uncaused* events, according to simple indeterminists, but the fact that free actions are uncaused does not mean they occur merely by chance or randomly. The occurrence of free actions, though uncaused, can be explained in terms of the reasons and purposes of agents.

Understanding this simple indeterminist view requires discussion of two topics that play an important role in debates about free will but have not to this point received enough attention: (1) the nature of *explanation* and (2) the nature of *action*. Many problems about free will discussed in chapters 4 and 5 concern the question of how free actions can be *explained* if they are undetermined or uncaused. Questions about how free actions can be explained in turn lead to deeper questions about what makes something an *action* in the first place rather than an event that merely happens (say, by chance or accident). We must now consider these questions about the nature of explanation and action.

An *explanation* of any kind is an answer to a *why* question: Why does something exist? Why did it occur? Why is it so? But in the case of events, there are two kinds of answers to the question "Why did it occur?"—an explanation in terms of causes (e.g., the fire was caused by an explosion) and an explanation in terms of reasons and purposes. And the explanations we usually give when talking about human *actions* are explanations in terms of reasons and purposes. For example, when we ask "Why did Mary enter the room?" we give her reasons in the form of her wants, desires, beliefs, intentions, and goals. Mary entered the room because she *wanted* to find her keys, *believed* she may have left the keys there, and had the *purpose* or *goal* of finding them. Citing these reasons and purposes explains *why* Mary acted as she did. But it does not follow that Mary was caused or determined to act that way, say simple indeterminists. For reasons and purposes are not causes of action, according to them; and explanations in terms of reasons are not causal explanations. Free actions may therefore be *uncaused* without occurring merely by chance or randomly. They occur for a reason or purpose.

But if free actions really are uncaused events, as simple indeterminists claim, what makes them "acts" or "actions" in the first place rather than mere "happenings" occurring out of the blue? (This was the second question just mentioned, about the nature of *action*.) One prominent simple indeterminist, Carl Ginet, answers this question by arguing that an action, such as Mary's entering the room, begins with a simple mental act, a *volition* or act of will that initiates the action. What makes this volition and the action initiated by it actions rather than things that merely "happen" to Mary, according to Ginet, is that the volition and action have a certain "actish phenomenal quality"—that is, the volition and the action are directly *experienced* by Mary as something she is doing rather than something that happens to her.[1]

We are all aware of this difference in things that occur in our minds. Some mental events, such as the sudden occurrence of a thought or memory or image, seem to merely come *upon* us or happen *to* us in a way that is not under our control. But other mental events, like concentrating in the attempt to solve a problem, or making a decision, are things we seem to be doing that are under our control. Mental events of the latter kind, those that seem to be under our control, according to Ginet, have this "actish phenomenal quality"; and it is the presence of this experienced quality that makes them actions rather than mere happenings. Of course, not all actions are *free* actions. Ginet's actish phenomenal quality guarantees only that something is an action. For an action to be *free,* he insists, it must not only have this actish phenomenal quality, it must be done for a reason or purpose *and* it must be undetermined.

2. Objections to Simple Indeterminism

Many philosophers question the simple indeterminists' claim that reasons for actions are not causes of actions. Mary's reasons for entering the room were that she *desired* to find her keys and *believed* she might have left them in the room she entered. Citing these reasons explains why Mary entered the room, to be sure. But why can't we also say that her having this desire and belief were among the causes of her entering the room—and that is *why* they explain her behavior? Maybe the desire and belief were not the *sole* causes of Mary's action; and perhaps they did not determine that she would enter the room. Our reasons may "incline without necessitating," as Leibniz said. They may make it more likely that we will act in certain ways. But when we do act in these ways, it is natural to say that our desires and beliefs causally influence our acting, even if they do not determine it.

By comparison, a crack in a bridge support may make a bridge collapse more likely. The crack alone will not cause the collapse in the absence of a strong wind. Yet if the bridge does collapse in a strong wind, the crack in the support will have been one of the causes of the failure. So it would also be with desires, beliefs, and other reasons for action, say these critics of simple indeterminism. When we do act on them, they are among the causes of our actions, though not necessarily the sole causes.

In response to this objection, simple indeterminists, such as Ginet, concede that desires, beliefs, and other reasons do *influence* actions, but not by causing them. To understand how desires and other reasons might influence actions without causing them, one must bring in two other notions that are important in free will debates—the notions of *intention* and *purpose*. Free actions are actions we do *intentionally* or on *purpose*, not by accident or mistake. Mary's action was intentional, not accidental. When she entered the room, she *intended* to find her keys. Her purpose was therefore "to find her keys." An *intention* is a state of mind; and what we call a *purpose* is the mental *content* of the intention—what the intention is *about*. Thus, if I am walking to the store and have in my mind "the *intention* <to buy a jacket>" then my *purpose* is "<to buy a jacket>"—what my intention is an intention *to do*.

Ginet now adds that desires and other reasons influence actions, not by causing them, but by entering into the *contents* of our intentions to perform the actions. Thus, Mary's desire to find her keys influenced her entering the room because she *intended* <to enter the room *in order to satisfy the desire* to find her keys>. Reference to the desire is included in the purpose (which is signified by the brackets). In this way, Mary's *intention* and *purpose* provide the explanatory link between the *action* (entering the room) and her *desire* (to find the keys). The desire influences the action, not by causing it, but by being referred to in the intention to perform the action. But does this *intention* itself cause the action? No, says Ginet. The intention *explains* the action not by causing it, but simply by *referring* to the action (it is the intention <*to* enter the room>) and by linking the action to the reason (<*to* satisfy the desire>). Thus Mary's acting can be explained and is not merely arbitrary, *even though it was undetermined.*

Critics object, however, that many of our reasons for acting never explicitly enter our intentions in the way Ginet describes, yet they still influence our actions. Freud and other psychoanalysts have made us aware, for example, that many of our desires and other reasons for acting are *unconscious* reasons. In addition, we often *repress* the real reasons for our actions or deceive ourselves about why we are doing something. Suppose Mary's real reason for entering the room was to wake up her brother, who was sleeping there, though she repressed that reason and deceived herself into thinking she was entering the room to find the keys. (In fact, the keys were more likely to have been in another room.) Since childhood, Mary had always resented the fact that her brother was an earlier riser and out of meanness woke her up on school days before she wanted to be wakened. In such a case, it is natural to say that wanting to wake her brother was a cause of Mary's entering the room even though it was not the reason referred to in her intention. There are many reasons (wants, desires, beliefs, preferences, aversions, likes, dislikes, etc.)—both conscious and unconscious—that influence our acting as we do. It is not credible, as Alfred Mele points out in his book *Motivation and Agency,* that all these reasons must be referred to in the contents of our intentions in order to influence our actions.[2] It is more natural to think that reasons can causally influence our actions even if they do not explicitly enter into our intentions.

A second related objection to simple indeterminism concerns Ginet's claim that volitions and other actions are distinguished from things that merely happen *to* us by an "actish phenomenal quality." This means we directly experience our actions as things we are doing rather than things that are happening to us. But could this experience be *illusory?* If our free actions really are uncaused, might we be experiencing them *as if* they were our actions when they really are not. One critic of simple indeterminism, R. E. Hobart, puts this objection in the following way:

> In proportion as an act of volition starts of itself without cause, it is exactly, so far as the freedom of the individual is concerned, as if it had been thrown into the mind from without—"suggested to him by a freakish demon."[3]

Another critic of simple indeterminism, Timothy O'Connor, puts the objection this way:

> The fact that free actions have uncaused volitions at their core is prima facie puzzling. If [a volition] is uncaused, if it is in no sense determined to occur by anything at all, then it is not determined to occur by me in particular. And if I don't determine it, then it's not under my control.[4]

3. Agent-causation Revisited

O'Connor argues that simple indeterminism is inadequate at this point unless we add to it a notion of non-event *agent-causation* like that of Chisholm and Reid discussed in chapter 5. Free actions may be uncaused *by prior events,* O'Connor says, but they cannot be uncaused by *anything.* If a free action was "uncaused . . . by anything," then it would not be caused "to occur *by me* in particular" and would not be "under my control." O'Connor does agree with simple indeterminists that explanations of actions in terms of *reasons* are not explanations in terms of *causes.* He also accepts Ginet's idea that desires and other reasons can explain actions by referring to the agent's intentions. Thus O'Connor agrees that we can explain why Mary entered the room by saying she had the intention <to satisfy her desire to find her keys>.

But O'Connor thinks we must also ask where this *intention* of Mary's came from. If Mary's intention to enter the room to satisfy the desire was not caused by her desire or other reasons, what caused it? This is where O'Connor thinks a notion of non-event agent-causation like that of Chisholm and Reid must be brought in. Mary's intention to enter the room was not caused by her desire or any other reasons and was not determined by any prior events. But the intention was nonetheless directly caused by the agent, Mary, herself; and it was caused by her in a special way that cannot be explained in terms of causation by prior events. In short, we must invoke what Chisholm called *immanent* or direct causation of events or states by agents rather than the *transeunt* causation of events by other events.

Simple indeterminists, such as Ginet, are suspicious of this addition of a special kind of non-event agent-causation. They think it is unnecessary to "complicate our picture of free agency" with this additional notion. Another simple indeterminist, Stewart Goetz, states this objection to agent-causation in the following way. Goetz says that, on his simple indeterminist view, a choice—such as Mary's choosing to enter the room—is an uncaused event that is directly under the control of the agent.[5] If Mary did not have direct control over her choice, says Goetz, it would not *be* her choice. O'Connor's response is that Goetz is getting this result "for free" by simply *defining* a choice as an event that is (a) uncaused and therefore undetermined and yet (b) under the control of the agent. The problem, according to O'Connor, is to explain *how* an event could be uncaused by prior events and yet under the control of the agent.

"But what is O'Connor's alternative?" asks Goetz. It amounts to interpreting a free choice as the agent-causing-of-an-intention in a special non-occurrent way and then *defining* this special relation of agent-causation so that it is (a) essentially undetermined and (b) also essentially under the control of the agent. Goetz then adds: If I am getting my result "for free," then agent-causalists, such as O'Connor, are getting their result for free as well; and they are adding an extra and obscure notion of non-event causation to do it. If it is illegitimate, Goetz asks, for the simple indeterminist to define *Mary's choosing* (to enter the room) as essentially an exercise of power that is uncaused by prior events, yet under the direct control of the agent, then why isn't it just as illegitimate for the agent-causalist to define *Mary's agent-causing her intention* (to enter the room) as an exercise of power that is uncaused by prior events, yet under the direct control of the agent?

This is a potent question. Compatibilists, such as Watson, are likely to say at this point that *both* parties—simple indeterminists and agent-causalists—are getting their results illegitimately: by definition or stipulation. But O'Connor has a response to Goetz's objection. He insists that the agent-causalist *is* adding something important. By interpreting *Mary's choosing* as *Mary's agent-causing-her-intention,* the agent-causalist is bringing out the fact that choices are not "simple" mental events, as Goetz and other simple indeterminists claim. Choices have a causal structure. A choice to do something is an *agent's-bringing-about-or-causing-an-intention* to do it. By thus noting that free choices are agent-causings and not simple events, O'Connor argues, agent-causalists, unlike simple indeterminists, can explain *why* free choices are essentially uncaused by prior events.[6]

To explain this, O'Connor asks us to consider that ordinary causation by events has the following structure: Event e' (e.g., the lighting of a match) causes event e'' (an explosion). He then argues that causal relations between events like this (e' causes e'') cannot themselves be caused—at least not directly. We *can* say that the *striking* of the match (e) caused the match's *lighting* (e') *to* cause the *explosion* (e''). But in that case we are saying that event e (the striking) causes the *first event* in the causal relation, namely e' (the lighting of the match), and *then* e' causes the second event, e'' (the explosion). In other words, O'Connor argues, a causal relation between events (such as e′ causes e″) can only be caused indirectly by causing the first event (e′) in the causal relation, which then causes the second event (e″).[7]

But in the case of *agent*-causation, he argues, the causal relation does not have the usual form of causation between events (e causes e′). Instead, agent-causation has the form "A causes e," where the first term is not an event at all, but an agent, an enduring substance. And, O'Connor argues, "there appears to be no way of getting a grip on the notion of an event of *this* sort" (agent A causes event e) having a sufficient cause. "Because of its peculiar causal structure [A causes e], there is no event at its front end, so to speak [that could be caused by some other event] but only an enduring agent."[8] So an agent-causal relation cannot in principle itself be caused by other events. By adding such a notion, agent-causalists can explain, as simple indeterminists cannot, *why* free choices cannot be determined.

4. Actions and Events

One difficulty with the preceding argument concerns the nature of *action*. O'Connor is bringing out something important when he says that choices are not simple events. They appear to have a causal structure. A *choice* to do something (such as enter a room) is an agent's-bringing-about-or-causing-the-intention to do that thing. But the problem is that something similar could be said about *actions* of many kinds, not merely choices. To *act*, in general, is to *bring about or cause some event or state of affairs*. For example, to *kill the king* is to bring about (or cause it to be the case) that *the king is dead*. To *raise your arm* is to bring about (or cause it to be the case) that *your arm goes up*. To *turn on the light* is to bring it about that *the light is on*, and likewise for other actions.

This is the feature that makes *actions* different from simple *events* or happenings. Actions have the form "Agent (A) brings about or causes an event or state (e)," where the first term of the causal relation is an agent and the second term is an event or state of affairs. This feature of actions is one of the things that lends plausibility to agent-causal theories. But this feature of actions also raises questions about O'Connor's argument. For, if it is true that a causal relation of the form " A causes e" cannot itself be causally determined by prior events *because its first term is an agent and not an event,* then this would be true of actions, in general, not merely of free actions. For actions, in general, have this agent-causal form. That is what distinguishes them from mere events. If the argument worked, it would show that for something to be an action, whether free or unfree, it could not in principle be determined.

Some people might want to accept this strong conclusion. They might say that all actions must of necessity be undetermined. Then, if we lived in a determined world, no one would really *do* anything. Things would merely happen. There would be a "flow of events," but no real agency. But most people do not want to go that far. Even libertarians and incompatibilists usually insist that it is only *free* actions that must be undetermined, not all actions whatsoever. When persons act compulsively or are forced to do certain things (say, hand over their money when a gun is held to their head), they *do* something, though not freely. In fact, O'Connor himself does not want to say that all actions are essentially undetermined: only free actions are. But then, it is not sufficient for him to argue that a causal relation of the form "A causes e" could not be causally determined because *its first term is an agent* rather than an event. (For, all actions having this agent-causal form need not be undetermined.) He must add that *free* actions are unique because they are agent-caused in the *special* non-event or non-occurrent way that by its nature cannot in principle be determined. This claim, however, goes well beyond, and is not supported by, the claim that free actions have an agent-causal structure (A causes e) alone. One might argue therefore as Goetz does, that this further claim amounts merely to stipulating that free actions involve an agent-causal relation of a special kind that is (a) essentially undetermined and (b) also essentially under the control of the agent.

It is an important fact about actions and choices, to be sure, that they have an agent-causal structure: John's raising his arm is bringing it about (or causing it to be the case) that his arm goes up; Mary's making a choice is bringing it about (or causing it to be the case) that she has an intention or purpose to do something. Agent-causalists, such as Chisholm and O'Connor, correctly draw our attention to this fact. But having such an agent-causal structure does not *alone* prove that actions or choices cannot in principle be caused or determined by prior events. Stronger arguments are needed to show that.

5. The Causal Theory of Action

This debate about the causal structure of action is related to another feature of the simple indeterminists' view discussed in section 1, namely, the claim that *reasons* for actions are not *causes* of actions. As noted, many philosophers question the simple indeterminists' claim that reasons cannot be causes. Mary's reasons for entering the room were that she *desired* to find her keys and *believed* she might have left them in the room. Citing these reasons explains why Mary entered the room. But why, these philosophers ask, can't we also say that Mary's having this desire and belief were among the causes of her entering the room? The desire and belief need not have been the sole causes of Mary's action, just as the structural defect in the bridge was not the sole cause of the bridge's collapse. But we could still say that Mary's desires, beliefs, and other motives were among the causes of her action.

Philosophers who take this line—who insist that desires, beliefs, and other reasons are causes of action—are often called *causal theorists of action*.[9] Causal theorists of action agree with agent-causalists that actions have an agent-causal structure: they agree that an action is an-agent's-bringing-about-or-causing-something to occur. But (in opposition to agent-causalists) causal theorists of action argue that the agent-causal structure of action *can* be explained in terms of causation by prior *events* or *states of affairs*. Mary's entering the room, they say, was caused by her *intention* to enter the room; and her intention was caused by her *choice* to enter the room; and her choice to enter the room was caused by her *desire* to find her keys and by her *belief* that her keys might be in the room. To explain actions, according to causal theorists, one does not have to postulate any additional form of non-event agent-causation over and above causation by mental states and processes, such as beliefs, wants, desires, and intentions. This is true of *choices* as well as of actions of other kinds, according to causal theorists: Mary's *choice* to enter the room was also caused by her desires and beliefs, together with other mental events, such as her memories and perceptions, that entered into her deliberation and, through her deliberation, causally influenced the choice she made.

As you might guess, many causal theorists of action tend to be compatibilists or even determinists about free will. They reason that, if choices and actions can be caused by the agent's reasons and other mental states, then choices and actions might also be *determined* by the agent's reasons and other mental states. In fact, the causal theory of action is often invoked to refute libertarian theories of free will, such as simple indeterminism, which claim that free actions or choices are not caused by reasons and therefore cannot in principle be determined.

6. Causation and Determinism

But one can agree with causal theorists that reasons may be causes of action without necessarily being a compatibilist or a determinist about free will. For the fact is that all causes need not be *determining* causes. Some causes are merely probabilistic; they make it more likely that certain events will occur without determining that those events will occur. And this might be the case with reasons and motives as well. Free choices and actions may be causally influenced by the agent's reasons or motives without being determined by those reasons or motives. As Leibniz said, reasons may "incline without necessitating." Mike's desire to surf along with other reasons may incline him to choose to vacation in Hawaii without necessitating or determining that choice; and his desire to ski along with other reasons may incline him to choose to vacation in Colorado without necessitating that choice.

But we may wonder what "tips the balance," if Mike might choose either Hawaii or Colorado and neither choice is determined by his reasons. Perhaps *this* is the point at which one must introduce some kind of agent-causation "over and above" causation by prior reasons and motives. That is the line taken by another agent-causalist, Randolph Clarke.[10] Clarke is unpersuaded by arguments of simple indeterminists and other agent-causalists, such as O'Connor, that reasons cannot be causes of actions. Clarke thinks that many reasons or motives, conscious and unconscious, may causally influence our actions even though they are not referred to in our intentions. But he still believes that non-event agent-causation is needed to explain what tips the balance between the reasons for one choice or the other when neither set of reasons is determining. Somehow Mike himself (the *agent*) must cause the choice of Hawaii (or Colorado) in a way that cannot be completely explained in terms of his prior reasons or his prior deliberation or in terms of any prior events whatsoever.

But how does appealing to agent-causation explain why Mike's tipping the balance in one way *rather than* the other is not arbitrary or random, since his reasons and motives may have inclined him in either direction? Clarke concedes that introducing non-event agent-causation at this point does not answer puzzles about arbitrariness of this sort concerning libertarian free agency. But introducing agent-causation, he argues, does at least account for the fact that the agent, Mike, has *control* over, and *produces,* the choice that is finally made, as opposed to one set of reasons simply "winning out" over the other set by mere chance. Yet critics of agent-causation, such as Watson, respond that postulating agent-causation at this point does not seem to explain *how* the agent controls or produces one choice rather than the other either.[11] The agent-causalist says that the agent controls or produces one outcome rather than the other without really explaining *how* the agent can do this except randomly or arbitrarily. This criticism reminds one of Watson's objection noted in the preceding chapter: that agent-causation merely "labels what libertarians need," rather than explaining it. Clarke might respond that agent-causation *does* nonetheless correctly represent what libertarians need—namely, something to tip the balance.

Ginet and O'Connor have a different objection to Clarke's agent-causal view. They argue that if libertarians concede, as Clarke does, that desires, beliefs, and other reasons can be causes of action (even indeterministic causes), then libertarians risk making agent-causation of a special non-event kind superfluous. Ginet asks: does the agent cause in Clarke's theory, supply some extra "oompf" or force that the reasons and other mental and physical events do not supply, an extra force that tips the balance?[12] Clarke admits that this cannot be what agent-causation adds. We cannot think of non-event agent-causation as some kind of extra *force,* either physical or mental, that tips the balance. To construe agent-causation in such mechanical "push/pull" terms would be to reduce it to another kind of event causation, which it is not.

But, says Ginet, that seems to be the picture we have, if we allow that reasons may be indeterministic or probabilistic causes of free actions. For then reasons would supply *some* of the force inclining us to make a particular choice, but not enough. The extra force or "oomph" would have to be supplied by the agent. Yet that picture cannot be right, Ginet argues, if agent-causation is not just another form of causation by forces and events. A similar criticism is made by O'Connor. He says that an agent-causation that is irreducible to event causation cannot "be fitted into or on top of an unbroken chain of event causation," including causation by reasons, as Clarke suggests. "Once we recognize free will to involve a type of undetermined, direct control" of the kind that non-event agent-causation requires, "we have to reject the completeness of the simple, continuous-flow-of-events picture of nature."[13]

But Clarke responds that such a view of agent-causation would require that agent-causation (and hence free will) must "interrupt" or "disrupt" the ordinary pattern of events in nature and perhaps that it would in some way violate the laws of nature. And this would make agent-causation (and libertarian free will) mysterious or something of a miracle. One possible reply suggested by O'Connor and others is that non-event agent-causation is a special capacity of organisms that *emerges* in nature but is no longer reducible to natural flow-of-events picture of nature.[14] This suggestion would require further development, however, to explain how, if at all, such an emergent capacity would not "interrupt" the ordinary pattern of events in nature or why it would not violate the laws of nature. Perhaps, to make ultimate sense of agent-causation, one might have to revert after all, to the dualistic picture of a mind and body, in which the mind is somehow outside the natural order of events but capable of intervening in the physical world to "tip the balance." Both Clarke and O'Connor would like to avoid a mind–body dualism of this kind, and they do not want to claim that free will must violate natural laws. But their debate makes some philosophers

wonder whether making sense of free will in agent-causationist terms
might require a dualist view of mind after all.[15]

7. Deliberation and Causal Indeterminism

The final libertarian theory I want to consider in this chapter takes a very
different approach to explaining libertarian free choices. This view rejects
both simple indeterminism and agent-causation. Instead it focuses on the
process of deliberation. When we deliberate, for example, about where to
vacation or which law firm to join, many different thoughts, images, feelings, memories, imagined scenarios, and other considerations pass
through our minds. Deliberation can be quite a complex process. When
Mike thinks about Hawaii, he pictures himself surfing, walking on sunny
beaches, eating in his favorite Hawaiian restaurants; and these various
thoughts incline him to choose Hawaii. But he also thinks about skiing,
sitting by a fireplace after a long day on the slopes, and visiting with
friends he knows in Colorado; and he leans toward Colorado. Back and
forth he goes, until after a period of time considerations on one side outweigh the others and he finally chooses one option. (Unless, of course he
is one of those indecisive types who finds it hard to make up his mind.)

In the course of such deliberations—which may sometimes take hours
or days and may be interrupted by daily activities—new thoughts, memories or images can often come to mind that influence our deliberations.
Mike may suddenly remember a lively nightclub he visited in Honolulu
when he was last there—great music, great girls—and the idea of going
back to this place gives him an added reason to favor Hawaii, a reason that
hadn't previously entered his deliberation. Other images that flit through
his mind may turn him against Hawaii. Imagining himself out on the
beach all day, suddenly he remembers his doctor's warning about not
getting too much sun if he wants to avoid skin cancer.

Now one could imagine that some of these various thoughts, memories,
and imagined scenarios that come to mind during our deliberations are
undetermined and arise by chance and that some of these "chance selected
considerations" might make a difference in how we decide. If this were to
happen in Mike's case, the course of his deliberation, hence his choice,
would be undetermined and unpredictable. A Laplacian demon could not
know in advance which way Mike would go, even if the demon knew all
the facts about the universe prior to Mike's deliberation, for these facts
would not determine the outcome. Yet Mike would still have control over
his choice in a certain sense. He could not control all the thoughts and

imagined scenarios that come to mind by chance. But he would be in control of how he reacted to those thoughts and imaginings once they did occur. And his choice of Hawaii in the end would be perfectly rational, not arbitrary, if the weight of all the considerations that did come to mind (some of them by chance) weighed in favor of Hawaii. In this way, choices could thus be controlled and rational even though indeterminism was involved in the deliberations leading up to them.

A view of this kind is called *causal indeterminism* or *event–causal libertarianism,* for it allows that our thoughts, images, memories, beliefs, desires, and other reasons may be causes of our choices or actions without necessarily determining choices and actions; and yet this view does not postulate any extra kind of agent-causation either. Two philosophers who have suggested causal indeterminist views of this kind (without endorsing them), Daniel Dennett and Alfred Mele, argue that a view of this kind would give libertarians at least some of the important things they demand about free will.[16] Such a view, for example, provides for an "open future," such as we think we have when we exercise free will. We would not have to think that our choices and the future direction of our lives had somehow been decided long before we were born. Nor would it be possible for behavioral engineers to completely control our behavior as in Walden Two or for Laplacian demons to know what we were going to do, if chance considerations might enter our deliberations.

Yet, as Dennett and Mele also admit, a causal indeterminist view of this deliberative kind does not give us everything libertarians have wanted from free will. For Mike does not have complete control over what chance images and other thoughts enter his mind or influence his deliberation. They simply come as they please. Mike *does* have some control *after* the chance considerations have occurred. But then there is no more chance involved. What happens from then on, how he reacts, is *determined* by desires and beliefs he already has. So it appears that he does not have control in the *libertarian* sense of what happens after the chance considerations occur as well. Libertarians require more than this for full responsibility and free will. What they would need for free will is for the agent to be able to control which of the chance events occur rather than merely reacting to them in a determined way once they have occurred.

Yet, as Mele points out, while this causal indeterminist view does not give us all the control and responsibility that libertarians have wanted, it does give us many of the things they crave about free will (an open future, a break in the causal order, etc.). And it is clearly a possible view. Perhaps it could be further developed to give us more; or perhaps this is as much as libertarians can hope for.

Suggested Reading

Carl Ginet's simple indeterminist view is developed in *On Action* (Cambridge, 1990). Other noncausalist views are Hugh McCann (*The Works of Agency: On Human Action, Will and Freedom,* Cornell, 1998) and Stewart C. Goetz (see references in note 5). Timothy O'Connor's agent-causal view can be found in *Persons and Causes: The Metaphysics of Free Will* (Oxford, 2000), and Randolph Clarke's agent-causal view appears in his *Libertarian Accounts of Free Will* (Oxford, 2003). The indeterminist view described in the final section is developed in Daniel Dennett, "On Giving Libertarians What They Say They Want" (in *Brainstorms,* MIT, 1978) and by Alfred Mele in *Autonomous Agents: From Self-Control to Autonomy* (Oxford, 1995). A different view of this causal indeterminist kind is defended by Laura Waddell Ekstrom *Free Will: A Philosophical Study* (Westview, 2000). *Agents, Causes, and Events: Essays on Free Will and Indeterminism* (Oxford, 1995) edited by O'Connor is a collection of readings for and against the different libertarian views discussed in this chapter. Two other libertarian theories that do not fit clearly into one or another of the categories of this chapter can be found in James S. Felt, *Making Sense of Your Freedom* (Cornell, 1994), and T. L. Pink, *Free Will: A Short Introduction* (Oxford, 2004). Still other libertarian views are mentioned in the readings suggested at the end of chapter 12.

CHAPTER 7

Is Free Will Possible?
Hard Determinists and Other Skeptics

1. Oklahoma City and Columbine

On April 15, 1995, a young man named Timothy McVeigh parked a truck loaded with explosives outside a federal office building in Oklahoma City, Oklahoma. The truck exploded, ripping off the front of the building, killing over 130 people, and injuring many others, including office workers, visiting citizens, and federal employees' young children in a day care center in the basement. Why did he do it?

Tim McVeigh had a fairly normal American upbringing in a midwestern town. He joined the army after high school and liked military life so much that he applied for the elite Special Forces. Then things started to turn bad. He was turned down by the prestigious unit, perhaps because of suspicions about his mental stability. This rejection was a bitter disappointment to a sensitive young man, and McVeigh eventually left the military in a state of frustration and resentment. Outside the military, his resentments were further fueled by association with antigovernment militia types and by reading fictional works that described revolts against the U.S. government initiated by bombings of federal buildings. Thus began a downward spiral that led him to allegedly plan and carry out the bombing of the Alfred P. Murrah Building in Oklahoma City.

These are the surface facts. They leave out the fact that McVeigh had help from others, though a wider conspiracy was never proven. But few doubt that he himself was involved. The surface facts also do not tell us what was going on in Tim McVeigh's mind, what demons were haunting him. They do not tell us about his early childhood experiences, or other factors that may have led him to contemplate and commit such a horrendous act. When most people think about free will in a case like this—when they wonder whether McVeigh was responsible for the act of which he was found guilty—they tend to have the following thoughts. It is understandable that he was disappointed and resentful because he was turned down for Special Forces. But many other young men have been turned down for this elite service and they did not become mass murderers.

Other people also have resentments against the government. But few join militia groups, and most who do join such groups do not actually commit violent acts, much less murder. No, it was said, McVeigh did what he did of his own free will. Others in the same circumstances and with the same experiences would not necessarily have done what he did. We all have difficulties in life, but we have the free choice to make the best of them or the worst. There is such a thing as moral evil; and people like McVeigh are responsible for choosing evil over good. The jury in McVeigh's trial obviously reasoned in this way. McVeigh was given the death penalty and was executed in 2001.

People reasoned similarly about the terrible massacre at Columbine High School in Colorado on April 20, 2000. Two young men, Eric Harris and Dylan Klebold, entered the school with an arsenal of weapons, killing fourteen fellow students and a teacher and injuring many others before turning the guns on themselves. Like McVeigh, Harris and Klebold harbored resentments—in their case because they were constantly ridiculed by classmates and treated as outsiders by most of their peers. Well, one might say, many teenagers are treated that way in high school without turning into mass murderers.

Harris and Klebold were also deeply influenced by violent films and video games. There was a lot of public debate in the press and on TV at the time about the effects of violence in the media and of violent video games on young people. But it was also said that most young people are subjected to violence in the media today and play these games from early ages, yet do not turn into killers like Harris and Klebold. Harris and Klebold were also obsessed with celebrity and wanted to be famous. Obsession with celebrity is another troubling trend among the young (and old) in modern society, but most people do not kill for it. No, it was said, these young men were evil and chose as they did of their own free wills. If Harris and Klebold had not killed themselves, it is not difficult to imagine a jury reasoning in this way and perhaps sentencing them to death.

But there is another way of thinking about these well-known cases, a way favored by *hard determinists*. Hard determinists believe that if you look more deeply into the psychological and other springs of action, you will see that all of us are determined to do what we do, whether it be good or evil; and so none of us is ultimately responsible. People are making a fundamental mistake, say hard determinists, when they reason that McVeigh, Harris, and Klebold must have acted of their own free wills because other persons in the same circumstances and with the same experiences would not have done what they did. For, no one ever is in exactly the *same* circumstances as anyone else. We all bring different backgrounds, histories, experiences, and temperaments to every situation; and it is naïve to think that people have free will simply because they act differently in *similar* circumstances. If we knew enough about their pasts to really *explain* why McVeigh, Harris, and Klebold did what they did, we would see that any persons who were exactly like them (not merely similar) would have acted as they did in these circumstances. If this were not true, we would not be able to truly explain *why* they did what they did *rather than* something else.

2. Hard Determinism

Such is the view of hard determinism, the third traditional position on free will. At the beginning of chapter 4, I noted that those who believe that free will and determinism are incompatible may take either of two opposing positions. They may deny determinism and affirm free will, as libertarians do. Or they may affirm determinism and deny free will, which is what hard determinists do. Hard determinism can also be distinguished from "soft" determinism, which was defined at the end of chapter 2. Both hard and soft determinists believe in determinism. But soft determinists are *compatibilists* who insist that determinism does not undermine any free will worth having, while hard determinists are *incompatibilists* who take a "harder" line: Since determinism is true, free will does not exist in the true sense required for genuine responsibility, blameworthiness, and desert for deeds and accomplishments. These traditional positions can be nicely summarized in figure 7.1, which returns us to the picture of Incompatibilist Mountain of chapter 4.

Compatibilists and *soft determinists* say you cannot get *up* Incompatibilist Mountain because you cannot show that free will and determinism are incompatible. Soft determinists add that you cannot get down either—you cannot show that an indeterminist free will exists—because

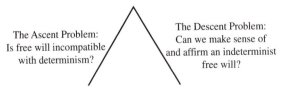

The Ascent Problem:
Is free will incompatible with determinism?

The Descent Problem:
Can we make sense of and affirm an indeterminist free will?

Figure 7.1   Incompatibilist Mountain and the Libertarian Dilemma

determinism is true. (Most other compatibilists also think you cannot get down Incompatibilist Mountain because they do not think an indeterminist free will makes sense.)

Libertarians and *hard determinists,* by contrast, say you *can* get up Incompatibilist Mountain—it can be shown that free will and determinism are incompatible. But hard determinists, in contrast to libertarians, say you cannot get back down because determinism is true. It is cold up there on Incompatibilist Mountain; and hard determinism is a cold view, according to most people, since it requires us to live without free will.

It is not surprising that few thinkers have been willing to embrace such a hard determinist position unqualifiedly, since it seems to require major changes in the way we think about human relations and attitudes, how we treat criminals and assess criminal behavior, and so on. This has not prevented hard determinism from being endorsed by some thinkers, such as Baron d'Holbach in the eighteenth century and Paul Edwards in the twentieth. The controversial American attorney Clarence Darrow was even known for defending hard determinism in the courtroom. Darrow gained fame in the 1931 Scopes trial, in which he defended a Tennessee high school teacher who had been fired for teaching the theory of evolution. But in other cases, such as the equally famous Leopold and Loeb trial, Darrow argued that his clients, Nathan Leopold and Richard Loeb, were not ultimately responsible for doing what they did—for murdering a young boy in cold blood for the sheer pleasure of it—because they were determined to do what they did by their formative circumstances. Few thinkers have been willing to go as far as Darrow, d'Holbach, or Edwards, however. Unqualified endorsement of hard determinism has been rare. The principle at work seems to be that of the Victorian lady who, upon first hearing of Darwin's theory of evolution, exclaimed, "Descended from the apes. Let's hope it isn't true. But if it is, let's hope it does not become generally known."

Nonetheless, a core or kernel of the traditional hard determinist position persisted throughout the twentieth century and continues to play an important role in free will debates. To understand this kernel of hard determinism, note first that traditional hard determinism is defined by three theses: (1) free will is incompatible with determinism and (2) free will does not exist because (3) determinism is true. Modern thinkers who hold the kernel of hard determinism accept theses 1 and 2, but they are not committed to thesis 3—the universal truth of determinism. Aware of developments in twentieth-century physics, these modern thinkers are less confident than traditional hard determinists were that determinism is universally true in the natural world. They prefer to leave the question of the truth of determinism to the scientists. Yet they remain convinced that (1) free will and determinism are incompatible and that (2) free will (of the incompatibilist or libertarian kind) does not exist.

This is the kernel of traditional hard determinism—theses 1 and 2. What is interesting about this kernel is that it *amounts to a rejection of both compatibilism and libertarianism.* For anyone who accepts thesis 1 holds *against compatibilists* that free will is incompatible with determinism; and anyone who also accepts thesis 2 holds *against libertarians* that there is no free will of the true libertarian or incompatibilist kind. In short, those who hold this kernel of hard determinism are *skeptics* about free will. They reject both compatibilism and libertarianism, the traditional solutions to the free will problem. One such skeptic, Derk Pereboom, has introduced a useful expression to characterize those who accept theses 1 and 2. He calls them "hard incompatibilists."[1] They are "incompatibilists" by virtue of thesis 1 (true free will is not compatible with determinism) and "hard" by virtue of thesis 2 (true free will does not exist).

The skeptical positions of hard determinism and hard incompatibilism constitute a "third rail" in contemporary free will debates, the rail most people do not want to touch for fear of being electrocuted. For both these skeptical positions require living without belief in free will and true moral responsibility. Yet, while they may be unpopular, these skeptical positions are important because they pose a significant challenge to the other two main positions on free will, compatibilism and libertarianism.

3. Strawson's Basic Argument: The Impossibility of Moral Responsibility

But, you might ask: Why do modern skeptics about free will who are not committed to the truth of determinism believe that free will of the libertarian kind does not exist? In other words, why do they accept thesis 2 (free will does not exist) if they remain noncommittal about thesis 3 (that determinism is true)? The answer for most modern skeptics about free will is that they think free will in the libertarian sense is *impossible, whether determinism is true or not.* The most widely discussed skeptical argument to show this impossibility is an argument by Galen Strawson, which he calls the Basic Argument.[2] The idea behind Strawson's Basic Argument is an ancient idea: Having true free will of the libertarian kind would require that one be a *causa sui*—a cause of oneself. But being a *causa sui* is impossible, at least for us human beings. Strawson supports this idea with the following argument:

1. You do what you do because of the way you are (your nature or character).
2. To be truly responsible for what you do, you must be truly responsible for the way you are (for your nature or character).

3. But to be truly responsible for the way you are, you must have done something in the past for which you were also responsible to make yourself, at least in part, the way you are.

4. But if you were truly responsible for doing something in the past to make yourself what you are now, you must have been responsible for the way you were then (for your nature or character) at that earlier time.

5. But to have been responsible for the way you were at that earlier time, you must have done something for which you were responsible at a still earlier time to make yourself the way you were at that earlier time, and so on backward.

"Here one is setting off on a regress," Strawson concludes, a regress that cannot go back forever in the case of human beings. Eventually you return to early childhood when your initial nature was not formed by you at all, but was the product of your heredity, early upbringing, and other factors beyond your control. Strawson then adds: "This argument goes through whether determinism is true or false. . . . Even if the property of being a *causa sui* is allowed to belong (entirely unintelligibly) to God, it cannot be plausibly supposed to be possessed by ordinary human beings."[3]

Strawson then approvingly quotes Friedrich Nietzsche, who said:

> The *causa sui* is the best self-contradiction that has been conceived so far; it is a sort of rape and perversion of logic. But the extravagant pride of man has managed to entangle itself . . . with just this nonsense. The desire for "freedom of the will" in the superlative metaphysical sense, which still holds sway, unfortunately, in the minds of the half-educated—the desire to bear the entire and ultimate responsibility for one's actions oneself, and to absolve God, the world, ancestors, chance and society—involves nothing less than to be precisely this *causa sui* and, with more than Baron Munchausen's audacity, to pull oneself up into existence by the hair, out of the swamps of nothingness.[4]

Baron Munchausen was the notorious teller of tales who claimed to have pulled himself from a ditch by his own hair. Needless to say, Nietzsche is another modern skeptic about free will who believes, along with Strawson, that the true free will of the ultimate libertarian kind is an illusion. Nietzsche thinks we should learn to accept our fate, even to learn to love our fate, and get on without the illusion of free will.

Is Strawson's Basic Argument compelling? Premise 1 seems sound: "You do what you do because of the way you are (your nature or character)." As Hume pointed out, if our actions happened merely by accident or chance, if they did not flow from our character and motives, they could not be imputed to us as "our" actions. How about premise 2? Is it the case that to be truly responsible for what you do, you must be truly responsible for the way you are (for your nature or character)? Think of McVeigh, Harris, and Klebold in connection with this premise. If we hold them responsible for their horrendous acts, it is because we think they were responsible, at least in part, for becoming the kinds of persons who would commit such acts. But this is what premise 2 requires—that McVeigh, Harris, and Klebold were at least in part responsible for becoming the kinds of persons who could commit such crimes. To hold them ultimately responsible we cannot think they were *entirely* shaped by psychological and social factors beyond their control.

Premise 3 seems sound as well: if McVeigh, Harris, and Klebold were responsible at least in part for being the way they were, it must have been because of something they *did* in the past for which they were responsible (some actions they performed or choices they made) to make themselves into the kinds of persons they became. But if premises 2 and 3 are sound, then steps 4 and 5 would seem to follow as well. For steps 4 and 5 simply reapply premises 2 and 3 to the past actions by which the agents made themselves what they are. If the agents are to be responsible for those past actions, they must also have been responsible for the characters and motives from which those past actions issued.

Is there any way to avoid Strawson's conclusion from these plausible premises? It may be true, as his argument claims, that we cannot be creators of our "original" characters and motives—the characters and motives we began with in childhood before we ever made any free choices. But as we get older and develop, are we powerless to *change* the original characters we started with in childhood? Compatibilists and libertarians both respond to skeptical arguments like Strawson's by saying that, although we are not the creators of our original characters, we can indeed freely change our natures and characters as we mature.

That seems like a piece of common sense. But Strawson replies that neither compatibilists nor libertarians give us an adequate account of *how* we could change our characters that accounts for true responsibility. If the *way* we change ourselves later in life, he argues, is *determined* by how *we already are,* as compatibilists allow, then that kind of change would not amount to true responsibility. But if the way we change ourselves later in life is *undetermined,* as libertarians require, then it would amount to mere luck or chance and that would not be true responsibility either. In other words, Strawson accepts the objections to *both* compatibilism and libertarianism that were considered in chapters 3 and 4. To answer his Basic Argument, compatibilists or libertarians must succeed in answering the objections against their views of these chapters; and in

doing so they must show that one or another of their views can account
for true responsibility.

4. Living Without Free Will: Crime and Punishment

We will be returning in later chapters to both compatibilist and libertarian
attempts to account for true responsibility and thereby answer Strawson's
challenge. But suppose, for the sake of argument, that skeptical arguments
against free will, such as Strawson's, cannot be answered. Can we live
without the illusion of free will, as Nietzsche says we must? Skeptics
about free will have addressed this question; and many of them have
argued that living without the illusion of free will would not have the dire
consequences that proponents of free will claim. Some skeptics about free
will have gone even farther, affirming, as Nietzsche does, that giving up
the illusion of free will would actually lead to a more positive, healthy, and
honest approach to life.

Ted Honderich is one such skeptic who has addressed the consequences
of living without free will.[5] Honderich concedes that if we believed, as he
does, that our behavior was sufficiently determined that we lacked free
will, we would have to give up some important "life-hopes," but not all
life-hopes. For example, we could no longer believe that our successes
and accomplishments were really "up to us" in the sense that we were the
ultimate "originators" of our actions. Nor could we believe that we were
ultimately responsible for the traits of character in which we took pride—
that we were hardworking, diligent, loyal, successful, and so on. To the extent that we had such characteristics, we would have to admit that we were
merely lucky in our heredity and formative circumstances.

But most everyday life-hopes would remain, says Honderich. Desires to
become a successful actor or dancer or writer, to start a business, to find
love, to have children, to be admired by others—these hopes that give
meaning to life would not be undermined by the belief that we are not the
"originating" causes of our own characters. What these everyday life-
hopes require is only that, if we make the appropriate voluntary efforts,
there is a good chance that nothing will prevent us from realizing our
cherished goals. Even if our behavior is determined, we cannot know in
advance how things are destined to turn out. So we must go on trying to
realize our life-hopes and dreams in the same manner as we would if we
did believe we had free will in the incompatibilist sense, though in fact we
do not.

How does this skeptical view of Honderich's differ from compatibilism?
Honderich says that compatibilists try to convince us that if determinism

were true, nothing of importance would be lost in the way of freedom and responsibility. But this, Honderich thinks, is mistaken. Life-hopes that depend on believing that we are the undetermined originators of our characters and actions *are* important to our self-image. We are in fact giving up something important when we take a hard determinist or hard incompatibilist position. We should be honest and not deceive ourselves about that. But enough life-hopes remain, he thinks, to permit us to go on living in meaningful ways.

How would we deal with criminal behavior if we took this skeptical position on free will? According to Honderich, we would have to give up a *retribution* theory of punishment. According to the retribution theory, punishment of criminal behavior is right because it is *deserved*. The criminal has done wrong and must repay in kind for the wrong inflicted. "An eye for an eye" is the motto of the retribution theory. But if persons lacked free will, they would not be ultimately blameworthy for their actions and therefore punishment would not be truly deserved. So if hard determinism or hard incompatibilism were true, the retribution theory of punishment would have to be given up.

But Honderich insists that giving up the retribution theory does not mean we have to stop punishing criminals. There are other justifications for punishment that remain valid even if free will is rejected. The most common of these alternative justifications is *deterrence*. We also punish criminals to discourage them from committing future crimes and, even more important, we punish them to deter other persons from committing similar crimes. Still another motive for punishment is to *reform* or *rehabilitate* criminals so that they will return from prison as productive members of society. These motives for punishment—deterrence and reform—remain legitimate, Honderich insists, even if we reject free will. So we need not fear that our prisons would be emptied if everyone came to believe that people lack free will. Indeed, Honderich suggests that, if we gave up a belief in free will, we would put more emphasis on the prevention of crime through deterrence and reform rather than on retribution and vengeance—and society would be better off as a result.

Another skeptic about free will, Derk Pereboom, takes Honderich's arguments about criminal punishment a step further. In his book, aptly titled *Living Without Free Will,* Pereboom introduces a quarantine analogy to justify criminal punishment:

> Ferdinand Schoeman has argued that, if in order to protect society, we have the right to quarantine people who are carriers of severe communicable diseases, then we also have the right to isolate the criminally dangerous to protect society. . . . This is true irrespective of the carriers' moral responsibility

for the disease. If a child is a carrier of the Ebola virus by virtue of its being passed on to her at birth from her parent, quarantine is nevertheless intuitively legitimate.

Furthermore, if we have the right to "quarantine" criminals, we have the right to tell people in advance that they will be isolated from society if they commit crimes. . . . This publicity itself has a powerful deterrent effect.[6]

An advantage of the quarantine model cited by Pereboom is that punishments would not be more severe than is needed to protect society and deter future crime, just as a quarantine of the sick should not be more restrictive than is needed to protect society from diseases. But a difficulty of the quarantine model is that it might allow us to jail persons who have not committed any crime but yet are thought to be a danger to society.

In response to this objection, Schoeman argues that it is more difficult to predict who will commit future crimes than it is to determine who has a dangerous communicable disease. But while this may usually be the case, is it always the case? There are some very bad and potentially dangerous people out there. (Consider the debates about how to treat child molesters who have been released from prison after serving time for their crimes.) Retributivists would argue, in response, that practices of punishment are bound to be unfair if we do not focus on who *deserves* to be punished, but instead focus only on what punishments will deter crime or protect society. If the focus is entirely on deterrence and protection rather than on retribution, injustices are bound to arise. Pereboom responds that the quarantine model works pretty well in most cases. If we reject free will, we would have to live with the few cases in which the quarantine model might be unfair. After all, those who are quarantined because they are sick are usually innocent as well. Also, if we place a high value on freedom, we will be reluctant for that reason alone to jail people who have not actually committed a crime.

5. Personal Relations: Love, Admiration, and All That

How would the rejection of free will affect our personal relations? Would the value of a person's love for you be deflated if you came to believe the person was determined to love you by heredity and environment? Many people think so because, as Pereboom says: "One might argue that we very much want to be loved by others as a result of their free will—we want freely willed love." But, he adds: "Against this, the love parents have for their children is typically engendered independently of the parents' will and we do not find this love deficient."[7] Also, when we fall in love romantically, it is rarely a matter of our free decision. Yet we do not find romantic love less satisfying for that reason. But is there not a mature kind of love we desire from lovers, spouses, friends, and even parents when we are older that would be deficient if we knew that factors beyond the others' control determined that they love us? To this objection, which I once posed to Pereboom's position, he responds as follows:

> If we indeed desire a love of this kind, then we desire a kind of love that is impossible if hard incompatibilism is true. Still the kinds of love that are invulnerable to hard incompatibilism are surely sufficient for good relationships. If we aspire to the sort of love parents typically have toward their children, or the kind romantic lovers ideally have . . . or the type shared by friends . . . whose relationship is deepened by their interactions, then the possibility of fulfillment in personal relationships is far from undermined [by hard incompatibilism].[8]

Similar questions arise about other attitudes besides love. Could we admire people for generous or heroic deeds if we did not think they were ultimately responsible for those deeds? Could we feel grateful to them? Could we resent them or blame them if they reacted treacherously or deceitfully toward us? Pereboom says that some of these reactive attitudes (such as blame and guilt) would have to be given up if we accepted hard determinism or hard incompatibilism. But other significant attitudes of these kinds would not have to be given up altogether. We could go on believing that acts of certain kinds, say, of generosity and heroism, are admirable and that acts of other kinds are despicable even if we not believe that persons are ultimately responsible. Gratitude, for example, he says, "typically involves joy occasioned by the beneficent act of another. But hard incompatibilism fully harmonizes with being joyful and expressing joy when others are considerate and generous on one's behalf."[9]

6. Illusion and Free Will

Thus, Honderich and Pereboom believe we can live meaningful lives without the illusion of free will, though some important hopes and attitudes would have to be changed. But another skeptic about free will is not so confident that we can live meaningfully without belief in free will. Saul Smilansky agrees with Honderich and Pereboom that free will and determinism are incompatible and that libertarian free will does not exist. That is, he also holds theses 1 and 2 of section 2, the kernel of hard determinism. But Smilansky thinks Honderich and Pereboom are too optimistic about the possibilities of living without belief in such a free will. So in his book *Free Will and Illusion,* Smilansky makes the provocative suggestion that even though we do not have true free will and moral responsibility in the deeper incompatibilist sense, we must foster the illusion in people that we do.[10] He says:

> To put it bluntly: People as a rule ought not to be fully aware of the ultimate inevitability of what they have done, for this will affect the way in which they hold themselves responsible. . . . We often want a person to blame himself, feel guilty and even see that he deserves to be punished. Such a person is not likely to do all this if he internalizes the ultimate hard determinist perspective, according to which . . . he could not strictly have done anything else except what he did do.[11]

Smilansky wonders whether society as we know it could survive if most people came to believe that they were not truly responsible for their behavior. Some people might become more humane and understanding in their treatment of others knowing that no one was ultimately responsible. But Smilansky suggests that most people might simply become more selfish and no longer feel restrained by the requirements of morality. The stability of civilized societies would then be threatened. Only force and fear of punishment would keep people from breaking the law. As one of America's founders, James Madison, argues in Federalist Paper 10, if society has no ethical foundation, the law alone will not protect us. Smilansky also argues that accepting the hard determinist or hard incompatibilist perspective would be "extremely damaging to our view of ourselves, to our sense of achievement worth and self-respect."[12] Contrary to the arguments of Honderich and Pereboom, he thinks that giving up certain reactive attitudes such as blame, guilt, and resentment would have dire effects for society and personal life.

All this suggests to Smilansky that we must foster the illusion of free will and moral responsibility. (As the Victorian lady said of Darwin's theory: "If it is true, let us hope it does not become generally known.") Smilansky does not mean that we should induce illusory beliefs in the masses, in the manner of the movie *The Matrix* in which almost everyone lives in a virtual, computer-created, illusory world. Rather he thinks the illusion of free will is already in place. For most people already think of themselves either as compatibilists or libertarians. But compatibilists believe we already have all the freedom and responsibility we need even if determinism is true. And libertarians believe we also have the deeper incompatibilist free will. Both are wrong, according to Smilansky. But he thinks these illusory beliefs play a largely positive social and moral role and we should leave them in place rather than undermining them.

I will leave the reader to judge who wins this debate. Can we live meaningful lives without the illusion of free will and ultimate moral responsibility, as hard determinists or hard incompatibilists such as Honderich, Pereboom, Strawson, and Nietzsche say we must? Would the moral foundations of society survive intact? If not, could we really live in illusion, as Smilansky counsels us to do, if we knew the truth? What if people in *The Matrix* all *found out* it was all a dream?

Suggested Reading

Galen Strawson's Basic Argument against the intelligibility of free will appears in *Freedom and Belief* (Oxford, 1986) and in his 1994 essay "The Impossibility of Moral Responsibility," reprinted in Gary Watson's edited volume, *Free Will,* 2nd ed. (Oxford, 2003). Ted Honderich's view is most clearly presented in *How Free Are You?* (Oxford, 1993). Derk Pereboom's hard incompatibilist view is developed in his book *Living Without Free Will* (Cambridge, 2001), and Saul Smilansky's illusionist view is developed in his *Free Will and Illusion* (Oxford, 2000).

CHAPTER 8

Moral Responsibility and Alternative Possibilities

1. The Principle of Alternative Possibilities (PAP)

Chapter 7 made clear how important the notion of moral responsibility is to the free will debate. Many philosophers actually define free will as the kind of freedom (whatever it may be) that is necessary to confer true moral responsibility on agents—the kind of responsibility that would make agents genuinely blameworthy or praiseworthy for their actions and deserving of punishment or reward. Defining free will in this manner is in fact a useful way of distinguishing *free will* from other ordinary kinds of *freedom*. Of course, philosophers and others disagree about just what kind of freedom *is* required for moral responsibility; hence they disagree about what free will really requires.

For example, most people believe that for agents to be morally responsible for their actions, they must have the power to perform the actions and the power to do otherwise. Harry Frankfurt has formulated this assumption in a principle that he calls the *Principle of Alternative Possibilities:*

(PAP) Persons are morally responsible for what they have done only if they could have done otherwise.

According to Frankfurt, this principle PAP lies behind the common belief (embodied in the Consequence Argument) that free will also requires the power to do otherwise. If *free will* is the kind of freedom required for *moral responsibility* and if moral responsibility requires the power to do otherwise, as PAP says, then it would also be the case that

(AP) Free will requires the power to do otherwise, or, alternative possibilities.

Now we know how crucial this principle of alternative possibilities (AP) was for the Consequence Argument. The Consequence Argument attempted to show that determinism rules out free will because it rules out the power to do otherwise. But then determinism would rule out free will only if it is also true that free will requires the power to do otherwise (i.e., only if one assumes AP). We did not question this principle (AP) in chapter 3 when we were discussing the Consequence Argument. We took it for granted that free will required the power to do otherwise, and we focused instead on whether determinism really rules out the power to do otherwise.

But if AP is false—if free will does *not* require alternative possibilities—then the Consequence Argument would fail from the start, whether determinism rules out the power to do otherwise or not. This is the position taken by Harry Frankfurt and other "new compatibilists." They deny that free will requires alternative possibilities (AP); and so they deny that determinism rules out free will. Moreover, the reason they reject AP is because they believe AP rests upon PAP *and PAP is false*. In other words, these new compatibilists argue that people tend to believe that free will requires alternative possibilities *because* they assume that moral responsibility requires alternative possibilities. But if moral responsibility does not require alternative possibilities, then free will does not require alternative possibilities either. So the major reason for thinking that determinism is incompatible with free will (because determinism rules out alternative possibilities) would be undermined.

2. The Luther Example

But why think moral responsibility does not require alternative possibilities or the power to do otherwise? Why think the Principle of Alternative Possibilities (PAP) is false? Two kinds of examples have been offered by new compatibilists to show the falsity of PAP. A good example of the first kind is Daniel Dennett's example of Martin Luther. When Luther broke with the church of Rome in the sixteenth century, initiating the Protestant Reformation, he made a famous statement: "Here I stand. I can do no other." Dennett asks us to assume for the sake of argument that Luther was speaking the literal truth at that moment. Luther's experiences and his reasoning, let us suppose, had brought him to the point where he *could* not have done otherwise at that moment than break with the church. As Dennett puts it: "His conscience made it *impossible* for him to recant." Would that mean we could not hold Luther responsible for his act? Not at all, says Dennett: "We simply do not exempt someone from blame or praise for an act because we think he could do no other."[1] In saying "I can do no other," Luther was not avoiding responsibility for his act, he was taking full responsibility for it. Indeed, it may have been the most responsible act of his life.

Dennett adds a personal example. Like most of us, he believes he could never torture an innocent person for a thousand dollars. His background and character make it completely out of the question. Yet he sees no reason why his refusing an offer to torture should not be regarded as a morally responsible act even though he could not have done otherwise given his background and character. And so it is also for the rest of us, he thinks. We can be praised or blamed for actions even when our consciences or characters make it impossible for us to do otherwise.

Thus Dennett concludes that PAP is false: moral responsibility does not require the power to do otherwise. If free will is the kind of freedom needed for moral responsibility, then AP is false as well: acting of one's own free will does not require the power to do otherwise either. So the main reason for thinking that free will and moral responsibility are incompatible with determinism (that both imply the power to do otherwise) is undermined.

How should we respond to examples like Dennett's, which have been called "character examples"? In my book, *The Significance of Free Will,* I make the following response to Dennett's Luther example. We may grant to Dennett that Luther's "Here I stand" might have been a morally responsible act done "of his own free will" even if Luther could not have done otherwise at the moment he made the statement. But this would be true only to the extent that we could assume other things about the background of Luther's action that made him responsible for it. If his act did issue from his existing character, then his moral accountability for it would depend on whether he was responsible by virtue of earlier choices and actions *for being the sort of person he had become at that time.* Those who know Luther's biography know the inner struggles and turmoil the religious leader had endured getting to that point in his life. Often we act from a will already formed, but it is "our own free will" by virtue of the fact that *we* formed it by other choices and actions in our past for which we could have done otherwise. If this were not so, *there is nothing we could ever have done to make ourselves different from how we are*—a consequence that is difficult to reconcile with the claim that we are ultimately morally responsible for being the way we are and hence for acting the way we do.

In other words, we can concede to Dennett that *not all* the morally responsible acts done of our own free wills have to be such that we could not have done otherwise with respect to *those particular actions* directly. Many of our responsible acts, like Luther's, flow from our wills already formed. Yet *some* of the choices or acts in our lifetimes must be such that we could have done otherwise or we would not be responsible for forming the wills from which we act. Our wills would not be "our own free wills." So if we take a broader view of an agent's life history, rather than focusing on individual acts like Luther's in isolation, it does not follow that free will and moral responsibility do not require alternative possibilities or the power to do otherwise *at all,* at *any* times in our lives. A stronger argument would be needed to show that. Examples like that of Luther, which we might call "character examples," do not alone show it.[2]

3. Frankfurt-type Examples

But many philosophers believe there is a second kind of example that goes beyond character examples and does provide the stronger argument needed to show that moral responsibility does not require the power to do otherwise at all. Examples of this stronger kind are called "Frankfurt-type examples," after Harry Frankfurt, who introduced such examples into recent free will debates to refute PAP (the principle which says that moral responsibility requires the power to do otherwise).

The first example of a Frankfurt type was actually proposed by the seventeenth-century philosopher John Locke. Imagine that a man is locked in a room but does not know the door is bolted and that he cannot get out. The man is enjoying the company in the room, however, and he stays of his own free will to converse with the others there. It appears that the man is responsible for staying in the room, since he stayed of his own volition or free choice, yet *he could not in fact have done otherwise.* He could not have left the room, since he was locked in. So it appears his responsibility for staying does not require that he had alternative possibilities.

Now we might object that the man in Locke's example did have *some* alternative possibilities for which he was responsible. Even though he could not have left the room, he could have *chosen* to leave or *tried* to leave, in which case he would have found out that he was locked in. But Frankfurt enters the picture at this point. He proposes a further example, similar to Locke's, but in which the agent has no alternative possibilities at all and yet is responsible for his act, thus refuting PAP. Suppose, says Frankfurt,

> Someone—Black let us say—wants Jones to perform a certain action. Black is prepared to go to considerable lengths to get his way, but he prefers to

avoid showing his hand unnecessarily. So he waits until Jones is about to make up his mind . . . and he does nothing unless it is clear to him . . . that Jones is going to do something *other* than what he [Black] wants him to do. If it does become clear that Jones is going to decide to do something else, Black takes effective steps to ensure that Jones . . . does what he wants.[3]

To guarantee Black's powers, Frankfurt says, we might imagine him to have a potion that can be administered to work his will or imagine him as a neurosurgeon with direct control over Jones's brain and intimate knowledge of Jones's inclinations. The point of the example is this: Jones *cannot do otherwise* because Black will not let him. But Jones might decide *on his own* to do what Black wants, in which case Black would not intervene. Frankfurt's claim is that if Jones does act on his own and Black does not intervene, then Jones would be responsible for what he did even though Jones could not have done otherwise. For if Jones did act on his own without Black intervening, Jones would have done so from his own motives and for his own reasons and no one would have interfered with his choice. The principle which says that moral responsibility requires alternative possibilities (PAP) would then be false: Jones would have acted responsibly though he could not in fact have done otherwise (because Black would not have let him).

Note that Frankfurt examples of this kind provide a stronger argument against PAP than do character examples, such as the Luther example. For we might imagine a "global" Frankfurt controller, like Black, who controls *all* Jones's choices and actions throughout Jones's entire lifetime. We might even imagine that on every occasion Jones in fact does what the global controller wants, with the result that the controller never has to actually intervene in Jones's actions. Jones acts on his own throughout his life, and the controller never interferes. It would seem in that case that Jones could be responsible for many acts in his lifetime because he would have done them on his own, for his own reasons, and on the basis of his own choices. Yet Jones could *never* have done otherwise because the controller would never have let him do otherwise. If Jones had chosen or tried to do something else, the controller would have intervened and stopped him (though in fact the controller never had to intervene). So a global Frankfurt case like this yields the stronger conclusion that being responsible need not require the power to do otherwise *ever* in one's life.

Could God be such a global Frankfurt controller? Since God is assumed to be good, it seems that we would have to suppose that God would not interfere if we were going to perform good acts but would intervene if we were about to do evil. But if we look around our world with all the evils in it, it seems obvious that God does not act that way. Though it also seems that God, being all-powerful, could act that way. Why then is there evil in the world and why does God permit it? We will return to this "problem of evil" in a later chapter and ask how it is related to the free will problem. (The two problems of evil and free will are indeed intimately related, as religious writers since Saint Augustine have shown.) For the present, however, we must ask whether Frankfurt's argument really does work in the first place and whether moral responsibility does or does not require alternative possibilities upon any occasion during the course of our lives. If Frankfurt's argument does work, we can consider its religious implications later.

4. Responses to Frankfurt: Flickers of Freedom

Frankfurt-type examples, like that of Black and Jones, have generated much discussion and many responses. One common objection is the following.

> Suppose Black wants Jones to perform an action A (say, voting for a presidential candidate) and Jones does A, as Black wanted, so that Black does not interfere. What makes us think Jones is responsible in such a case is that Jones did A *on his own* (that is, of his own free choice) without interference from Black. But if that is why we think Jones is responsible, then Jones did have an alternative possibility after all. For Jones could have done other than A-on-his-own by not choosing to vote for the presidential candidate Black wanted and thus forcing Black to intervene. Of course, if Black had intervened, Jones would still have done A (voted for the candidate Black wanted) but Jones would not have done A-on-his-own. So it seems that responsibility requires the power to do otherwise after all. Jones is responsible for doing A-on-his-own because he could have done other than that. But Jones is not responsible for doing A itself (voting for the candidate Black wanted), because he could not have done other than A. Black would not have let him.

Unfortunately, this tempting response to Frankfurt will not work. The response is correct in saying that when Black does not intervene, Jones is responsible for doing A-on-his-own and Jones *could* have done other than A-on-his-own. But the response goes wrong when it says that Jones is *not* responsible for doing A itself, since Jones could *not* have done other than A. For if Black does not intervene, how can Jones be responsible for doing A-on-his-own and yet *not* be responsible for doing A itself? That makes no sense. If someone is responsible for voting for the presidential candidate on his own, then he or she is responsible for voting for the presidential candidate. That was the point the Frankfurt-type examples were trying to make in the first place: we are responsible for the things we do on our own when no one interferes. So if Jones is responsible for doing A-on-his-own, he is also responsible for doing A. But he could *not* have done otherwise than A. So Frankfurt's conclusion stands: PAP is false. Being responsible for an action (in this case, A) does not necessarily require having the power to avoid doing it.

Well, perhaps moral responsibility requires that we be able to do *something* otherwise, though not necessarily the action itself. This thought leads to a second common objection to Frankfurt-type examples, which focuses on the controller Black. For Black to know whether to intervene in Jones's action, Black must have some prior indication of what Jones is going to do. If Black detects a certain neurological pattern in Jones's brain, for example (or a blush or a furrowed brow), that reliably indicates Jones is going to do what Black wants, Black will not intervene. But the need for this prior sign suggests another way in which Jones might have some alternative possibilities after all. For Jones might exhibit a different prior sign: for example, he might exhibit a different neurological pattern (or he might not blush or not furrow his brow).

In response to this objection, defenders of Frankfurt-type examples first note that if Jones exhibits a different neurological pattern or other prior sign, he must do so either *voluntarily* or *nonvoluntarily*. Defenders of Frankfurt-type examples have an answer to this objection either way. If Jones *voluntarily* exhibits one sign rather than another that indicates he will vote a certain way, they say, then Black can simply concentrate on controlling this earlier voluntary action of exhibiting one sign or another. If, for example, Jones is going to voluntarily exhibit a neurological pattern that will lead to the vote Black wants, Black will not interfere. But if Jones is going to exhibit a different neurological pattern, Black will intervene and not let Jones do it. Frankfurt's argument will then simply be shifted back to this earlier act of exhibiting a prior sign without losing its force. Jones would not be able to do otherwise than exhibit the prior sign he does exhibit because Black would not have let him. Yet, if he voluntarily exhibits the prior sign Black wants, Black will not interfere and Jones will be responsible.

Suppose, by contrast, that Jones's exhibiting a prior sign about how he will vote is *nonvoluntary* or *involuntary* (something he may do, like blush or furrow his brow, that merely happens to him and is not under his voluntary control). This would be an alternative possibility of sorts for Jones. But would it be an alternative possibility for which Jones could be held *responsible?* It seems not. One prominent defender of Frankfurt-type cases, John Martin Fischer, puts the argument this way:

> It may be objected that . . . although Jones cannot choose or vote differently, he can still exhibit a different neurological pattern in his brain. . . . I have called such an alternative possibility a "flicker of freedom." . . . But I contend that the mere involuntary display of some sign—such as a neurological pattern in the brain, a blush or a furrowed brow—is too thin a reed on which to rest moral responsibility. The power involuntarily to exhibit a different sign seems to me to be insufficiently robust to ground our attributions of moral responsibility.[4]

Fischer is saying that if you are going to claim that Jones really has alternative possibilities in the Frankfurt example, those alternative possibilities cannot merely be occurrences like neurological patterns or blushes over which the agent has no voluntary control. How much free will do we have if the only way we can do otherwise is involuntarily, by accident or mistake, rather than voluntarily or on purpose? To refute Frankfurt, Fischer is arguing, you must not only show that Jones has alternative possibilities of *any* kinds; you must show that these alternative possibilities are not mere involuntary "flickers of freedom" but are robust enough voluntary acts to ground moral responsibility.

5. The Indeterministic World Objection

While the "flicker of freedom" strategy will not suffice to refute Frankfurt, it does lead to a third objection that is more powerful. This third objection is one that has been developed by several philosophers, including myself, David Widerker, Carl Ginet, and Keith Wyma.[5] We might call it the Indeterministic World Objection. I discuss this objection in my book *Free Will and Values*. Following is a summary of this discussion:

> Suppose Jones's choice is *undetermined* up to the moment when it occurs, as many incompatibilists and libertarians require of a *free* choice. Then a Frankfurt controller, such as Black, would face a problem in attempting to control Jones's choice. For if it is undetermined up to the moment when he chooses whether Jones will choose A or B, then the controller Black cannot know *before* Jones actually chooses what Jones is going to do. Black may wait until Jones actually chooses in order to see what Jones is going to do. But then it will be too late for Black to intervene. Jones will be responsible for the choice in that case, since Black stayed out of it. But Jones will also have had *alternative possibilities,* since Jones's choice of A or B was undetermined and

therefore it could have gone either way. Suppose, by contrast, Black wants to *ensure* that Jones will make the choice Black wants (choice A). Then Black cannot stay out of it until Jones chooses. He must instead act *in advance* to bring it about that Jones chooses A. In that case, Jones will indeed have no alternative possibilities, but neither will Jones be responsible for the outcome. Black will be responsible since Black will have intervened in order to bring it about that Jones would choose as Black wanted.

In other words, if free choices are *undetermined,* as incompatibilists require, a Frankfurt controller like Black cannot control them without *actually* intervening and making the agent choose as the controller wants. If the controller stays out of it, the agent will be *responsible* but will also have had *alternative possibilities* because the choice was undetermined. If the controller does intervene, by contrast, the agent will *not* have *alternative possibilities* but will also not be *responsible* (the controller will be). So responsibility and alternative possibilities go together after all, and PAP would remain true—moral responsibility requires alternative possibilities—*when free choices are not determined.*[6]

If this objection is correct, it would show that Frankfurt-type examples will not work in an indeterministic world in which some choices or actions are undetermined. In such a world, as David Widerker has put it, there will not always be a *reliable* prior sign telling the controller in advance what agents are going to do.[7] Only in a world in which all of our free actions are determined can the controller always be certain in advance how the agent is going to act. This means that, if you are a compatibilist, who believes free will could exist in a determined world, you might be convinced by Frankfurt-type examples that moral responsibility does not require alternative possibilities. But if you are an incompatibilist or libertarian, who believes that some of our morally responsible acts must be undetermined, you need not be convinced by Frankfurt-type examples that moral responsibility does not require alternative possibilities.

6. New Frankfurt-type Examples

This "indeterministic world" objection to Frankfurt-type examples has inspired many new and more sophisticated Frankfurt-type examples attempting to show that moral responsibility does not require alternative possibilities, *even if* choices are undetermined right up to the moment they occur. All these new Frankfurt-type examples cannot be considered in an introductory work of this kind. The debate about them has become very complex. But I will mention a few new Frankfurt-type examples to give you an idea of the direction of the current debates about moral responsibility and alternative possibilities. Those who want to pursue the issues further may look into the suggested readings at the end of this chapter.

As we have seen, when Jones's choice is undetermined, the controller Black's problem is that he does not have a *reliable* prior sign indicating what Jones is going to do. How then can Black prevent Jones from having alternative possibilities, while at the same time allowing Jones to act on his own? One way a Frankfurt controller might do this, suggested by David Hunt and others, involves *blockage*.[8] Suppose Jones is deliberating about whether to vote for presidential candidate A or presidential candidate B. Since Black wants Jones to choose A, he places a barrier at the end of the neural pathway in Jones's brain leading to choice B, so that Jones could not choose B if he were about to so. But Jones can still choose A on his own anyway. So the barrier need not come into play.

Here is a simple example that helps to clarify this blockage idea. Imagine Jones is walking down a dark corridor in a castle. He comes to a fork, where there is a door on the left (A) and door on the right (B). He goes through door A. But, unknown to Jones, door B was locked (by Black). So Jones could not have gone through door B. Nonetheless, Jones did go through door A on his own, not knowing door B was blocked. Black did not interfere with the deliberation process that led to Jones going through door A, even though Jones could not have done otherwise.

Note that blockage cases like this are not like the original Frankfurt-type examples. In the original examples, Black is what Fischer calls a mere "counterfactual intervener" rather than an actual intervener. He *could* intervene in Jones's brain, but he does not *in fact* or *actually* intervene. In blockage cases, however, Black does *actually* intervene to block one of the outcomes; and he does so in advance by locking the door or blocking the neural pathway leading to choice B. Does Jones have any alternative possibilities as a result? Well, choosing A or B might not have been his only options. Jones might also have decided not to vote for either candidate (C) or to postpone a decision till later (D). Suppose Black blocked choice B, but not the others. Then Jones would still have *some* alternative possibilities, namely, C and D. Jones's *responsibility* would then be less, however. Jones could be blamed for not choosing C, if C was the morally right thing to do, because C was a possible option. But he could not be blamed for not choosing B, if B were the morally right thing to do, because B was not a possible option for him. (Note how the *extent* of Jones's responsibility does seem to depend on what, and how many, alternative possibilities he has.)

To take away *all* Jones's alternative possibilities, of course, Black would have to block not only option B, but options C and D as well. But if

Black did *that*—if he eliminated *all* Jones's alternatives but one—it looks as if the outcome would be *determined* in advance by Black's actions (of blocking all alternative pathways in Jones's brain). In other words, complete blockage looks like *predetermining* or *predestining* the outcome to only one possibility. Are free will and moral responsibility compatible with such predestination?

A more sophisticated blockage example, suggested by Alfred Mele and David Robb, tries to avoid this charge of predetermining or predestining the outcome.[9] Suppose Jones is again engaging in an undetermined deliberation process (call it P) about whether to vote for candidate A or candidate B. In this case, Black introduces into Jones's brain a separate process P* that does not interfere in any way with Jones's own deliberation process P. Black's process P* is deterministic, however, and will inevitably produce the choice of A if Jones's own deliberation process does not. Still, Jones's own deliberation process P is undetermined, so on its own it *might* result in the choice of A (the choice Black wants). If Jones's process does result in the choice of A on its own, then it will "preempt" or "override" Black's process, so that Jones will make the choice of A on his own and Black's process will be inoperative. Jones would then be responsible for choosing on his own, according to Mele and Robb, even though Black's deterministic process would have made Jones choose A anyway, if Jones's own process had not.

Note that, in this scenario, Black's process does not predetermine or determine in advance how Jones's own deliberation process P will turn out. The two processes proceed independently of each other (until the end). If Jones's process ends in the choice of A, then it preempts or overrides Black's process (which becomes inoperative). If Jones's process does not result in the choice of A, Black's process preempts or overrides Jones's and makes Jones choose A anyway. So in this Mele–Robb example, Black does not need a prior sign to know what Jones is going to do. Instead, Black's process will *automatically* override Jones's process at the very end, if Jones does not choose what Black wants.

While Mele and Robb claim that Black's implanted process P* does not interfere with Jones's own deliberation process P in any way, one may wonder whether the mere fact that Black has implanted this additional deterministic process P* in Jones's brain does not somehow "make a difference" to Jones's own deliberation. To test this possibility, ask the following question: what would have happened if Black had never implanted his additional deterministic process in Jones's brain? If Black had never implanted anything in Jones's brain, Jones own deliberation process, which was supposed to be indeterministic, might have had different outcomes. For example, Jones might have made choice A or B or C or D. But with Black's deterministic process implanted things are different. Jones can still make choice A as a result of his own deliberative process. But he can no longer make alternative choices B or C or D as a result of his own deliberative process, for if Jones does not make choice A on his own, Black's implanted deterministic process will "preempt" Jones's deliberation and determine that Jones will make choice A.

Could Jones still make choice B (or C or D) as a result of his own deliberation process *at the same time* that Black's deterministic process was making him choose A? The answer is no. For then Jones would be making contradictory choices; and Mele and Robb do not allow that. They cannot allow Jones to choose B or C or D by his own deliberation process at the same time that Black's process is making him choose A for another reason as well: for then Jones would have some alternative possible choices that he could make on his own after all, which is just what Black's implanted process is suppose to prevent.

So the mere presence of Black's implanted process does seem to "make a difference" to Jones's deliberation. It looks as if, by merely implanting his process, Black has in effect *blocked* all other possible outcomes (B or C or D) of Jones's own deliberation process but A. Indeed it seems that, as a result of Black's implanted process, Jones's own deliberation process is no longer even *indeterministic,* since it can have only one outcome. So this looks like another case of complete blockage.

Not so, say Mele and Robb. Black's process does block all Jones's *robust* alternative possibilities (those under his voluntary control) such as voluntarily *choosing* candidate B or voluntarily *choosing* not to vote at all (C) or voluntarily *choosing* to postpone his vote (D). But Black's process does not block every alternative possibility for Jones's own deliberation process whatsoever. For example, Jones might *involuntarily* become distracted and just stop deliberating rather than choosing anything. So Jones's own deliberation process remains indeterministic, Mele and Robb insist, unlike cases of complete blockage. Jones's own deliberative process might have outcomes other than the choice of A, though these other outcomes would not be voluntary *choices* of Jones.

Let us grant to Mele and Robb that this is not a case of complete blockage and that Jones's deliberative process remains indeterministic. But critics of Mele and Robb have posed the following question: if the only alternative possibilities left to Jones by Black's implanted process are *non*voluntary ones, is that good enough for true responsibility? Recall that Fischer, who is a prominent defender of Frankfurt-type examples, says that only *robust* alternative possibilities—those that are under the voluntary control of the agent—are good enough to ground moral responsibility. Could Jones be responsible for choosing A, if the choice of A issued from his deliberation process, when the only alternative was that he might become involuntarily distracted and stop deliberating? Our immediate intuitions suggest not. But Mele and Robb say their example shows otherwise. If Jones does choose A on his own in their scenario, they argue, Black's implanted process will not come into play. So why can't we hold Jones responsible for his choice, since Jones made it on his own—even if the only alternatives to his choosing A on his own were involuntary? Jones still made the choice on his own without the interference of Black's process.

Is Frankfurt thus vindicated after all? Is moral responsibility consistent with not having any robust alternative possibilities? Or must agents at least *sometimes* be able to *voluntarily* do otherwise if they are to be truly responsible? These are questions we will be returning to in later chapters.

Defenders of Frankfurt-type examples have proposed even more elaborate new examples to show that PAP is false (that moral responsibility does not imply the power to do otherwise). (See the suggested readings.) And many new compatibilists are convinced by these new examples that moral responsibility does not require alternative possibilities. We will look more closely at the positive views of these new compatibilists in the next chapter.

Suggested Reading

The most comprehensive collection of readings on Frankfurt-type examples and the debate surrounding them is David Widerker and Michael McKenna, eds., *Moral Responsibility and Alternative Possibilities* (Ashgate, 2003). This volume covers Frankfurt-type examples as discussed in this chapter as well as other new Frankfurt-type examples put forward by Eleonore Stump, David Hunt, Derk Pereboom, and others. Another collection partially dealing with Frankfurt-type examples is John Martin Fischer and Mark Ravizza, eds., *Perspectives on Moral Responsibility* (Cornell, 1993). Frankfurt-type examples are also discussed at length in Fischer's *The Metaphysics of Free Will: A Study of Control* (Blackwell, 1994) and Ishtiyaque Haji's *Moral Appraisability* (Oxford, 1998).

CHAPTER 9

Higher-order Desires, Real Selves, and New Compatibilists

1. *Hierarchical Motivation Theories: Frankfurt*

If new compatibilists, such as Frankfurt, do not think free will and moral responsibility require the power to do otherwise, or alternative possibilities, what *do* they think free will and moral responsibility require? What is their positive account of free will? In this chapter, we consider some new compatibilist theories of free will, beginning with Frankfurt's own theory, which has been very influential. Frankfurt, like many other new compatibilists, thinks that *classical* compatibilism—the view of Hobbes, Hume, Mill, and others discussed in chapter 2—is deficient because classical compatibilists give us only a view of *freedom of action,* but not an adequate view of *freedom of will.* (Recall that this was one of the criticisms of classical compatibilism discussed in chapter 2.) But Frankfurt thinks it would be a mistake to reject compatibilism just because the classical version was deficient. What is needed is a new and improved view of free will and free action without the defects of classical compatibilism.

Classical compatibilists viewed freedom as the *absence of constraints* preventing us from doing what we want. But they tended to focus on *external* constraints on freedom, such as physical restraint (being in jail or tied up), coercion or threats (holding a gun to someone's head), and physical disabilities (such as paralysis). Less attention was given by classical compatibilists to constraints that are *internal* to our wills, such as addictions, phobias, obsessions, neuroses, and other kinds of compulsive behavior. Freedom to do what we want is also impaired if we are addicted to drugs or have irrational fears of heights, an obsessive need to wash our hands, neurotic anxieties, and the like. Psychoanalysis and other modern psychological theories have made us aware of the importance of these internal constraints in people's lives. And note that these internal psychological afflictions are especially relevant for free will because they not only affect our freedom to do what we want. They also affect our freedom to *will* what we want.

To deal with internal constraints on the will, Frankfurt introduces a distinction between first-order and second-order desires.[1] Second-order desires are desires about *other* desires. For example, a drug addict may have a first-order desire to use a drug. He wants it badly. But he may also want to overcome his addiction in order to save his job and his marriage. In other words, he has a second-order desire *that the (first-order) desire* for the drug *not move him* to actually use the drug. This second-order desire is thus a desire *about* another desire. Because this second-order desire is a desire that the first-order desire for the drug not be "effective in action," Frankfurt also calls it a *second-order volition.*

Frankfurt thinks that the ability to have higher-order desires and volitions is one of the things that make us human. To be more specific, it makes us *persons* or *selves.* Nonrational animals also have desires or wants and even purposes. The tiger desires to protect itself from the cold, so it looks for a warm resting place. What makes persons or selves, such as humans, different is that we are capable of thinking *about* what kinds of desires and purposes we have and *ought* to have. In other words, persons or selves (we could also call them *rational* animals) are capable of "reflective self-evaluation"—of reflecting upon and perhaps changing the desires and purposes they do have rather than merely acting instinctively on their desires.

Consider the unwilling drug addict again. He desires the drug. But to save his job and marriage, he also desires to resist his desire to take the drug. As Frankfurt puts it, he has a second-order desire (or volition) that his first-order desire for the drug not "move him to action." Alas, for the addict, this second-order desire to avoid being moved to take the drug is ineffective. He cannot resist taking the drug. His behavior is therefore *compulsive* or *addictive;* and compulsive or addictive behavior is not free.

What the unwilling addict lacks, according to Frankfurt, is freedom *of will* because he cannot make his will (his first-order desire for the drug) conform to his second-order volition to resist taking the drug. According to Frankfurt, the unwilling addict lacks the will (first-order desire) that he wants (second-order volition) to have. When persons do not have *the will they want to have,* they lack free will. Consider, by contrast, a person who can resist his desire to take the drug. He may also have a first-order desire for the drug. Perhaps he took this drug on an earlier occasion and liked it.

But he knows the dangers of the drug and, unlike the addict, he *can* resist his desire to take the drug and does resist. This person has free will.

To illustrate further how free will is connected to the capacity for higher-order desires and reflective self-evaluation, Frankfurt introduces the idea of a *wanton*. Wantons are persons who act impulsively on their desires without reflecting on what desires they should or should not have. You probably know many persons who are like that with respect to some of their desires. But few persons act impulsively on *all* their desires. Such complete wantons, as Frankfurt notes, would not be *persons* at all. They would not be capable of having second-order volitions about which of their first-order desires should move them to act. Such beings, says Frankfurt, would lack the conditions for freedom of will. They would simply be pulled about by their first-order desires, never reflecting on the desires they should or should not act upon.

Theories of free will, such as Frankfurt's, are called "hierarchical theories" because they refer to "higher-order" desires and motives (desires and motives *about* other desires and motives). Hierarchical theories are an improvement in many ways over classical compatibilism because they provide a novel account of freedom of *will* (as well as freedom of action) and a richer account of the human person capable of higher levels of motivation. But note that hierarchical theories, such as Frankfurt's, are still *compatibilist* theories of free will even though they go beyond classical compatibilism. As Frankfurt says, it is "conceivable that it should be causally determined that a person is free to want what he wants to want" or "has the will he wants to have" (unlike the unwilling addict). And "if this is conceivable, then it might be casually determined that a person enjoys a free will."[2]

Indeed, on Frankfurt's theory it is not even required for free will that the agent "could have done otherwise" or had alternative possibilities. (Recall from the preceding chapter that Frankfurt argues by way of "Frankfurt examples" that responsibility does not require the power to do otherwise.) Indeed, if you have free will in Frankfurt's sense—if you have the will you want to have and you could act in accordance with your higher-order desires without internal or external constraints, why would you want to do otherwise? Frankfurt has thus provided a novel "hierarchical" account of free will that is compatible with determinism and does not require the power to do otherwise.

2. Identification and Wholeheartedness

While many people believe that Frankfurt's theory overcomes some of the objections to classical compatibilism, his theory also introduces a new set of problems about free will. For example, critics of Frankfurt have posed the following problem. Suppose that our first-order desires did conform to our second-order desires, but we were wantons (and therefore unreflective) about our *second-order* desires. Would we then have free will? Consider the following example suggested by a critic of Frankfurt's, Richard Double, in *The Non-Reality of Free Will.*

Suppose a young man has joined a religious cult and is completely devoted to the cult's leader. So complete is the young man's devotion that he has the first-order desire to sacrifice his life if the religious leader asks him. In addition, this first-order desire conforms to his second-order volition: the young man wants his desire to sacrifice his life to actually "move him to act," if the leader asks. He does not want to lose his nerve at the last minute. Suppose also that this desire is strong enough to move him to sacrifice his life. The young man thus has "the will he wants to have." But suppose he is also completely unreflective about this second-order desire to be moved by the desire to do whatever the cult leader asks. The young man is so completely under the influence of the cult leader that he never questions this second-order desire and is no longer capable of questioning it.

Double argues that this young man seems to have all the requirements of free will in Frankfurt's sense: his first-order desire conforms to his second-order volition and his first-order desire will be effective in action. Yet, "it is difficult to see how the young man has any more freedom than a wanton," says Double, since he is no longer capable of reflecting on his second-order desires.[3] Would not free will demand that one also be reflective about one's second-order desires and bring them into conformity with one's *third-order* volitions, and so on indefinitely? Why stop at the second, or any higher, order of desires? It seems that we would have to make an infinite number of higher-order reflections to have free will.

Frankfurt answers by appealing to a notion of *identification* or "decisive commitment" to some higher-order desire. Rather than reflecting indefinitely, he says, agents at some point simply identify with, or decisively commit to, certain higher-order desires and decide that no further questions about them need to be asked. But this answer has not satisfied Frankfurt's critics. In the words of another critic, Gary Watson: "We wanted to know what prevents wantonness with regard to one's higher-order desires. What gives these desires any special relation to 'oneself'? It is unhelpful to answer that one makes a decisive commitment where this just means that an interminable ascent to higher orders is not going to be permitted. This *is* arbitrary."[4]

To avoid the charge of arbitrariness, Frankfurt appeals to an additional notion of *wholeheartedness*. Persons are "wholehearted" when there are no conflicts in their wills and they are not ambivalent about what they want to do. Ambivalent persons, by contrast, are of two (or more) minds about what they want to do and cannot make up their minds. Reflection on our desires stops, says Frankfurt, when we reach desires to which we are wholeheartedly committed and to which we have no ambivalence. It is not arbitrary, he insists, to identify with such wholehearted desires because they are the desires with which we are "fully satisfied" and we have no "active interest in bringing about a change in them. Why then should we not identify with them? It is not irrational or arbitrary to stop our reflections, Frankfurt says, when we reach higher-order desires with which we are fully satisfied and about which have no doubts. He thus concludes that to have free will is to be able to act on higher-order desires to which we are wholeheartedly committed.

Frankfurt's appeal to wholeheartedness answers some objections to his theory, but it leads to another deeper objection. For all Frankfurt's account tells us, says Watson, a person's wholehearted commitment to certain desires may be the result of brainwashing or severe conditioning. Suppose the young man in Double's example has been brainwashed by the cult leader into being wholeheartedly willing to sacrifice his life if the leader asks. Would the young man then have free will simply because he is wholeheartedly committed to sacrificing his life and has no ambivalence or doubts about acting on this desire? Does it not also matter for free will how he came to have the wholehearted commitments he does have?

Recall the citizens of Skinner's community Walden Two, described in chapter 1. They can have and do everything they want, but only because they were conditioned by behavioral engineers since childhood to want only what they can have and do. The citizens of Walden Two are marvelously "wholehearted" in their attitudes and engagements in Frankfurt's sense. They are "satisfied" with themselves and "have the wills they want to have." Not only are they free to do whatever they want, they can *will* whatever they *want*. Their first-order desires always conform to their second-order volitions. So they not only have freedom of *action* but also freedom of *will* in Frankfurt's sense. It seems that the founder of Walden Two, Frazier, *can* truly say it is "the freest place on earth" in Frankfurt's sense. But do the citizens of Walden Two really have free will if their wholeheartedness came about entirely by behavioral engineering? Or are they more like the young man in the religious cult, if he was brainwashed into being wholeheartedly committed to the point of sacrificing his life? Or is there a difference, perhaps, between engineering the upbringings of persons so they will be happy (as in Walden Two) and brainwashing them so they will sacrifice their lives if you desire—a difference that might account for why the brainwashed cult member may lack free will while the citizens of Walden Two may have it?

A further problem for Frankfurt's theory is this. If free will is being wholeheartedly committed to one's desires or engagements and having no ambivalence about them, then it seems that persons can never get *from* ambivalence *to* wholeheartedness *of their own free will*. For note that we do not have free will in Frankfurt's sense *until* we have already attained wholeheartedness and are no longer ambivalent about what to do. This is an odd consequence of Frankfurt's view. For ambivalence is a common feature of everyday life. We often find ourselves in states of ambivalence—about what career to pursue (doctor or lawyer or cabinetmaker), whom to marry, where to live, which course of study to pursue. It seems that what we call free will is often making choices about these things and trying to bring ourselves *from* states of ambivalence *to* being wholeheartedly committed to what we think is important in life—a career, marriage, or whatever. Yet, on Frankfurt's view, it seems we cannot go from ambivalence to wholeheartedness of our own free wills because we do not have free will until we have become wholehearted.

Frankfurt's answer to these criticisms is to bite the bullet. He says it does not matter *how* we got to be wholehearted in our commitments or how we came to have the wills we want (whether by our own free wills or in some other way). People may come to have the wills they want in all sorts of ways, he notes, by luck or fortunate circumstances, even by social conditioning. It does not matter how they came to have the wills they want. What matters for free will is *how we are now,* not how we got that way. What matters is that we *are* wholehearted in our commitments and are not ambivalent and torn up about what to do and how to live. When we are in such a condition and do have the wills we want to have, then we are not compulsive like the addict, or obsessed like the neurotic, or ambivalent and confused like persons not completely committed to or wholehearted about their jobs, careers, or other things. Then we have free will.

3. Values and Desires: Watson

Many people are attracted to Frankfurt's novel account of free will and find it an interesting way of defending compatibilism. But they also wonder whether Frankfurt has accurately captured *all* that we mean by free will. Gary Watson is another new compatibilist who has criticized Frankfurt's theory, as we have just seen. Watson thinks Frankfurt is right about many things, including the belief that "reflective self-evaluation" is crucial for free will. But Watson does not think that what is important about free will and reflective self-evaluation can be understood in terms of higher-order desires alone. Reflective self-evaluation involves practical reason, according to Watson, which in turn depends on a fundamental distinction between *desires* and *values*.[5]

What we *value* is what our practical reasoning tells us is the *best* thing to do or what goals we should pursue—that is, what we have good *reasons* to do. Often our *values* in this sense conflict with our *desires* and *passions*. A disgruntled worker may feel like punching his obnoxious boss in the nose. But his practical reason tells the worker that this is not something he should do if he wants to keep his job; and keeping his job is an important *value* of his. A woman may want to watch TV but knows she must get up and exercise if she wants to heal her injured knee; and healing that knee is an important *value* for her. In such cases, and in many other similar cases we experience daily, our values conflict with our desires and passions. Sometimes in such conflicts, desires, and passions win out and we act against our better judgment. The worker cannot restrain himself and punches his boss; the woman lazily sits in front of the TV and cannot bring herself to get up to exercise.

In such cases, we say the persons are guilty of *weakness of will*. They do what they immediately desire to do against their better judgment. In Watson's terms, their *desires* win out over their *values*. The ancient Greek philosophers called such weakness of will *akrasia*—literally "no" (*a-*) "power" (*krasia*). Its opposite is *self-control*. One has self-control when one can make one's desires conform to one's reason and better judgments. The ancients believed that to act from weakness of will—to give in to desires against our better judgment—was to be unfree. By contrast, when we can make our desires and passions conform to our reason and better judgment, we are free. Watson pursues this theme. He distinguishes between persons' *valuational systems*—their values and reasoned judgments about what they should do—and their *motivational systems*—the desires, passions, and other psychological states that move them to act. When these two systems are in harmony, when persons' desires conform to their values and reason, they have free will. When the two systems are not in harmony, when persons' desires impel them to act against their better judgment and their actions are due to weakness of will, they are unfree.

4. Plato: Reason and Desire

Watson has thus revived a distinction between reason and desire that goes back to the ancient Greek philosopher Plato. Plato imagined that Reason and Desire were two parts of the soul that could be at war with one another. In one of his dialogues, he imagined we were drivers of chariots pulled by two horses, one white, one black.[6] The white horse represents

Reason, the black horse represents unruly Desire. When the two horses pull together, the soul is in harmony. Our desires conform to our Reason and we have *self-control* or *self-discipline*. When the two horses pull in different directions, we lack harmony in the soul and our desires are uncontrolled. Lacking control, we are unfree.

Watson's theory is thus like Frankfurt's in some respects. He says:

> Frankfurt's position resembles the Platonic conception in its focus on the structure of the 'soul.' But . . . whereas Frankfurt divides the soul into higher and lower orders of desire, the distinction for Plato—and for my thesis—is among independent sources of motivation.[7]

Reason and Desire (the valuational system and the motivational system) are independent sources of motivation for Watson, as for Plato; and when Reason rules over Desire rather than being overrun by Desire, we have freedom of will.

Like Frankfurt's theory also, Watson's theory is *compatibilist*. He adds:

> It can now be seen that one worry that blocks the acceptance of . . . compatibilism . . . is unfounded. . . . It is false that determinism entails that all our actions and choices have the same status as 'compulsive choosers,' such as kleptomaniacs. . . . The compulsive character of the kleptomaniac's thievery has nothing at all to do with determinism. Rather it is because his desires express themselves independently of his valuational judgments that we tend to think of his actions as unfree.[8]

The kleptomaniac cannot control his desire to steal, just as the unwilling addict cannot resist his desire for the drug. Frankfurt would say here that first-order desires do not conform to persons' second-order volitions. Watson thinks a more accurate thing to say is that the desires and reason— the persons' motivational systems and their valuational systems—are out of synch. Their desires do not conform to their reason. That is why they lack free will. And yet determinism, Watson is saying, does not imply that we are all like kleptomaniacs and unwilling addicts, that our reason and desires are always out of synch. So determinism alone does not rule out free will.

One problem for Watson's theory, and for Plato's, is embodied in the following question. Do we always act *unfreely* when we act from weakness of will? If being free means that Reason rules over Desire, then presumably we must be unfree whenever Desire wins out over Reason and we act from weakness of will. But is this always so? Suppose the woman who knows she should exercise her injured knee nonetheless succumbs to the temptation to continue watching TV. Or, suppose a student who knows he should study for an exam nonetheless succumbs to the temptation to go to a party. We think it is reasonable to say that in many such cases of weakness of will, the agents succumbed to temptation *freely,* or of their own free wills. Otherwise we could never hold persons responsible for their weakwilled behavior. When we give in to temptation it is not always a matter of compulsion. But to say that we have free will when Reason rules over Desire and that we are unfree when Desire is uncontrolled by Reason seems to imply that weak-willed behavior is not a matter of free will. It seems that Watson needs a principled way of distinguishing compulsive and addictive behavior from other cases of weak-willed behavior where people give in to their desires of their own free wills and could have done otherwise.

In addition, according to some critics, Watson's theory, like Frankfurt's, seems to be subject to the objection about behavioral engineering and manipulation. If persons could be behaviorally engineered to always act on their values or better judgments and never succumb to their unruly desires, it seems that they would be truly free in Watson's (and Plato's) sense. This is in fact the condition of the citizens of Walden Two, whose values were implanted in them by their behavioral controllers. Their reason and their desires were engineered to always be in harmony. Such harmony of Reason and Desire is also the condition Plato tried to bring about in the ideal state of his famous work *The Republic,* in which citizens were trained so that their desires would as much as possible conform to their reason. Yet we wondered whether the citizens of Walden Two really had free will. And we might also wonder whether the citizens of Plato's ideal state would have free will if they were so well trained that they could no longer act except as reason dictated.

5. Real or Deep Selves and Sanity: Wolf

Susan Wolf is another new compatibilist who thinks that the compatibilist theories of Frankfurt and Watson are on the right track but that both are incomplete.[9] Wolf calls theories such as Frankfurt's and Watson's "Real Self (or Deep Self)" theories. Our "real" or "deep" selves are the selves with which we "identify" or want to affirm as what we really are. For Frankfurt, our Real or Deep Self is represented by higher-order volitions that express the will we want to have and to which we are wholeheartedly committed. For Watson, our Real or Deep Self is represented by our values or what we think we ought to be, rather than by what we merely desire. But, on both views, we have free will and are responsible when our actions are in conformity with (and express) the Real or Deep Selves with which we reflectively identify.

Wolf is sympathetic to Real Self views, but she thinks they leave something out. For true freedom and responsibility, on Wolf's view, it is not good enough that we act from our Real or Deep Selves if our Real or Deep Selves are so messed up that we cannot appreciate the True and the Good and thereby lack the capacity to do "the right thing for the right reasons." Consider the notorious serial killer David Berkowitz, known as "Son of Sam." Berkowitz heard alien voices that he ascribed to a dog, named Sam, telling him to kill. He felt compelled to obey these voices, much as people might feel they had to do things they thought were being commanded by the voice of God. Son of Sam was insane and, in his delusional state, he was incapable of conforming his behavior to ordinary moral and legal norms. Or, consider another notorious serial killer, Jeffrey Dahmer, who had a compulsion to kill people and eat his victims. When Dahmer was finally apprehended, police found body parts of his latest victims in his refrigerator, apparently stored for future meals. Dahmer's pathology was strange, and it was never made clear what made him the way he was. But few doubted he was insane and incapable of conforming his behavior to ordinary moral and legal norms.

On Wolf's view, Berkowitz and Dahmer lacked the normative competence required to make them truly free and responsible agents. In her words, they were incapable of doing "the right thing for the right reasons" or incapable of appreciating and conforming their behavior "to the True and the Good."[10] To claim this is not to say that insane persons, such as Berkowitz and Dahmer, who cannot do the right thing for the right reasons and commit heinous crimes, should go free. Far from it. Since such moral deviants are an obvious danger to society, they could legitimately be confined to an institution, perhaps for the rest of their lives. Schoeman's analogy about disease and quarantine is helpful here. People like Berkowitz and Dahmer are as dangerous to society (in utterly different ways, of course) as carriers of a deadly virus for which there is no known cure. Those who commit heinous crimes, as they did, could therefore be confined against their wills if a cure is unlikely and uncertain. But to say this is not to say that the truly insane are morally responsible for their actions, any more than carriers of a newly discovered deadly virus are responsible for their illness. Nor is it to say that all insane persons are truly dangerous like Berkowitz and Dahmer.

What shall we say about Wolf's theory? She is no doubt right to emphasize that *sanity* and *normative competence* (the ability to appreciate and conform one's behavior to moral and legal norms) are important requirements for responsibility. These requirements for responsibility play an important role in courtrooms, and they have not received as much attention as they deserve in our earlier discussions. But Wolf's view—she calls it the "Reason View—also has some unusual consequences that many people find problematic. For example, she says:

> According to the Reason View, responsibility depends on the ability to act in accordance with the True and the Good. If one is psychologically determined to do the right thing for the right reasons, this is compatible with having the requisite ability. . . . But if one is psychologically determined to do the wrong thing, for whatever reason, this seems to constitute a denial of that ability. For if one *has* to do the wrong thing, then one *cannot* do the right thing, and so one lacks the ability to act in accordance with the True and the Good.[11]

In other words, as Wolf admits, her

> Reason View is committed to the curious claim that being psychologically determined to perform good actions is compatible with deserving praise for them, but that being psychologically determined to perform bad actions is not compatible with deserving blame.[12]

In defense of this curious "asymmetry thesis," as she calls it, Wolf points out that we often praise persons for doing the right thing (say, saving a drowning child) even if we know that their character and mental makeup was such that they could not have done otherwise in the circumstances. Yet we are reluctant to *blame* persons for doing the wrong thing (say, a kleptomaniac for stealing) if we know their mental makeup was such that they could not have resisted doing what they did. There is some truth to these claims. But they do not alone establish Wolf's asymmetry thesis. For, when we praise persons for good acts (such as saving a child) that flow from their characters, do we not assume, as Aristotle suggested, that they were in some ways responsible for the good characters from which those acts flow? And when we are reluctant to blame persons (such as kleptomaniacs for their acts of thievery), is it not because we believe they have a psychological illness for which they are *not* responsible and so they are *not* responsible for the mental makeup from which their acts flow?

6. Darth, the Hit Man: Good and Evil

To see why these questions may pose a problem for Wolf's asymmetry thesis, consider the following example. Suppose Darth is a vicious criminal who works as a hit man and enforcer for the mob. Darth is cruel and has no moral qualms about torturing or killing anyone who gets in his way. (Perhaps it is an indictment of modern moviemakers that a large percentage of villains in Hollywood movies turn out to be like Darth: vicious criminals without any redeeming features.) Darth's character is such that he is not capable of acting in accordance with the True and the Good in Wolf's sense, or of doing the right thing for the right reasons in the moral sense she intends. So Darth is not responsible for his vicious behavior, according to Wolf's theory.

But are we supposed to exempt all vicious criminals like Darth from moral responsibility simply because they can no longer do the right thing for the right reasons, without knowing anything more about them or how they became vicious? It is possible, to be sure, that Darth is a true psychopath whose childhood was so horrible (perhaps he experienced vicious child abuse and received no love) that he *could not help* becoming the kind of person he is. But we do not know this without knowing more about his background. It is also possible that his background was fairly normal, yet he was selfish and deliberately "hardened his heart" whenever he was required to be self-less. In other words, it is also possible, as Jonathan Jacobs has argued in his book *Choosing Character,* that agents like Darth intentionally made themselves into the vicious persons they now are, and they are responsible for doing so.[13] The point that critics of Wolf's view would make here is that whether Darth is responsible may not only be a matter of whether he can now act in accordance with the True and the Good, as she contends. It may also be a question of how he got to this point where he can or cannot act in accordance with the True and the Good.

Now look at another side of the picture. Suppose someone invented a drug we could give to Darth (without his knowledge) that would turn him overnight into a saintly Mother Teresa–like figure. He gives up being a hit man and begins helping the sick and the poor. Darth is now acting in accordance with the True and the Good, in Wolf's sense. So after being given this drug, he would be responsible for his behavior, according to her theory. Whereas before he was given the drug, he was not responsible because he was not capable of acting in accordance with the True and the Good. This is implausible, according to many of Wolf's critics. Ordinary intuitions suggest that it might be just the other way around. If Darth had deliberately and selfishly made himself into the vicious criminal he was before taking the drug, he would be responsible for his actions before taking the drug (contrary to Wolf's theory), And since he had nothing to do with the change in his behavior after taking the drug (because it was administered to him without his knowledge or consent), it seems that he would not be responsible for his behavior after taking the drug.

Now suppose that the drug later began to wear off, and Darth was tempted to go back to his vicious ways. Yet he resisted the temptations and deliberately chose to continue doing good when he could have chosen to go back to criminality. Then, it seems, Darth would be responsible for his behavior once again. But it seems that his responsibility would not be due *merely* to the fact that he could now choose to act in accordance with the True and the Good, as Wolf says. It would also be due to the fact that, when the drug wears off, he has a choice between doing good *or* evil. He can now choose to continue doing good works, but he can also choose to do otherwise—choose to go back to his earlier evil ways. This line of reasoning has suggested to critics of Wolf that being able to act in accordance with the True and the Good may not be all that is required for responsibility. We must not only be able to choose the Good, it would seem, we must be able to choose *between* Good and Evil. And if free will is the kind of freedom we associate with moral responsibility, as suggested in chapter 8, then free will would not just be the capacity to choose the Good. It would be the capacity to choose between Good and Evil.

Wolf and her defenders would question some of the intuitions behind the foregoing arguments. They might, for example, argue that Darth's behavior before taking the drug was so lacking in awareness of right and wrong that he was a psychopathic personality and therefore not responsible. (Psychopaths, for whatever reason, lack a moral conscience and have no remorse for their deeds.) So, in the end, you will have to decide for yourself whether the arguments presented work against Wolf's view or whether they do not. It is also worth noting, in Wolf's defense, that the capacity to understand the difference between Good and Evil ("to understand the difference between right and wrong"), which she emphasizes, is an important condition for moral responsibility. We do not have the capacity to freely choose *between* good and evil, right and wrong, if we are incapable of understanding the difference between right and wrong in the first place. Wolf has therefore drawn our attention to important and often neglected issues in the debate about moral responsibility and free will, whatever the final verdict may be on her view.

In conclusion, new compatibilists, such as Frankfurt, Watson, and Wolf, have introduced interesting new ideas into debates about free will and moral responsibility in the attempt to defend compatibilism and overcome the objections to classical compatibilism. Frankfurt is surely correct in saying that free will requires the capacity for *reflective self-evaluation* and perhaps also the possibility of higher-order motivations. Watson reminds us that there is some truth to the ancient Platonic notion that we are most free when our Reason is in control of our Desire and our values are in harmony with our passions, so we do not suffer from weakness of will. Wolf is correct in pointing out that *sanity* and *normative competence* are essential requirements for moral responsibility, hence for free will. These conditions would all seem to be necessary requirements for free will and moral responsibility, so the views of Frankfurt, Watson, and Wolf give us important parts of the picture of free will and moral responsibility. The question raised by the discussion of their views in this chapter is whether they give us the whole picture of what free will and responsibility require, or only a part of it.

Suggested Reading

Frankfurt's hierarchical view is put forth in "Freedom of the Will and the Concept of a Person," in the following edited volumes: Gary Watson, *Free Will,* 2nd ed. (Oxford, 2003); Robert Kane, *Free Will* (Blackwell, 2002); and Laura Waddell Ekstrom, *Agency and Responsibility: Essays on the Metaphysics of Freedom* (Westview, 2000). Essays examining Frankfurt's views on freedom and other topics can be found in Sarah Buss and Lee Overton, eds., *The Contours of Agency* (MIT, 2002). Watson's view appears in his article "Free Agency" (in Watson, ed., *Free Will* and Ekstrom, ed., *Agency and Responsibility*). Wolf's reason view is developed in her *Freedom Within Reason* (Oxford, 1990) and "Sanity and the Metaphysics of Responsibility" (in Watson, ed., *Free Will* and Kane, ed., *Free Will*).

CHAPTER 10

Reactive Attitude Theories

1. Freedom and Resentment: P. F. Strawson

The views of the preceding chapter were attempts to provide new and more sophisticated compatibilist versions of free will that would avoid the difficulties of classical compatibilism. In this chapter, we consider a second group of new compatibilists who try to defend the compatibility of free will and determinism in a different way. According to this group of new compatibilists, to understand free will properly, we must focus on the *practices* of everyday life in which we hold each other responsible and on the *attitudes* we take to others as a result of these everyday practices.

This new "reactive attitude" approach to free will, as it is often called, was initiated by an influential 1962 essay, "Freedom and Resentment," by British philosopher P. F. Strawson. Strawson argued that free will issues are about the conditions for holding people responsible. He further argued that to regard people as responsible agents is to be ready to treat them in certain ways, to adopt various attitudes toward them, such as resentment, admiration, gratitude, indignation, guilt, blame, approbation, and forgiveness. Strawson called attitudes of these kinds *reactive attitudes* because they are evaluative reactions to people's behavior. To be responsible, he argued, is to be a "fit" subject of such reactive attitudes. It is to be part of a "form of life" or moral community in which people can appropriately take such reactive attitudes to one another and thus hold each other responsible. This is what we do when we *admire* other people or *resent* or *blame* them for their behavior.

Consider the young man of chapter 1 who had committed a brutal murder. At his trial, our initial reaction was one of anger and resentment at what he had done. We blamed him for the crime and held him responsible.

But when we learned about the young man's sordid past, some of our anger, resentment, and blame was transferred to his parents and others who had abused him so horribly in childhood. We felt they shared some of the responsibility. If we did not feel this, it would not be appropriate to feel these reactive attitudes toward them as well as toward the young man himself. Similarly, when we are *grateful* toward persons who have done us a good deed, it is partly because we believe they did not *have* to do what they did. They had a choice about it and did it of their own free will.

Now many people have recognized these connections between free will and responsibility on the one hand, and reactive attitudes—such as resentment, blame, admiration, and gratitude—on the other. But what is unique about Strawson's theory is his belief that responsibility is *constituted* by our adopting such reactive attitudes toward one another. What justifies us in holding people responsible is that they are part of a *practice* or *form of life* in which it is appropriate to have such reactive attitudes toward one another. This practice or form of life is justified in turn by the fact that it expresses elementary human needs and concerns. "It matters to us," Strawson says, "whether the actions of other people . . . reflect attitudes toward us of good will, affection or esteem on the one hand, or contempt, indifference or malevolence on the other." Accordingly, the reactive attitudes are "natural human reactions to the good or ill-will . . . of others toward us as displayed in *their* attitudes and actions."[1]

Having said all this, Strawson turns to the issue of determinism. He notes that some people, namely incompatibilists, claim that if determinism were true, we would have to abandon the reactive attitudes and the practices associated with these attitudes because no one would ever really be responsible for what he or she did. But Strawson thinks that would be a crazy reaction. First, according to our ordinary practices of holding people responsible, he argues, we excuse or exempt them from responsibility under certain conditions, such as having acted in ignorance or having done what they did by accident or unintentionally or insanity. But determinism does not imply that *all* our actions are done out of ignorance or by accident or with some other such excuse or exempting condition. So, determinism does not imply that no one is ever responsible for his or her actions.

Strawson then goes farther, arguing that if we found out determinism is true, we should not give up the form of life in which we take reactive attitudes toward one another because we *could* not give up such a form of life and remain truly human. Our human commitment to the reactive attitudes is so "thoroughgoing and deeply rooted" in our nature, he says, that it would be psychologically impossible to abandon the reactive attitudes if we found determinism is true. He further argues that even if we could suspend the reactive attitudes, it would be *irrational* to do so, since the losses to human life in suspending these attitudes would far outweigh any reasons we would have to suspend them. Why should esoteric discoveries of physicists or chemists or neurologists about the behavior of electrons or amino acids or nerve cells lead us to abandon attitudes of admiration, gratitude, resentment, and blame toward other human beings in our everyday practices? These everyday practices involving the reactive attitudes are justified, according to Strawson, by the fact that they fulfill fundamental human needs. It would be irrational to give up feeling and expressing such attitudes toward one another because of what scientists might discover about physical particles or biological phenomena in a laboratory.

2. Excuses and Blame: Wallace

Strawson's idea that to be responsible is to be a fit subject of reactive attitudes has had a significant influence on debates about free will and responsibility. But what exactly is required for someone to be a "fit" or appropriate subject of resentment or blame, admiration or gratitude? On Strawson's view, to answer that question one has to look at ordinary practices of holding people responsible. Yet, when we look at these practices, we find that we often *excuse* people from responsibility or blame when they "couldn't help" doing what they did or "could not possibly have done" what we expected of them. But if determinism is true, it may seem that no one ever "could help" doing what they did or "could have done" what we expected of them. So it might appear that our ordinary practices of holding people responsible *themselves* imply that, if all our actions were determined, we would not be "fit" subjects of the reactive attitudes after all. This was in fact the conclusion drawn by many hard determinists and other skeptics about free will, as we saw in chapter 7. It is one reason, for example, why Smilansky argued that we would have to foster the illusion of free will if we came to believe that determinism is true.

Strawson rejects this incompatibilist conclusion, as you might guess. But his essay does not provide a sufficiently developed account of ordinary practices of holding people responsible that would show *why* determinism poses no threat to these practices. So other philosophers sympathetic to Strawson's view have attempted to supply just such an account of responsibility. R. Jay Wallace is one such philosopher.[2] Wallace argues that if we look more closely at ordinary practices of *excusing* and *exempting* people from responsibility and blame, we find that these practices are not undermined by determinism, just as Strawson claims. Moreover, Wallace thinks the reason why ordinary practices of holding people responsible are not undermined by determinism is that these practices do not require that agents could have done otherwise or that they had alternative possibilities. To make his case, Wallace focuses on responsibility of a moral kind. For persons to be "fit" subjects of moral reactive attitudes such as resentment, indignation, and blame, he argues, it must be *fair* to hold them responsible or blame them for what they have done. But it is fair to hold persons responsible or blame them, Wallace adds, only if they have done something wrong or violated a moral obligation we can reasonably have expected them to obey. For example, consider ordinary situations in which we excuse someone from blame. Suppose Molly blames John for not picking her up on the way to a party. John responds, "I'm not to blame. No one told me I was suppose to pick you up." Molly says, "But I also left a message on your answering machine," to which John replies: "But I didn't stop at home, I went directly to the party from work, so I didn't get the message." If John is telling the truth, it would not be *fair* to blame him, since there was no way he could have known what he was supposed to have done. He therefore violated no obligation and has a valid excuse.

Now it may *seem* that John is excusing himself by saying he *could not have done otherwise* in the circumstances, since he could not have known Molly expected to be picked up. But Wallace argues that even if this is so, even if John could not have done otherwise, that is not the *reason* we excuse him. The reason we absolve persons from blame in cases of legitimate excuses, Wallace argues, is that the persons did not *choose* to do what they did; they did not do what they did *deliberately* or *on purpose*. That is why we say they did not do anything wrong or did not violate any obligation. The fact that they could not have done otherwise is not a legitimate excuse *if* they chose to do what they did and did it deliberately.

In other words, it's the *attitude* of persons that counts when we are blaming or excusing them, not whether they could have done otherwise or had alternative possibilities. It would be *unfair* to hold persons responsible, or to blame them, if they did not *choose* to do what they did or did not do it *deliberately*. Recall Strawson's claim that the reactive attitudes are about whether persons display "ill-will" or "good-will" toward us in their attitudes and actions. When Molly learns that John did not deliberately fail to pick her up, that he did not do it out of ill will, it would be unfair for her to continue blaming him or feeling resentment toward him. And the same is true, says Wallace, about all our ordinary practices of offering excuses (ignorance, accident, coercion, etc.). A person excuses herself by saying "I did not *mean* to knock over your lamp (I did not do it on purpose), it was an *accident*." Or, "I did not *choose* to give him your money, he *forced* me to do it. He was holding a gun to my head."

Having considered our reasons for *excusing* persons from responsibility or blame, Wallace turns to the reasons why we *exempt* some persons from responsibility for such general conditions as childhood, retardation, insanity, and addiction. Often when we exempt persons from responsibility for such conditions as insanity, the persons also could not have done otherwise. But again, according to Wallace, that is not why we exempt them from responsibility. The reason is that very young children, the retarded, the insane, and the addicted lack what he calls the power of *reflective self-control*—"the power to grasp and apply moral reasons and . . . to control . . . [their] behavior in the light of such reasons."[3] But satisfying this condition, Wallace argues, also does not require the power to do otherwise. For we may have the power to understand what is morally required of us and to do it even when we could not have done otherwise. So ordinary practices of both excusing and exempting persons from blame or responsibility, Wallace argues, do not require alternative possibilities, hence do not require the falsity of determinism.

In summary, Wallace has attempted to provide support for Strawson's view that our ordinary practices of holding people responsible and taking moral reactive attitudes toward them would not be undermined even if determinism were true. Compatibilist views, such as Strawson's and Wallace's, are often called "*reactive attitude theories.*" Reactive attitude theorists hold (1) that to be responsible is to be an appropriate subject of reactive attitudes, such as resentment, admiration, indignation, and blame; and (2) that being an appropriate subject of such attitudes is compatible with determinism.

Notice that in defending this reactive attitude approach to compatibilism, Wallace takes a line similar to Frankfurt's in *some* ways. Like Frankfurt, he rejects the Principle of Alternative Possibilities (PAP), which says persons are morally responsible for doing something *only if* they could have done otherwise. But Wallace does not argue that responsibility does not require alternative possibilities by appealing to Frankfurt-type examples like those of Frankfurt and others in chapter 8. Wallace proceeds instead in the manner suggested by Strawson. He focuses on *ordinary practices* of holding people responsible and excusing or blaming them. Thus we have a "new compatibilist" theory (one that rejects the claim that responsibility requires alternative possibilities) that is different from Frankfurt's and from other new compatibilist theories considered in earlier chapters.

3. Challenges to Reactive Attitude Compatibilism

It seems correct to say that the *attitudes* of persons count when we are blaming or excusing them. Whether persons *chose* or meant to do what they did or did it *deliberately* and *on purpose* does matter when we are assessing responsibility. But critics of Wallace have questioned whether he is *also* right in saying that being able to do otherwise, or having alternative possibilities, has nothing to do with holding people responsible and blaming or excusing them. Isn't it also *unfair* to blame a person for not doing something the person *could not have done?* Can we blame a man for failing to save a drowning child if the man *cannot* swim? Is it true, as Wallace claims, that "the conditions of moral responsibility do not include *any* condition of alternative possibilities" at all?[4]

We know what Wallace would say in reply: often when we excuse persons from blame, it turns out that in fact they could not have done otherwise. But not being able to do otherwise is not *why* we excuse them. The reason we excuse them, according to Wallace, is that they have not "done anything wrong." That is, they have not "violated a moral obligation" that we could reasonably have required them to honor. John did not violate a moral obligation in failing to pick up Molly if he had no way of knowing she expected him to pick her up. So John rightly claims that he "didn't do anything wrong." (How often do we hear that excuse when friends and lovers quarrel!) Similarly, if Molly does not know how to swim, she does not *have* an obligation to swim to the middle of a lake to save a drowning man. So she does not violate any obligation by failing to do it.

Fair enough, say the critics. But isn't not being able to do otherwise sometimes the *reason why* we say persons have not violated a moral obligation, hence have not done anything wrong? Suppose an elderly man walking down the street at dusk sees an assault taking place in an alley. He chooses not to come to the aid of the victim himself and he chooses not to look for police or to seek help from others, not wanting to get involved. Most people would not blame the man for failing to come to the aid of the victim himself, since he was old and frail and the assailant was young and strong. They would feel he did not have a moral obligation to do that. But they would blame him for not choosing to look for help from police or elsewhere, since it seems he did have an obligation to do that. What accounts for this difference? It cannot be that he *chose* not to do one and not the other. For he chose not to aid the victim himself *and* he chose not to seek help. The difference seems rather to be that he *could not have done otherwise* in the one case (prevent or stop the attack himself), but he could have done otherwise in the second case (he could have looked for police or sought help from others). So we feel he did have an obligation to look for police or to seek help and is blameworthy for not doing at least that.

The principle at work in cases like this is something like the following: it is unfair to hold persons to moral obligations, if they could not possibly have fulfilled the obligations. (Thus we feel the elderly man did not *have* an obligation to stop the assault himself, since he could not have done so.)

Ishtiyaque Haji, a critic of Wallace's, has argued that this is a plausible principle of ordinary practices of holding people to moral obligations.[5] Haji also argues that this principle (taken together with other principles Wallace holds) entails the belief that it is unfair to blame persons for failing to fulfill a moral obligation if they could not have fulfilled the obligation (in other words, if they could not have done otherwise than fail to fulfill it). Wallace might reject one or another of the principles leading to this conclusion. But on the surface at least, they seem to be plausible principles of our *ordinary practices* of assessing people's behavior. So the burden of proof would be on anyone who rejects these principles to show where, if at all, they go wrong.

Another move Wallace might make is to concede that being able to do otherwise, or having alternative possibilities, is sometimes relevant to judgments about what moral obligations we have. But Wallace might contend that the sense in which we must be able to do otherwise in order to have a moral obligation *has nothing to do with determinism*. To say there is nothing the elderly man could have done to save the assault victim or to summon the police is to say that he lacked the *capacities* to do these things. But our judgments about whether he had these capacities depend on ordinary facts, such as whether the man was frail as well as old or whether he had a cellular phone and it was properly charged. And establishing whether these ordinary facts are true, Wallace might argue, does not depend on establishing whether determinism is true or not. Such a response leads us, however, to a second possible objection to Wallace's theory that directly involves the issue of determinism.

4. "Judas Set Up?"

This further objection to Wallace's theory is similar to an objection made against the new compatibilist theories of Frankfurt and Wolf. For Wallace, persons are blameworthy when they have violated a moral obligation and they have the capacity for *reflective self control*—the "power to grasp and apply moral reasons and to control their behavior in the light of those reasons" (as the insane and the severely retarded cannot). But it seems that one might satisfy these conditions for blameworthiness even if one's behavior was completely controlled or manipulated by others.

An objection of this kind is made to Wallace's theory in a striking way by Gideon Rosen with the following biblical example.

Acting from greed and envy, Judas conspires to deliver Jesus to the Romans. Let us stipulate that the act is one of loathsome betrayal and that in doing it

Judas possessed the "general capacity to see the reasons for acting differently and to act in the light of them." According to Wallace's account, we have all we need to hear. Judas is responsible for his act. It is perfectly fair to blame him for it.

But now suppose the whole thing was a setup. God's plan for salvation required that Jesus be betrayed, so he deliberately arranged the initial state of the universe and the laws of nature in such a way that Judas would betray him as he did with probability 1. That is to say, God saw to it that Judas would not exercise his capacity to do the right thing . . . by seeing to it that it would be physically impossible for him to exercise this capacity in the circumstances. When we hear this it is hard not to be shaken by the initial conviction that Judas is not responsible for his act. It's not just that we come to think that God is *also* responsible. Something in the story tends to absolve Judas.[6]

In response to Rosen, Wallace says we must distinguish "between the familiar notions of capacity, ability, power and difficulty, on the one hand, and . . . the technical notion of physical necessity or impossibility" given the laws of nature, on the other.[7] When we ask whether Judas was incapable of remaining loyal "in the ordinary sense," Wallace argues, we have to ask questions like the following: Did he act in ignorance? Did he do what he did by accident (did he have any excuse)? Was he insane or retarded or a child lacking the capacity to grasp moral reasons and to control his behavior accordingly? If the answer to all these questions is no, then Judas did not lack the *general capacity* to remain loyal in the ordinary sense that matters to us in everyday life; and so Judas was responsible. To think otherwise, Wallace contends, is to confuse impossibility given the laws of nature "with more familiar notions of incapacity, incompetence, difficulty and lack of power," which have to do with ordinary conditions that make things impossible or difficult to do.[8] It is these ordinary conditions that are relevant when we blame or excuse persons, he argues, and not abstract notions of physical impossibility and necessity connected with the laws of nature.

Wallace thus sticks to his guns, arguing along Strawson's lines, that theoretical issues about determinism are not relevant to our ordinary practices of holding people responsible. In defense of Strawson and Wallace, it must be conceded that thoughts about determinism, such as those raised by Rosen, do not usually enter our everyday discussions about whether persons are or are not responsible for their behavior. For example, almost everyone would be reluctant to accept the implications of Clarence Darrow's plea on behalf of Loeb and Leopold that *no* defendant is responsible because *everyone* is determined. Yet it is hard also to be unmoved by Rosen's intuition that it would be "profoundly unfair" to blame Judas if, "thanks to factors independent of [him], it was . . . impossible [given the laws of nature] that he should exercise his powers of reflective self-control" differently than he actually did. Is it enough to have the powers of reflective self-control if you cannot *exercise* those powers differently in the particular circumstances? We will come back to that question in the next chapter.

5. Semi-compatibilism

There is one other influential reactive attitude theory we must consider that gives at least some weight to Rosen's intuition and in the process puts a whole new twist on debates about free will. This is a view called "semi-compatibilism," whose chief advocate is John Martin Fischer. Fischer agrees with Wallace and Strawson that to be responsible is to be an appropriate subject of reactive attitudes, such as resentment, admiration, gratitude, and blame. Fischer also agrees with Wallace that moral responsibility in this reactive attitude sense does not require alternative possibilities and so is compatible with determinism. But, unlike Wallace or Strawson, Fischer arrives at the conclusion that responsibility is compatible with determinism by appealing to Frankfurt-type examples rather than relying entirely on ordinary practices of holding people responsible.

The most striking feature of Fischer's view, however, is that he makes a concession to incompatibilists that no other compatibilist makes. Fischer challenges an assumption that nearly everyone makes when discussing the free will problem—the assumption that freedom and responsibility necessarily go together: either both freedom and responsibility must be compatible with determinism or both must be incompatible. Most of our discussions in earlier chapters have made this assumption. But Fischer thinks it should be rejected. To be *free,* he thinks, does require forking paths into the future; and freedom is the power to go down one of these paths *or* another; so freedom requires alternative possibilities. In addition, Fischer is convinced by the Consequence Argument that determinism rules out alternative possibilities. So he concludes that *freedom* (in the sense that requires alternative possibilities) is not compatible with determinism. But responsibility is another matter. Reflections on Frankfurt examples among other considerations convince Fischer that responsibility does not require alternative possibilities and so responsibility is compatible with determinism. Hence the name "*semi*-compatibilism" that Fischer gives to his view: responsibility is compatible with determinism, but freedom (in the sense that requires alternative possibilities) is not compatible with determinism.

Fischer's semi-compatibilism has appeal for those who were convinced by the Consequence Argument of chapter 3 and other considerations that freedom is incompatible with determinism, but were also convinced by appeals to Frankfurt-type examples in chapter 8 or other considerations that responsibility is compatible with determinism. Such persons would be in a quandary—having some good arguments for incompatibilism and some good arguments for compatibilism. But this is a problem only if one assumes that freedom and responsibility necessarily go together, so that both must be compatible with determinism, or both incompatible. The semi-compatibilist view asks us to question this assumption.

To defend semi-compatibilism, however, Fischer must address a question that other compatibilists about responsibility, such as Frankfurt and Wallace, must also answer: if responsibility does not require alternative possibilities, or the freedom to do otherwise, what does responsibility require? Fischer's answer, in a word, is that responsibility requires *control*. To be held responsible for their behavior, persons must have control over their actions. But there are two kinds of control, according to Fischer: *regulative control* and *guidance control*. Regulative control requires alternative possibilities, but guidance control does not; and it is guidance control that is necessary for responsibility.

To illustrate the difference between these two kinds of control, suppose Mary is driving a car and comes to an intersection. Unknown to Mary, the steering mechanism of her car has temporarily locked so that the car will only turn to the left; it will not turn right or go straight. As it happens, however, Mary was planning to turn left anyway since she was intending to go to a shopping mall that required a left turn. So she does turn left. Mary does not have *regulative* control over which way she turns because she had no alternative possibilities: she could not have turned right or gone straight. Yet she does have *guidance* control, according to Fischer, because she intentionally "guides" her car to the left by steering it that way. According to Fischer, such guidance control is what one needs for responsibility. Mary is responsible for guiding her car to the left because she herself does it by turning the steering wheel in that direction, even though she could not have done otherwise (because the steering mechanism was locked). If, for example, in turning left she had hit a pedestrian, she could be blamed for hitting the pedestrian because she chose to turn left and proceeded with the turn deliberately.

Note that this line of reasoning is similar to Wallace's: responsibility has to do with what we *choose* to do or *deliberately* do on our own and not with whether we could have done otherwise. But note also that the reasoning is also similar to Frankfurt-type examples: Mary could not have done otherwise than turn left because the locked steering wheel would not have let her. But this constraint did not actually come into play because she chose on her own to turn left. So guidance control is what we need for responsibility, according to Fischer, and it does not require alternative possibilities. By contrast, *freedom* does require regulative control or the possibility of doing otherwise. Intuitively, Mary is not *free* to turn right or go straight. She does not have the power to do either one. So she lacks regulative control. Yet she is *responsible* for turning left because she was able to guide her car to the left and deliberately did so.

But if guidance control does not require the actual power to do otherwise, what does it require? In a book written, with Mark Ravizza, another semi-compatibilist, Fischer develops the view that guidance control requires *reasons-responsiveness*.[9] First, Fischer and Ravizza argue that agents have guidance control only if they act for reasons or motives and are able to guide their behavior in accordance with their reasons or motives. Thus, Mary had a reason to turn left (she wanted to go to the mall), and she guided her behavior in accordance with that reason. That is *why* she turned left, not because she could not have done otherwise. This much is necessary for guidance control, but it is not enough. Compulsives, addicts, and neurotics also guide their behavior in terms of their reasons or motives. But they cannot resist acting as they do even if they have good reasons to do otherwise. So compulsives, addicts, and neurotics are not "reasons-responsive" in the way that guidance control and responsibility require, according to Fischer and Ravizza.

To see what else is required for reasons-responsiveness and guidance control, we have to imagine what would have happened if the steering wheel had not been locked. Then, if Mary had had different reasons (if, for example, she believed the mall was on the right rather than the left), she might have turned to the right instead of turning left. Her behavior would be *responsive* to a difference in her reasons. But if, on the other hand, her turning to the left was compulsive, she could not have resisted turning left even if she had good reasons to turn right. Her behavior would not be responsive to a difference in her reasons, and she would not have true guidance control. In actual fact, of course, she could not have turned to the right anyway because the steering wheel was locked. Thus to determine whether she had guidance control and was reasons-responsive, we must *subtract* in our imagination the fact that the steering wheel was locked and *then* ask what would have happened. If Mary would have responded to different reasons and turned right (had the steering wheel not been locked), then she had guidance control and was responsible. If she would have compulsively turned left anyway, then she lacked guidance control.

If Fischer and Ravizza are right in saying that responsibility requires only guidance control in the foregoing sense, then responsibility would not require alternative possibilities. Even though Mary was responsible because she was reasons-responsive and was not turning left compulsively, she could not have done otherwise (for the steering wheel was in fact locked). So responsibility would be compatible with determinism. But then, wouldn't Fischer and Ravizza's semi-compatibilist view also be subject to Rosen's objection? Judas could understand the reasons for betraying Jesus and was able to guide and control his behavior in accordance with those reasons. Thus, Judas would seem to have had guidance control in Fischer and Ravizza's sense, and so he would be responsible for his behavior, even though he could not have done otherwise because God had set up the whole thing so that Judas would act exactly as he did.

Fischer and Ravizza do not answer Rosen's objection directly. But they do insist that it *does* often matter for responsibility whether persons were behaviorally engineered or manipulated by others into having a certain mind-set. For example, they argue against compatibilists like Frankfurt who think *historical* conditions of responsibility (such as how persons came to have the reasons or motives they do have) do not matter in judging whether persons are responsible. But Fischer and Ravizza also maintain that being manipulated or controlled by other agents, such as the behavioral engineers of Skinner's Walden Two, is not the same thing as merely being determined. They thus revert to a familiar classical compatibilist distinction: complete control by other agents may rule out responsibility, but *mere determinism* without control *by other agents* does not rule out responsibility. Perhaps all compatibilists have to make this distinction. But how is it to be made?

Fischer and Ravizza answer that in addition to "reasons-responsiveness," guidance control requires that the agents "take responsibility" for acting on the motives they do act on and so view themselves as fair targets for reactive attitudes. Suppose, for example, that the citizens of Walden Two said: "We know we have been behaviorally engineered to be the way we are. But we like what we are and we take responsibility for what we do and want to be held responsible for it." Wouldn't it be proper to "hold" them responsible for what they did from that point onward since they had just taken personal responsibility for what they were? To take them at their word and hold them responsible thereafter does seem to make sense. But Fischer and Ravizza face a further problem. Suppose the citizens of Walden Two were *also* behaviorally engineered or manipulated to "take responsibility" for themselves in this way. We might wonder in that case whether they would still be responsible. Fischer and Ravizza concede that it might be possible for persons to be engineered to take responsibility as well.[10] So they concede that their notion of "taking responsibility" is not complete and needs further development. But they are convinced that the idea of agents "taking responsibility" for what they are (when added to reasons-responsiveness and guidance control) is the key to understanding how responsibility can ultimately be reconciled with determinism.

Suggested Reading

Peter F. Strawson's "Freedom and Resentment" is reprinted in two edited volumes: Gary Watson, *Free Will,* 2nd ed. (Oxford, 2003); and Laura Waddell Ekstrom, *Agency and Responsibility: Essays on the Metaphysics of Freedom* (Westview, 2000). R. Jay Wallace's reactive attitude view is developed in his book *Responsibility and the Moral Sentiments* (Harvard, 1994). Fischer's semi-compatibilism is developed in *The Metaphysics of Free Will: A Study of Control* (Blackwell, 1994) and in Fischer and Mark Ravizza's *Responsibility and Control: A Theory of Moral Responsibility* (Cambridge, 1998). We have considered only a sampling of new compatibilist views in the past two chapters. Many other and different modern compatibilist views are discussed in essays by Tomis Kapitan, Bernard Berofsky, Ishtiyaque Haji, and Paul Russell and in an essay jointly written by Christopher Taylor and Daniel Dennett in Robert Kane's edited volume, *The Oxford Handbook of Free Will* (Oxford, 2002).

CHAPTER 11

Ultimate Responsibility

1. Two Conditions for Free Will: AP and UR

The past two chapters described the latest attempts by compatibilists to answer objections to their view and to provide more sophisticated compatibilist accounts of free will and responsibility. It is now time to return to incompatibilists or libertarians and to ask how they might deal with the objections to incompatibilist or libertarian accounts of free will discussed in chapters 4, 5, and 6. As noted in chapter 4, libertarians must solve two problems to defend their view. They must find a way to ascend Incompatibilist Mountain and get down the other side. The Ascent Problem consists in showing that free will is incompatible with determinism. The Descent Problem consists in showing how a free will that requires indeterminism or chance can be made intelligible and how such a free will might exist in the real world. In this chapter and the next, we take another look at these two problems, beginning with the Ascent Problem.

Recall from chapter 1 that there were two reasons why people were led to believe that free will must be incompatible with determinism. (1) Free will seems to require that *open alternatives* or *alternative possibilities* lie before us—a garden of forking paths—and it is "up to us" which of these alternatives we choose. (2) Free will also seems to require that the *sources* or *origins* of our actions are "in us" rather than in something else (such as the decrees of fate, the foreordaining acts of God, or antecedent causes and laws of nature) outside us and beyond our control. Both requirements seem to conflict with determinism.

Our focus up to this point, however, has been almost exclusively on the first requirement—on the requirement of Alternative Possibilities, or AP. We have said very little, by contrast, about the second requirement for free will mentioned in chapter 1—that the sources or origins of our actions must be in us and not in something else. It is time to remedy this omission. For a case could be made for saying that this second requirement for free will is even more important than alternative possibilities, or AP, for resolving issues about free will and determinism. Having alternative possibilities is not enough for free will, as we shall see in this chapter, even if the alternative possibilities are undetermined. And as a result, AP, or the power to do otherwise, may provide too thin a basis on which to rest the case for incompatibilism: there are reasons to believe that the incompatibility of free will and determinism cannot be settled by focusing on alternative possibilities alone.

Fortunately, there is another place to look. In the long history of debates about free will, there is another criterion fueling intuitions about the incompatibility of free will and determinism. This criterion is related to the second requirement for free will mentioned in chapter 1, namely, the requirement that the sources or origins of our actions be in us and not in something else. I call this second criterion for free will the condition of Ultimate Responsibility, or UR. The basic idea is this: to be *ultimately responsible* for an action, an agent must be responsible for anything that is a sufficient reason, cause, or motive for the action's occurring. If, for example, a choice issues from, and can be sufficiently explained by, an agent's character and motives (together with background conditions), then to be *ultimately* responsible for the choice, the agent must be in part responsible by virtue of choices or actions performed in the past for having the character and motives he or she now has. Compare Aristotle's claim that if a man is responsible for the good or wicked acts that flow from his character, he must at some time in the past have been responsible for forming the good or wicked character from which these acts flow.

Thus, we said that even if Luther's assertion "Here I stand, I cannot do other" was determined by his character and motives when he made it, Luther could still be responsible for his assertion to the extent that he was responsible for forming his present character and motives by many earlier struggles and choices in the past that brought him to this point. Often we act from a will already formed, but it is *our own free will* by virtue of the fact that we formed it by past free choices and actions. This is the idea behind the condition of Ultimate Responsibility or UR. UR does not rule out the possibility that our choices and actions might be determined by our wills, characters, and motives. But it does require that whenever this is so, to be *ultimately* responsible for what we are, and therefore to have free will, we must be responsible for forming the wills or characters that now determine our acts.

The Columbine killers, Harris and Klebold, may have been determined to act as they did by their wills and characters on that fateful day at the high school. But they might still be ultimately responsible for their acts to the extent that their wills and characters were formed by their own previous choices and actions and not merely by society or genes or other factors over which they had no control.

2. A Regress? UR and Determinism

This condition of Ultimate Responsibility, or UR, thus makes explicit something that is often hidden in free will debates—namely, that free will, as opposed to mere freedom of action, is about the forming and shaping of character and motives that are the *sources* or *origins* of praiseworthy or blameworthy actions. If persons are responsible for wicked (or noble, shameful, heroic, generous, treacherous, kind, or cruel) acts that flow from their wills, they must at some point be responsible for forming the wills from which these acts flow.

But it takes no great insight to see that this condition of UR is also problematic. For it seems to lead to a regress. To trace the regress: if we must have formed our present wills (our characters and motives) by voluntary choices or actions in our past . . . then . . . UR requires that if any of these earlier choices or actions *also* had sufficient causes or motives when we performed *them* . . . then . . . we must have also been responsible for those earlier sufficient causes or motives by virtue of forming them by still earlier voluntary choices or actions. We thus regress on backward indefinitely into our past. Eventually we would come to infancy or to a time before our birth when we could not have formed our own wills.

We saw in chapter 7 that such a regress plays a role in skeptical arguments against libertarian free will, such as Strawson's Basic Argument. Such skeptical arguments show us that there is a *possibly* vicious regress here, but it is an actual vicious regress only if *every* one of our voluntary choices and actions in the past had sufficient causes or motives for occurring. Then the regress would continue backward requiring that we be responsible for those sufficient causes or motives. So the potential regress tells us that free will is possible only if *some* voluntary choices or actions in our life histories did *not* have sufficient causes or motives that would have required us to have formed them by still earlier choices and actions.

Therein lies the connection of UR to determinism. If determinism were true, *every* act would have sufficient causes in the past, given the laws of nature. So the potential regress tells us that *if* free will requires ultimate responsibility in the sense of UR, then *free will must be incompatible with determinism.* Some choices of acts in our life histories must lack sufficient causes, and hence must be undetermined, if we are to be the *ultimate* sources or grounds of, and hence ultimately responsible for, our own wills.

Now it may be that this notion of being an "ultimate source or ground" of one's own will, which lies behind UR, is incoherent and impossible. We saw in chapter 7 that skeptics about free will, such as Nietzsche and Galen Strawson, think such a notion is incoherent and impossible, since it would require one to be a "prime mover unmoved" or "uncaused cause of oneself" or a *causa sui*—something the skeptics regard as absurd. But regardless of whether one can make sense of the notion of being an ultimate source of one's own will, one thing is clear from the preceding argument: if free will requires such an idea, free will would have to be incompatible with determinism.

A significant feature of this argument for incompatibilism from UR is that it does not mention the condition of *alternative possibilities, or AP.* The argument for incompatibilism from UR focuses on the *sources* or *grounds* or *origins* of what we actually do rather than on the power to do otherwise. When one argues for the incompatibility of free will and determinism from alternative possibilities or AP, as we have seen, the focus is on notions of "necessity," "possibility," "power, " "ability," "can," and "could have done otherwise." The argument from UR, by contrast, focuses on a different set of concerns about the "sources," "grounds," "reasons," and "explanations" of our wills, characters, and purposes. Where did our motives and purposes come from? Who produced them? Who is responsible for them? Are *we* ourselves responsible for forming our characters and purposes, or is it someone or something else—God, fate, heredity and environment, nature or upbringing, society or culture, behavioral engineers or hidden controllers? Therein lies the core of the traditional problem of free will.

Aristotle said that the goal of metaphysics, the central branch of philosophy, was to discover the "sources" or "grounds" (*archai* in Greek) and the "reasons" or "explanations" (*aitiai* in Greek) of all things. In this sense, the free will issue is deeply metaphysical, for it is about the *sources* and *reasons*—the *archai* and *aitiai*—of some important things in the universe that matter most to us, namely, our own choices and actions. To have free will, these choices and actions must be "up to us." And, as Aristotle said, the concept of an action's being "up to us" is connected with the idea that the "origin" (*arche*) of the action is "in us" and not in something else. This is the idea that UR expresses.

3. Austin-style Examples

But if one can argue for incompatibilism directly from UR, does that mean that alternative possibilities, or AP, have nothing to do with free will or with the question of incompatibility of free will and determinism? We have seen that many *compatibilists,* such as Frankfurt, think that AP is irrelevant to free will. Surprisingly, it turns out that some incompatibilists also think that AP is irrelevant because they think that UR is the source of the incompatibility of free will and determinism rather than AP.[1] But to infer that AP is entirely irrelevant to the free will problem or the incompatibility question if UR is involved would be a mistake. For UR not only entails indeterminism, as we have just seen. It turns out that UR also entails AP, or alternative possibilities, for at least *some* acts in an agent's life history. UR and AP are thus connected after all, and both have something to do with free will. Indeed, as we shall now see, the connection between these two pivotal criteria for free will is an interesting and unusual connection, showing us something significant about the free will problem that we have not discussed before.

To understand the connection between AP and UR (alternative possibilities and ultimate responsibility) we have to return to a claim made earlier in this chapter—that having alternative possibilities is not *sufficient* for free will, even if the alternative possibilities are undetermined. Some incompatibilists have thought that all one needs for free will is alternative possibilities *plus* indeterminism: in other words, it is sufficient for free will that we be able to do otherwise in a way that is not determined by our past.

But even if these two requirements—alternative possibilities and indeterminism—are both necessary for free will, it can be shown that they are not sufficient, even taken together. For there are examples of possible actions in which the agents have alternative possibilities, and in addition the actions are undetermined, *yet the agents lack free will.* I call examples of such actions "Austin-style examples" after the British philosopher J. L. Austin, who introduced one of the first such examples into free will discussions.[2] These Austin-style examples have implications for the free will issue that even Austin did not foresee.

Here are three Austin-style examples to serve as illustrations. The first example is Austin's own. He imagined needing to hole a three-foot putt to win a golf match, but owing to a nervous twitch in his arm, he misses the putt. The other two examples are my own. An assassin is trying to kill the prime minister with a high-powered rifle, but owing to a nervous twitch in his arm, he misses and kills the minister's aide instead. The third example is this: I am standing in front of a coffee machine intending to press the button for black coffee when, owing to a brain cross, I accidentally press the button for coffee with cream. In each of these examples, we can suppose, as Austin suggests, that an element of genuine chance or indeterminism is involved. Perhaps the nervous twitches of Austin and the assassin and in my brain were brought about by actual undetermined quantum jumps in our nervous systems. We can thus imagine that Austin's holing the putt is a genuinely undetermined event. He might miss it by chance and, in the example, does miss it by chance. (Likewise, the assassin might hit the wrong target by chance and I might press the wrong button by chance.)

Now Austin asked the following question about his example: can we say in these circumstances that "he could have done otherwise" than miss the putt? Austin's answer is that we can indeed say he could have done otherwise than miss it, for he had succeeded in holing many similar putts of this short length in the past (he had the capacity and the opportunity to hole the putt). But even more important, since the outcome of this putt was genuinely *undetermined,* he might well have succeeded in holing the putt and winning the golf match, as he was trying to do, rather than missing it.

But this means we have an action (missing the putt) that is (1) undetermined and (2) such that the agent could have done otherwise. (In other words, we have indeterminism *plus* AP.) Yet missing the putt is not something we regard as *freely* done in any normal sense of the term because it is not under the agent's voluntary control. Austin missed the putt all right; and he *could* have holed it—he could have done otherwise. But he did not miss it *voluntarily* and *freely.* He did not choose to miss it. The same is true of the assassin's missing the prime minister and killing the aide and my accidentally pressing the wrong button on the coffee machine. Both of us could have done otherwise (the assassin could have hit his target and I could have pressed the right button) because our actions were undetermined and they might have gone the other way. Yet the assassin did not miss his target voluntarily and as a result of his own free choice; and I did not press the wrong button voluntarily and as a result of my own free choice.

One might be tempted to think that these three occurrences (missing the putt, killing the aide, pressing the wrong button) are not *actions* at all in such circumstances because they are undetermined and happen by accident. But Austin correctly warns against drawing such a conclusion. Missing the putt, he says, was clearly something he *did,* even though it was not what he wanted or chose to do. Similarly, killing the aide was something the assassin did, though unintentionally; and pressing the wrong button was something I did, even if only by accident or inadvertently. Austin's point is that many of the things we do *by accident* or *mistake, unintentionally* or *inadvertently,* are nonetheless things we *do.* We may sometimes be absolved of responsibility for doing them (though not always, as in the case of the assassin). But it is for *doing* them that we are absolved of responsibility; and this can be true even if the accidents or mistakes are genuinely undetermined.

4. Will-setting and K-worlds

But we can now draw a further conclusion from these Austin-style examples that Austin himself did not consider. These examples also show that alternative possibilities *plus* indeterminism are not sufficient for *free will* even if they should be necessary for free will. To see why, consider the following scenario. Suppose God created a world in which there is a considerable amount of indeterminism of the kind that occurs in Austin-style examples. Chance plays a significant role in this world, in human affairs as well as in nature. People set out to do things and often succeed, but sometimes they fail in the Austinian way. They set out to kill prime ministers, hole putts, press buttons on coffee machines, thread needles, punch computer keys, scale walls, and so on—usually succeeding, but sometimes failing by mistake or accident in ways that are undetermined.

Now imagine further that in this world all actions of all agents, whether they succeed in their purposes or not, are such that their reasons, motives, and purposes for trying to act as they do are always predetermined or preset by God. Whether the assassin misses the prime minister or not, his intent to kill the prime minister in the first place is predetermined by God. Whether or not Austin misses his putt, his wanting and trying to make it rather than miss it are preordained by God. Whether or not I mistakenly press the button for coffee with cream, my wanting to press the button for coffee without cream is predetermined by God; and so it is for all persons and all their actions in this imagined world. Their reasons, motives, and purposes for acting as they do are always predetermined by God.

I would argue that persons in such a world lack free *will*, even though it is often the case that they can do otherwise—thus having alternative possibilities—in a way that is undetermined. The reason is that they can do otherwise, but only in the limited Austinian way—by mistake or accident, unwillingly or unintentionally. What they cannot do in any sense is *will* otherwise than they do; for all their reasons, motives, and purposes have been preset by God. We may say that the wills of persons in this world are always already "set one way" before and when they act, so that if they do otherwise, it will not be "in accordance with their wills." There is no name for worlds like this in which persons can do otherwise in undetermined ways, yet lack free will. So let me call them K-worlds.

The possibility of K-worlds shows in a striking way why, to have free will, it is not only necessary to be the ultimate source of one's *actions,* but to be the ultimate source of one's *will* to perform the actions as well. It would not be enough to have free will for agents to be unhindered in the pursuit of their motives and purposes if all their motives and purposes were created by someone or something else (God or fate or whatever). Even one's motives or purposes for wanting to change one's motives or purposes would be created by someone or something else in such a world.

Now it turns out that UR captures this additional requirement of being the ultimate source of one's *will* that is lacking in a K-world. For UR says that we must be responsible by virtue of our voluntary actions for anything that is a sufficient cause or a sufficient *motive* or *reason* for our acting as we do. We have a sufficient motive or reason for doing something when our will is "set one way" on doing it before and when we act—as the assassin's will is set on killing the prime minister. Among the available things he might do, only one of them (killing the prime minister) would be voluntary and intentional. Anything else he might do (such as miss the prime minister and kill the aide) would be done only by accident or mistake, unintentionally or unwillingly.

But UR says that if you have a sufficient motive for doing something in this sense—if your will is "set one way" on doing it rather than anything else available to you—then to be ultimately responsible for your *will,* you must be to some degree responsible by virtue of past voluntary acts for your will's being *set* the way it is. This is important because when we look to the responsibility of the assassin for what he did, we look to his evil motives and intentions. They are the source of his guilt, whether he succeeds in killing the prime minister or fails and kills the aide instead. Luther too, we assumed, had a sufficient motive for his final affirmation, "Here I stand," for his will was firmly set on making it. Yet, we said that if Luther's will was firmly set one way by the time he made his affirmation, the set state of his will would not count against his being ultimately responsible, *as long as he was responsible for his will's being set that way.* That is what UR requires.

But now it looks as if we have another regress on our hands. If it should turn out that our wills were already set one way when we performed the earlier voluntary actions *by* which we set our present wills, then UR would require that we must have been responsible by virtue of still earlier voluntary actions for our wills' being set the way they were at that earlier time, and so on backward indefinitely. But, once again, this is only a *potential* regress. Just as the regress discussed earlier in section 3 could be stopped by assuming that some actions in an agent's history lacked *sufficient causes,* so this regress can be stopped by supposing that some actions in an agent's past also lacked *sufficient motives*. Actions lacking sufficient motives would be actions in which the agents' wills were *not* already set one way before they performed the actions. Rather, the agents would set their wills one way or another in the performance of the actions themselves.

We may call such actions in which agents "set their wills" in one way or another in the performance of the actions themselves "will-setting" actions. Will-setting actions occur, for example, when agents make choices or decisions between two or more competing options and do not settle on which of the options they want more, all things considered, until the moment of choice or decision itself. They thus "set" their wills in one way or the other in the act of choosing itself and not before. The regress of sufficient motives can be stopped only by supposing that some voluntary actions in the agent's past are *will-setting* in this sense and not already *will-settled*. If all actions were like the assassin's killing of the prime minister, where the agent's will was already set one way, we would have to ask how the agent's will got to be set that way (by the agent or by something else?), and the regress would continue backward. So if we are to be ultimately responsible for our wills as well as for our actions, as free *will* requires, some actions in our lives must lack sufficient *motives* as well as sufficient *causes*. They must be will-setting actions that are not already will-settled.

5. Plurality Conditions

The need for will-setting actions tells us something further about free will. When we wonder about whether agents have freedom of will (rather than merely freedom of action), what interests us is not merely whether they could have done otherwise, even if the doing otherwise is undetermined, but whether they could have done otherwise *voluntarily* (or *willingly*), *intentionally,* and *rationally*. Or, more generally, we are interested in whether they could have acted in *more than one way* voluntarily, intentionally, and rationally, rather than *only in one way* voluntarily, and so on, and in other ways merely by accident or mistake, unintentionally or irrationally, as seen in the Austin-style examples. ("Voluntarily" means here "in accordance with one's will"; "intentionally" means "knowingly" and "on purpose"; and "rationally," means "having good reasons for acting and acting for those reasons.")

Let us use the term "plurality conditions" to describe these requirements of *more-than-one-way* (or plural) voluntariness, rationality, and intentionality. Such *plurality conditions* seem to be deeply embedded in our intuitions about free choice and action. Most of us naturally assume that freedom and responsibility would be deficient if it were always the case that we could do otherwise only by accident or mistake, unintentionally, or involuntarily. Free will seems to require that if we acted voluntarily, intentionally, and rationally, we could also have done otherwise voluntarily, intentionally, and rationally. But *why* do we assume this so readily? And why are these plurality conditions so deeply embedded in our intuitions about free will?

The argument of the preceding section from UR provides the clue. If (1) free will requires (2) ultimate responsibility for our wills as well as for our actions, then it requires (3) will-setting actions at some points in our lives; and will-setting actions require (4) these plurality conditions. To see why will-setting actions require these plurality conditions, consider a variation on the assassin example that would make his choice to kill the prime minister a will-setting one. Suppose that just before pulling the trigger, the assassin has doubts about his mission. Pangs of conscience arise in him, and a genuine inner struggle ensues about whether to go through with the killing. There is now more than one motivationally significant option before his mind. So his will is no longer clearly set one way (he is no longer sure he wants to pull the trigger); and he will resolve the issue one way or the other only by consciously deciding and thereby setting his will in one direction or the other. Unlike the original assassin example, neither outcome in this case would be a mere accident or mistake; either outcome would be a voluntary and intentional decision to go through with the killing or to stop. Will-setting actions are therefore voluntary, intentional, and rational *whichever* way they go, and so they satisfy the plurality conditions.

So we have the following chain of inferences: (1) *free will* entails (2) *ultimate responsibility* [UR] for our wills as well as for our actions, which entails (3) *will-setting* actions at some points in our lives, which in turn entail that some of our actions must satisfy (4) the *plurality conditions*. But if actions satisfy the plurality conditions, the agents could have done otherwise voluntarily, intentionally, and rationally, which in turn entails that (5) the agents *could have done otherwise* or had alternative possibilities.

Therein lies the connection between UR and AP. If free will requires ultimate responsibility in the sense of UR, then at least some actions in our life histories must be such that we could have done otherwise. Note, however, that this argument from free will to alternative possibilities (AP) is not direct. It goes *through* ultimate responsibility (UR), will-setting, and plurality; and UR is the key to it, since it is UR that implies will-setting and plurality. If we are to be ultimately responsible for our own wills, some of our actions must be such that we could have done otherwise *because* some of them must have been such that we could have done otherwise voluntarily, intentionally, and rationally.

6. Self-forming Actions (SFAs) and the Dual Regress of Free Will

UR thus entails both indeterminism and AP. But it entails them by different argumentative routes. Two separate regresses are involved. The first regress begins with the requirement (of UR) that agents be responsible by virtue of past voluntary actions for anything that is a *sufficient cause* of their actions. Stopping this regress requires that if agents are to have free will, some actions in their life histories must be undetermined (must lack sufficient causes). The second regress begins with the requirement that agents be responsible by virtue of past voluntary actions for anything that is a sufficient *motive* or reason for their actions. Stopping this regress requires that some actions in an agent's life history be will-setting (so they do not have sufficient motives already set), and hence must satisfy the plurality conditions. These actions will be such that the agents could have done otherwise, or had alternative possibilities.

The first of these two regresses results from the requirement that we be ultimate sources of our *actions;* the second regress results from the requirement that we be ultimate sources of our *wills* (to perform those actions). If the second requirement were not added, we might have worlds in which all the will-setting was done by someone or something other than the agents themselves, as in the imagined K-world in which all the will-setting was done by God. Agents in such a world might be unhindered in the pursuit of their purposes or ends, but it would never be "up to them" what purposes or ends they pursued. They would have a measure of free action, but not freedom of will. You may recall that what was worrisome about Walden Two was that, while persons there had a good deal of freedom to pursue their purposes, all their purposes had been designed by someone else, the behavioral controllers.

One might say that to have free will in the sense required by UR is to be the ultimate designer of at least some of one's own purposes. And to be such an ultimate designer, some actions in our life histories must be both will-setting and undetermined.[3] We might call these undetermined will-setting actions *"self-forming actions,"* or SFAs for short. For they would be the actions in our lives by which we *form* our character and motives (i.e., our wills) and make ourselves into the kinds of persons we are. All actions done *of our own free wills* do not have to be undetermined self-forming actions (SFAs) of this kind. (Luther's "Here I stand" could have been uttered "of his own free will" even if Luther's will was already settled when he said it.) But if *no* actions in our lifetimes were of this undetermined self-forming or will-setting kind, then our wills would not be our own free wills and we would not be ultimately responsible for anything we did.

This chapter has considered an alternative argument for the incompatibility of free will and determinism that does not rely on alternative possibilities alone, but relies instead on the second criterion for free will mentioned in chapter 1—the requirement that the *sources* or *origins* of our purposes and actions be ultimately "in us" rather than in something else. This requirement was spelled out in terms of a condition of Ultimate Responsibility or UR. Such a condition of Ultimate Responsibility, however, is an unusually strong condition. Is it something humans can really have or an impossible ideal? We turn to that question in the next chapter.

Suggested Reading

The account of ultimate responsibility presented in this chapter is further developed in my book *The Significance of Free Will* (Oxford, 1996). Discussions that take different perspectives on ultimate responsibility include Martha Klein, *Determinism, Blameworthiness and Deprivation* (Oxford, 1990); Galen Strawson "The Bounds of Freedom," in my edited volume *The Oxford Handbook of Free Will* (Oxford, 2002); and Derk Pereboom *Living Without Free Will* (Cambridge, 2001). All three of these authors think ultimate responsibility may be required for free will, but they argue that it is an impossible ideal or cannot be realized. So they provide a challenge to the view presented in this chapter and the next.

CHAPTER 12

Free Will and Modern Science

1. Introduction

Can we make sense of a free will that requires Ultimate Responsibility of the kind described in the preceding chapter? Many philosophers think not. They argue (in the manner of Nietzsche and Strawson in chapter 7) that being the *ultimate* source of one's will and actions is an incoherent and impossible ideal, since it would require us to be "prime movers unmoved" or "uncaused causes of ourselves"—"the best self-contradiction that has been conceived so far," as Nietzsche put it. Ultimate Responsibility, or UR, requires that there be some acts in our lifetimes that do not have sufficient causes or motives. But how could acts having neither sufficient causes nor motives be free and responsible actions?

In chapter 5, I noted that traditional libertarian theories of free will have usually appealed to "extra factors" in response to these problems. Realizing that free will cannot merely be indeterminism or chance, libertarians have introduced additional and often mysterious forms of agency or causation to make up the difference, such as immaterial minds, noumenal selves outside space and time or non-event agent-causes. The idea behind such extra-factor strategies is easy enough to understand: since indeterminism leaves it open which way an agent will chose or act, some "extra" kind of causation or agency must be posited over and above the natural flow of events to account for the agent's going one way or the other—something else must tip the balance. This is a tempting way to think. But introducing extra forms of causation or agency beyond the natural flow of events has invited charges that libertarian theories of free will are obscure and mysterious and cannot be reconciled with modern scientific views about human beings.

Libertarians in general have not done a good job explaining how their view of free will can be reconciled with modern scientific views about human beings and the cosmos. This is the challenge I want to take up in the present chapter. Can a libertarian view of free will requiring Ultimate Responsibility be made intelligible without appealing to obscure or mysterious forms of agency or causation? Can such a free will be reconciled with what we know about human beings in the modern physical, biological, and human sciences? To answer these questions, I believe we have to rethink issues about freedom, responsibility, and indeterminism from the ground up, without relying on appeals to extra factors unless absolutely necessary. What follows is my own attempt to do this. Consider it a proposal meant to stimulate thinking about how free will might exist in the natural world where we humans exist and must exercise our freedom.

2. Physics, Chaos, and Complexity

We must grant, first of all, that if any libertarian theory of free will is to succeed there must be some genuine indeterminism in nature to make room for it. As the ancient Epicurean philosophers said, the atoms must sometimes "swerve" in undetermined ways if there is to be room in nature for free will. Moreover, it would be no use if the atoms swerved in outer space somewhere far from human affairs. They must swerve where it would matter for human choice and action, for example, in the brain. This is true even if one postulates special kinds of agent-causes or a nonmaterial self to intervene in the brain. If these special forms of agency are to have any room to operate, the indeterminism must be there to begin with.

This is the point, as we have seen, where some scientists want to bring modern quantum physics into the picture to help account for free will. Suppose there were quantum jumps or other undetermined quantum events occurring in the brain. We know that information processing in the brain takes place through the firing of individual neurons or nerve cells in complex patterns. Individual firings of neurons in turn involve the transmission of chemical ions across neuronal cell walls, stimulated by various chemicals, called neurotransmitters, and by electrical stimuli coming from other neurons. Some neuroscientists have suggested that quantum indeterminacies in the transmission of these chemical ions across the cell walls of neurons might make the exact timing of the firings of individual neurons uncertain, thus introducing indeterminism into the activity of the brain and making "room" for free will.

Such suggestions are speculative. But even if they were correct, how would they help with free will? It was noted earlier that if choices were to occur as the result of quantum jumps or other undetermined events in the brain, the choices would not be under the control of the agents and would scarcely count as free and responsible actions. A similar criticism was made of the ancient Epicurean view. How could the chance swerve of atoms help to give us free will? Another problem about using quantum indeterminacy to defend free will was also mentioned in chapter 1. Determinists, such as Honderich, point out that quantum indeterminacy is usually insignificant in the behavior of larger physical systems like the human brain and body. When large numbers of particles are involved, as in the transmission of chemical ions across cell walls, any quantum indeterminacies would most likely be "damped" out and would have negligible effects on the larger activity of the brain and body.

Maybe so. But there is another possibility suggested by some scientists. Quantum theory alone will not account for free will, they concede. But perhaps quantum physics could be combined with the new sciences of "chaos" and "complexity" to help make sense of free will. In "chaotic" physical systems, very small changes in initial conditions lead to large and unpredictable changes in the system's subsequent behavior.[1] You may have heard the narrative in which the fluttering of a butterfly's wings in South America initiates a chain of events that affects weather patterns in North America. Perhaps that famous example is something of an exaggeration. But chaotic phenomena, in which small changes lead to large effects, are now known to be far more common in nature than previously believed, and they are particularly common in living things. There is growing evidence that chaos may play a role in the information processing of the brain, providing some of the flexibility that the nervous system needs to adapt creatively—rather than in predictable or rigid ways—to an ever-changing environment.

Determinists, to be sure, are quick to point out that chaotic behavior in physical systems, though unpredictable, is usually deterministic and does not itself imply genuine indeterminism in nature. But some scientists have suggested that a combination of chaos and quantum physics might provide the genuine indeterminism one needs. If the processing of the brain does "make chaos in order to make sense of the world"(as one recent research paper puts it[2]), then the resulting chaos might magnify quantum indeterminacies in the firings of individual neurons. These chaotically magnified indeterminacies in the firings of neurons would have large-scale indeterministic effects on the activity of neural networks in the brain as a whole. The indeterminacy at the neuron level would no longer be "damped out," but would have significant effects on cognitive processing and deliberation.

But once again we might ask how even this would help with free will. If indeterminacy in our neurons were amplified to have significant effects on our mental processing and deliberation, would that give us any greater control and freedom? More likely it would give us less control and freedom. Wouldn't deliberation become something like spinning a roulette wheel in one's mind to make a choice? Maybe. But before we jump to conclusions, we need to look more deeply into the situation. If there were some significant indeterminism available in the brain, could we make more sense of it than simply spinning roulette wheels? Let us see. What is required to answer these questions, as I suggested, is a thorough rethinking of issues about freedom, responsibility, and indeterminism.

3. Conflicts in the Will

The first step in this rethinking is to note that indeterminism does not have to be involved in *all* acts done "of our own free wills" for which we are ultimately responsible, as noted in chapter 11. Not all acts done of our own free wills have to be undetermined, only those acts by which we made ourselves into the kinds of persons we are—namely, the "will-setting" or "self-forming actions" (SFAs) that are required for ultimate responsibility.

Now I believe that these undetermined self-forming actions, or SFAs, occur at those difficult times of life when we are torn between competing visions of what we should do or become. Perhaps we are torn between doing the moral thing or acting from ambition, or between powerful present desires and long-term goals; or we may be faced with difficult tasks for which we have aversions. In all such cases of difficult self-forming choices in our lives, we are faced with competing motivations and have to make an effort to overcome the temptation to do something else we also strongly want. There is tension and uncertainty in our minds about what to do at such times, let us suppose, that is reflected in appropriate regions of our brains by movement away from thermodynamic equilibrium—in short, a kind of "stirring up of chaos" in the brain that makes it sensitive to micro-indeterminacies at the neuronal level. The uncertainty and inner tension we feel at such soul-searching moments of self-formation would thus be reflected in the indeterminacy of our neural processes themselves. What we experience internally as uncertainty about what to do on such occasions would correspond physically to the opening of a window of opportunity that temporarily screens off complete determination by influences of the past.

When we do decide under such conditions of uncertainty the outcome is not determined, thanks to the indeterminacy that preceded it. Yet the outcome can be willed either way we choose, rationally and voluntarily, because in such self-formation, the agents' prior wills are divided by conflicting motives. Consider a businesswoman who faces a conflict of this kind. She is on her way to an important meeting when she observes an assault taking place in an alley. An inner struggle arises between her conscience on the one hand (to stop and call for help for the assault victim) and her career ambitions, on the other hand, which tell her she cannot miss this important business meeting. She has to make an effort of will to overcome the temptation to do the selfish thing and go on to the meeting. If she overcomes this temptation, it will be the result of her effort to do the moral thing; but if she fails, it will be because she did not *allow* her effort to succeed. For while she willed to overcome temptation, she also willed to fail. That is to say, she had strong reasons to will the moral thing, but she also had strong reasons, ambitious reasons, to make the selfish choice that were different from, and incommensurable with, her moral reasons. When we, like the woman, decide in such circumstances, and the indeterminate efforts we are making become determinate choices, we *make* one set of competing reasons or motives prevail over the others then and there *by deciding*. Thus the choice we eventually make, though undetermined, can still be rational (made for reasons) and voluntary (made in accordance with our wills), whichever way we choose.

Now let us add a further piece to the puzzle. Just as indeterminism need not undermine the rationality and voluntariness of choices, so indeterminism in and of itself need not undermine control and responsibility. Suppose you are trying to think through a tough math problem. Say there is an indeterminacy in your neural processes complicating the task. This indeterminacy would make your task more difficult, in much the same way that low background noise would be slightly distracting if you were trying to solve a tough math problem. Whether you are going to succeed in solving the problem is uncertain and undetermined because of the distracting neural noise. Yet, if you manage to concentrate and solve the problem nonetheless, we have reason to say you did it and are responsible for it— even though it was undetermined whether you would succeed. The indeterministic noise would have been an obstacle that you overcame by your effort.

There are many examples supporting this idea of indeterminism functioning as an obstacle to success without precluding responsibility. Included among these examples are the Austin-style examples discussed in chapter 11. Recall the assassin, who was trying to shoot the prime minister but might miss because undetermined events in his nervous system might lead to a jerking or wavering of his arm. If the assassin did succeed in hitting his target, despite the indeterminism, can he be held responsible?

The answer is clearly yes because he intentionally and voluntarily succeeded in doing what he was *trying* to do—kill the prime minister. Yet his action, killing the prime minister, was undetermined. The indeterminism here functioned as an obstacle to his success but did not rule out his responsibility *if* he succeeded.

Here is another example. A husband, beside himself with rage while arguing with his wife, swings his arm down on her favorite glass-top table, intending to break it. Again, we suppose that some indeterminism in his outgoing neural pathways makes the momentum of his arm indeterminate, so that it is undetermined whether the table will break right up to the moment it is struck. Whether the husband breaks the table is undetermined, and yet he is clearly responsible if he does break it. (It would be a poor excuse to offer his wife if he claimed, "Chance did it, not me." Though indeterminism was involved, chance didn't do it, *he* did.) In this example as in the preceding one, the agent can be held responsible for an action even though the action is undetermined.

Now these examples—of the math problem, the assassin, and the husband—are not all we want for free will. They do not amount to genuine exercises of self-forming actions (SFAs) like the businesswoman whose will is divided between conflicting motives. The businesswoman wants to help the assault victim, but she also wants to go on to her meeting. By contrast, the assassin's will is not equally divided. He wants to kill the prime minister, but he does *not* also want to fail. (If he fails therefore, it will be *merely* by chance.) So while the examples of the assassin, the husband, and the like do not tell us all we need to know about free will, they do provide some clues to what free will requires. To go further, we have to appeal to some additional ideas.

4. Parallel Processing

Imagine in cases of conflict characteristic of self-forming actions or SFAs, like the businesswoman's that the indeterministic noise, which is providing an obstacle to her overcoming temptation, is coming not from an external source but from her own will, since she also deeply desires to do the opposite. Imagine that two crossing recurrent neural networks are involved, each influencing the other, and representing the woman's conflicting motivations. (These neural networks are complex networks of interconnected neurons in the brain, circulating impulses in feedback loops that are generally involved in higher-level cognitive processing.[3]) The input of one of these neural networks consists of the woman's reasons for acting morally and stopping to help the victim; the input of the other network comprises her ambitious motives for going on to the meeting. The two neural networks are connected, so that the indeterministic noise, which is an obstacle to the woman's making one of her choices, is coming from her own desire to make the opposite choice. In these circumstances, when either of the pathways "wins" (i.e., reaches an activation threshold, which amounts to choice), the woman will be making her choice in spite of the indeterministic noise she had to overcome. Her choosing in spite of the noise obstacle will be like your solving the tough math problem in spite of distracting background noise. And just as we can say, when you solved the math problem by overcoming the distracting noise, that you did it and are responsible for it, so we can say this as well, I would argue, in the woman's case, *whichever way she chooses*. The pathway through which the woman succeeds in reaching a choice threshold will have overcome the obstacle in the form of indeterministic noise generated by the other pathway.

Note that under such conditions of indeterminism arising from conflicting alternatives, choices going either way will not be "inadvertent," "accidental," "capricious," or "merely random" (as critics of indeterminism say). On the contrary, the choices will be *willed* by the agents either way when they are made, and done for reasons either way—reasons that the agents then and there *endorse*. But these are the conditions usually required to say that something is done "on purpose" rather than accidentally, capriciously, or merely by chance. Moreover, these conditions for saying the actions were done on purpose, taken together, I would argue, rule out each of the reasons we have for saying that agents act but do not have *control* over their actions. The agents need not have been acting under compulsion, coercion, constraint, inadvertence, accident, control by others, and so on.[4] To be sure, we must grant that when choices are undetermined SFAs, agents do not control or determine which choice-outcome will occur *before* it occurs. But it does not follow that, because one does not control or determine which of a set of outcomes is going to occur before it occurs, one does not control or determine which of them occurs, *when* it occurs.

When the preceding conditions for SFAs are satisfied, and the agents exercise control over their future lives *then and there* by deciding, they have what I call *plural voluntary control* over the options in the following sense: the agents are able to bring about *whichever* of the options they will, *when* they will to do so, *for* the reasons they will to do so, *on* purpose, rather than accidentally or by mistake, *without* being coerced or compelled in doing so or in willing to do so, or otherwise controlled in doing or in willing to do so by any other agents or mechanisms. Each of these conditions can be satisfied for SFAs, like the businesswoman's, as I have described them. The conditions can be summed up by saying that the agents can choose either way *at will*. In other words, the choices are "will-setting": we set our wills one way or the other in the *act* of deciding, and not before.

Note also that this account of self-forming choices amounts to a kind of "doubling" of the difficulty seen in the math problem example, where the agent had to make an effort to overcome indeterministic background noise. It is as if an agent faced with a self-forming choice is *trying* or making an effort to solve *two* cognitive problems at once, or to complete two competing (deliberative) tasks at once. In our example the businesswoman is trying to make a moral choice and to make a conflicting self-interested choice. The two competing choices correspond to two competing neural networks in her brain. Each task is being thwarted by the indeterminism coming from the other, so it might fail. But if it succeeds, then the agents can be held responsible because, as in the case of solving the math problem, the agents will have succeeded in doing what they were knowingly and willingly trying to do. Recall the assassin and the husband. Owing to indeterminacies in their neural pathways, the assassin might miss his target or the husband might fail to break the table. But if these two agents *succeed,* despite the probability of failure, they are responsible, since they will have succeeded in doing what they were trying to do. And so it is, I suggest, with self-forming choices like the businesswoman's. The agents will be responsible *whichever way they choose* because whichever way they choose they will have succeeded in doing what they were trying to do. Their failure to do one thing is not a *mere* failure, but a voluntary success in doing the other.

Does it make sense to talk about an agent's trying to do two competing things at once in this way, or to solve two cognitive problems at once? Well, we now know that the brain is a "parallel processor"; it can simultaneously process different kinds of information relevant to tasks such as perception or recognition through different neural pathways. Such a capacity, I believe, is essential to the exercise of free will. In cases of self-formation (SFAs), agents are simultaneously trying to resolve plural and competing cognitive tasks. They are, as we say, of two minds. Yet they are not two separate persons. They are not dissociated from either task. The businesswoman who wants to do something to help the victim is the same ambitious woman who wants to go to her meeting and make a sale. She is torn inside by different visions of who she is and what she wants to be, as we all are from time to time. But this is the kind of complexity needed for genuine self-formation and free will. And when she succeeds in doing one of the things she is trying to do, she will endorse that outcome as *her* resolution of the conflict in her will, voluntarily and intentionally, not by accident or mistake.

5. Challenges to This View: Responsibility, Luck, and Chance

Obviously, many questions arise about the preceding view and a number of objections may be made to it. We cannot address all these questions and objections here, but let us consider some of the more important ones. Some people have objected that if choices like the businesswoman's really are undetermined, they *must* happen merely by chance—and so must be "random," "capricious," "uncontrolled," "irrational," and all the other things usually charged. The first step in responding to this objection is to question the assumption that if indeterminism is involved in an occurrence, that occurrence must happen *merely* as a matter of chance or luck. "Chance" and "luck" are terms of ordinary language that carry the meaning of "its being out of my control." So using them already begs certain questions. "Indeterminism," by contrast, is a technical term that merely rules out *deterministic* causation, but not causation altogether. Indeterminism is consistent with nondeterministic or probabilistic causation, where the outcome is not inevitable. It is therefore a mistake (in fact, one of the most common mistakes in debates about free will) to assume that "undetermined" means "uncaused" or "*merely* a matter of chance."

A second objection is related to the first. One might argue that in the case of the businesswoman, since the outcome of her effort (the choice) is undetermined up to the last minute, she must have first made the effort to overcome the temptation to go on to her meeting and then at the last instant "chance takes over" and decides the issue for her. But this is a mistaken image. On the view just presented, one cannot separate the indeterminism from the effort of will, so that *first* the woman's effort occurs, to be *followed* by chance or luck. One must think of the effort and the indeterminism as fused; the effort *is* indeterminate and the indeterminism is a property of the effort, not something separate that occurs after or before the effort. The fact that the effort has this property of being indeterminate does not make it any less the woman's *effort*. The complex recurrent neural network that realizes the effort in the brain is circulating impulses in feedback loops, and there is some indeterminacy in these circulating impulses. But the whole process is the woman's effort of will, and it persists right up to the moment when the choice is made. There is no point at which the effort stops and chance "takes over." The woman chooses as a result of the effort, even though she might have failed. Similarly, the husband breaks the table as a result of his effort, even though he might have failed because of the indeterminacy. (That is why his excuse, "Chance broke the table, not me," is so lame.)

A third objection has to do with the notion of luck. If the business-woman's efforts were undetermined, so that either effort might have failed, some critics argue, then it was just a matter of luck which effort succeeded. To address this by-now familiar objection, we need to look more closely at the issue of luck. Recall that one might say of the assassin and the husband that "they got lucky" in killing the prime minister and breaking the table, because their actions were undetermined and might have failed. Yet the surprising thing is that we still say the assassin and the husband were *responsible* if they succeeded in killing the prime minister or breaking the table. So we should ask ourselves the following question: why is it wrong to say "He got lucky, *so he was not responsible*" in the cases of the husband and the assassin? For it *is* wrong to say this, since they did get lucky and yet they were *still* responsible. (Imagine the assassin's lawyer arguing in the courtroom that his client is not guilty because his killing the prime minister was undetermined and might therefore have failed by chance. Would such a defense succeed?)

The first part of an answer to why the assassin and the husband are still responsible has to do with the point made earlier about "luck" and "chance." These two words have question-begging implications in ordinary language that are not necessarily implications of "indeterminism" (for indeterminism implies only the absence of deterministic causation). The core meaning of "he got lucky" in the assassin and husband cases is "he succeeded *despite the probability or chance of failure*"; and this core meaning does not imply lack of responsibility *if he succeeds*. If "he got lucky" had other meanings in these cases, meanings that are often associated in ordinary usage with "luck" and "chance," the inference that a person "got lucky so he was not responsible" would not fail, as it clearly does. For example, if "luck' in these cases meant that the outcome was not his doing, or had occurred by mere chance, or that he was not responsible, then the inference "he got lucky so he was not responsible" would hold for the husband and assassin. But the point is that these further meanings of "luck" and "chance" do not follow *from the mere presence of indeterminism.*

The second reason why the inference "he got lucky, so he was not responsible" does not work in the cases of the assassin and the husband is that *what* they succeeded in doing was what they were *trying* and wanting to do all along (kill the minister and break the table, respectively). The third reason is that *when* they succeeded, their reaction was not "Oh dear, that was a mistake, an accident—something that *happened* to me, not something I *did*." Rather they *endorsed* the outcomes as something they were trying and wanting to do all along, knowingly and purposefully, not by mistake or accident.

But these conditions are satisfied in the businesswoman's case as well, *either way* she chooses. If she succeeds in choosing to return to help the victim (or in choosing to go on to her meeting), then (1) she will have "succeeded *despite the probability or chance of failure,*" (2) she will have succeeded in doing what she was *trying* and *wanting* to do all along (she wanted both outcomes very much, but for different reasons, and was trying to make those reasons prevail in both cases), and (3) when she succeeded (in choosing to return to help) her reaction was not "Oh dear, I did that by mistake, it was an accident; it was something that happened to me, not something I did." Rather she *endorsed* the outcome as something she was trying and wanting to do all along; she recognized the choice as her resolution of the conflict in her will. And if she had chosen to go on to her meeting, she would have endorsed that outcome, recognizing it as her resolution of the conflict in her will.

6. Choice and Agency

Here is a fourth objection that may have occurred to you. Perhaps we are begging the question by assuming that the outcomes of the woman's efforts are *choices* to begin with. If indeterminism is involved in a process (such as the woman's deliberation) so that its outcome is undetermined, one might argue that the outcome must merely *happen* and therefore cannot be somebody's *choice.* But there is no reason to assume that such a claim is true. A choice is the formation of an intention or purpose to do something. It resolves uncertainty and indecision in the mind about what to do. Nothing in such a description implies that there could not be some indeterminism in the deliberation and neural processes of an agent's preceding choice corresponding to the agent's prior uncertainty about what to do. Recall from our earlier arguments that the presence of indeterminism does not mean the outcome happened *merely* by chance and *not* by the agent's effort. Self-forming choices are undetermined but not uncaused. They are caused by the agent's efforts.

Well, say some critics, perhaps indeterminism does not undermine the idea that something is a *choice,* but rather that it is *the agent's* choice. This objection raises some important questions about agency. What makes the woman's choice her own on the foregoing account is that it results from her efforts and deliberation, which in turn are causally influenced by her reasons and her intentions (e.g., her intention to resolve indecision in one way or another). And what makes these efforts, deliberations, reasons, and intentions *hers* is that they are embedded in a larger motivational system realized in her brain in terms of which she defines herself as a practical reasoner and actor. A choice is the agent's when it is produced intentionally by efforts, by deliberations, and by reasons that are part of this self-defining motivational system and when, in addition, the agent *endorses* the new intention or purpose, created by the choice, into that motivational system, making it a further purpose that will guide *future* practical reasoning and action.

Well then, say other critics, perhaps the issue is not whether an undetermined SFA, such as the businesswoman's, is a *choice,* or even whether it is the *agent's* choice, but rather how much *control* she has over it. For while it may be true, as argued earlier (in the discussion of plural voluntary control), that the presence of indeterminism need not eliminate control altogether, wouldn't it be the case that the presence of indeterminism at least *diminishes* the control persons have over their choices and actions? Is it not the case that the assassin's control over whether the prime minister is killed (his ability to carry out his purposes and do what he is trying to do) is lessened by the undetermined impulses in his arm? This criticism is related to a problem about libertarian freedom encountered in chapter 4. The problem is that indeterminism, wherever it occurs, seems to be a *hindrance* or *obstacle* to our realizing our purposes and hence is an obstacle to our freedom rather than an *enhancement* of it.

There is some truth to this objection. But I think what is true in it may reveal something important about free will. Perhaps we should concede that indeterminism, wherever it occurs, *does* diminish control over what we are trying to do and *is* a hindrance or obstacle to the realization of our purposes. But recall that in the case of the businesswoman (and SFAs generally), the indeterminism that is admittedly diminishing the agent's control over one thing she is trying to do *is coming from her own will*—from her desire and effort to do a different thing that she also wants to do. And the indeterminism that is diminishing her control over that different thing (in this case the selfish thing) is coming from her desire and effort to do its opposite (to be a moral person who acts on moral reasons). So, in each case, the indeterminism *is* in fact functioning as a hindrance or obstacle to her realizing one of her purposes—a hindrance or obstacle in the form of resistance within her will which has to be overcome by effort.

If there were no such hindrance—if there were no resistance in her will—the woman would indeed in a sense have "complete control" over one of her options. There would no competing motives to stand in the way of her choosing it. But then also she would not be free to rationally and voluntarily choose the other option because she would have no good competing reasons to do so. Thus, by *being* a hindrance to the realization of some of our purposes, indeterminism paradoxically opens up the genuine possibility of pursuing other purposes—of choosing or doing *otherwise* in accordance with, rather than against, our wills (voluntarily) and reasons (rationally). To be genuinely self-forming agents (creators of ourselves)— to have free will—there must at times in life be obstacles and hindrances in our wills of this sort for us to overcome.

Another objection to the preceding theory is that we are not consciously aware of making two competing efforts when we engage in self-forming choices. But the theory does not require that we be consciously aware of these competing efforts. The idea was to compare exercises of free will to other cases of parallel processing in the brain, such as vision. Neuroscientists tell us that when we see a visual object, such as a red barn, the brain actually processes different properties of the object (like shape and color) separately, through parallel pathways whose results are eventually brought together in the visual image. We are not introspectively aware of processing the redness of the barn and its shape separately and in parallel. In fact, this information about parallel processing in the brain comes as a surprise to us. But if these neurological theories are correct, that is what we are doing.

The preceding account of free will is suggesting that something similar may be going on when we make self-forming choices. We are not introspectively aware that our efforts (our efforts to make one or another of our competing choices succeed) are being processed on separate, though interacting, pathways in the brain; but that process may in fact be what is going on. If we actually introspected all that was going on when we made free choices, free will would be less mysterious and the problem of free will would be a lot easier to solve than it is. To solve it, we have to consider what may be going on behind the scenes when we are conscious of trying to decide about which of two options to choose and either choice is a difficult one because there are resistant motives pulling us in different directions.[5]

Let us conclude with one final objection to the account of free will presented in this chapter. This objection is perhaps the most telling and has not yet been discussed. It goes like this: even if one grants that persons, such as the businesswoman, could make genuine self-forming choices that were undetermined, isn't there something to the charge that such choices would be *arbitrary*? A residual arbitrariness seems to remain in all self-forming choices, since the agents cannot in principle have sufficient or conclusive *prior* reasons for making one option and one set of reasons prevail over the other.

There is considerable truth to this objection as well, but again I think it may be a truth that tells us something important about free will. It tells us that every undetermined self-forming free choice is the initiation of what might be called a *value experiment* whose justification lies in the future and is not fully explained by past reasons. In making such a choice we say, in effect, "Let's try this. It is not required by my past, but it is consistent with my past and is one branching pathway in the garden of forking paths my life can now meaningfully take. Whether it is the right choice, only time will tell. Meanwhile, I am willing to take responsibility for it one way or the other."

It is worth noting that the term "arbitrary" comes from the Latin *arbitrium,* which means "judgment"—as in *liberum arbitrium voluntatis,* "free judgment of the will" (the medieval philosophers' designation for free will). Imagine a writer in the middle of a novel. The novel's heroine faces a crisis and the writer has not yet developed her character in sufficient detail to say exactly how she will act. The author makes a "judgment" about this that is not determined by the heroine's already formed past which does not give unique direction. In this sense, the judgment (*arbitrium*) of how she will react is "arbitrary," but not entirely so. It had input from the heroine's fictional past and in turn gave input to her projected future. In a similar way, agents who exercise free will are both authors of and characters in their own stories all at once. By virtue of "self-forming" judgments of the will (*arbitria voluntatis*) (SFAs), they are "arbiters" of their own lives, "making themselves" out of a past that, if they are truly free, does not limit their future pathways to one.

Suppose we were to say to such persons, "But look, you didn't have sufficient or *conclusive* prior reasons for choosing as you did since you also had viable reasons for choosing the other way." They might reply, "True enough. But I did have *good* reasons for choosing as I did, which I'm willing to stand by *and take responsibility for.* If these reasons were not sufficient or conclusive reasons, that's because, like the heroine of the novel, I was not a fully formed person before I chose (and still am not, for that matter). Like the author of the novel, I am in the process of writing an unfinished story and forming an unfinished character who, in my case, is myself."

To sum up, in this chapter I have suggested how a libertarian free will requiring ultimate responsibility and indeterminism might be reconciled with current scientific knowledge. There is much to debate about the theory of this chapter and many objections can and have been made to it.[6] I have tried to answer some of these objections here; but many other objections that also deserve answers have not been addressed. (Those who wish to pursue the issues further can look at the suggested readings that follow.) Many persons believe libertarian free will can never be reconciled with science and cannot exist in the natural order. Perhaps they will turn out to be right. But we should not conclude too hastily that free will of the deeper kind that libertarians believe in cannot be reconciled with science without first trying our best to see how it might be done.

Suggested Reading

The view presented in this chapter is further developed in my *The Significance of Free Will* (Oxford, 1996). Objections to this theory and further debates about it can be found in the references cited in note 6. An interesting collection of essays relating current research in the neurosciences, psychology and physics to free will is *The Volitional Brain,* edited by Benjamin Libet, Anthony Freeman, and Keith Sutherland (Imprint Academic, 1999). Other different attempts to reconcile free will with modern science include (from a libertarian perspective) David Hodgson "Hume's Mistake" (in *The Volitional Brain,* pp. 201–24) and Storrs McCall, *A Model of the Universe* (Oxford: Clarendon, 1994) and (from a compatibilist perspective) Henrik Walter, *Neurophilosophy of Free Will* (MIT, 2001), and Daniel Dennett, *Freedom Evolves* (Vintage, 2003).

CHAPTER 13

Predestination, Divine Foreknowledge, and Free Will

1. Religious Belief and Free Will

Debates about free will are impacted by religion as well as by science, as noted in chapter 1. Indeed, for many people, religion is the context in which questions about free will first arise. The following personal statement by philosopher William Rowe nicely expresses the experiences of many religious believers who first confront the problem of free will:

> As a seventeen year old convert to a quite orthodox branch of Protestantism, the first theological problem to concern me was the question of Divine Predestination and Human Freedom. Somewhere I read the following line from the Westminster Confession: "God from all eternity did . . . freely and unchangeably ordain whatsoever comes to pass." In many ways I was attracted to this idea. It seemed to express the majesty and power of God over all that he had created. It also led me to take an optimistic view of events in my own life and the lives of others, events which struck me as bad or unfortunate. For I now viewed them as planned by God before the creation of the world—thus they must serve some good purpose unknown to me. My own conversion, I reasoned, must also have been ordained to happen, just as the failure of others to be converted must have been similarly ordained. But at this point in my reflections, I hit upon a difficulty, a difficulty that made me think harder than I ever had before in my life. For I also believed that I had chosen God out of my own free will, that each of us is responsible for choosing or rejecting God's way. But how could I be responsible for a choice which, from eternity, God had ordained I would make at that particular moment of my life? How can it be that those who reject God's way do so of their own free will, if God, from eternity, destined them to reject his way?[1]

147

The problem of divine predestination and human free will that Rowe is describing has troubled most thoughtful religious believers at one time or another. Debates about this problem have been a feature of all the world's theistic religions, including Christianity, Judaism, and Islam. It was this problem of predestination and free will that led Muslim scholars (about a century after Muhammad's death) to ask the Caliphs if they could look into the scrolls of the ancient Greek philosophers left hidden in the libraries of the Middle East since the time of the conquests of Alexander the Great. The main concern of these Muslim scholars was to see if they could get some insight from the "pagan" Greek philosophers into the vexing problem of predestination and free will, which the *Qur'an* (Koran) did not resolve. The Hebrew and Christian scriptures also describe an omnipotent (all-powerful), omniscient (all-knowing), and all-good personal God, who created the universe, without entirely resolving the problem of how the omnipotence and omniscience of God could be reconciled with human freedom.

2. Predestination, Evil, and the Free Will Defense

One simple way to solve the problem of predestination that has tempted many thinkers in different religious traditions is to argue that divine predestination and human freedom are *compatible*. This solution was developed most fully by the American Calvinist theologian Jonathan Edwards (1703–1758). Edwards took the classical compatibilist line discussed in chapter 2 that freedom is the ability to do what we want without constraints or impediments; and Edwards argued that we could have such freedom to do as we want even if everything in the world was determined by the foreordaining acts of God. Though God has created the good or corrupt natures from which we act, Edwards argued, our acts are nonetheless our free acts, imputable to us, since they flow without impediments from *our* natures.

Predestination in this form is difficult to accept, as Rowe notes; and the reasoning of chapter 11 suggests why. If humans were predestined in the way Edwards describes, they would not be ultimately responsible for their actions in the sense of UR. For God's creation of the world, including creating different humans with good or evil natures, would be a *sufficient cause* of everything that happens, including the good and evil acts of humans. Since humans are not in turn responsible for God's creating the world as God did, then humans would not be ultimately responsible for their actions in the sense of UR. Worse still, the ultimate responsibility for good *and evil* acts would lie with God, who knowingly created a world in which those acts would inevitably occur. Such consequences are unacceptable for most theists, who believe that God is not the cause of evil and who also believe that God *justly* punishes *us* for our sins.

At this point, the problem of predestination and free will becomes entangled with the religious "problem of evil": if God is all-powerful and all-good, then why does God allow horrendous evils in the world? Either God cannot eliminate evil, in which case God is not all-powerful; or God can eliminate evil but chooses not to, in which case God is not all-good. One standard solution to this problem of evil due to Saint Augustine is called "the Free Will Defense." God is not the source of evil, according to the Free Will Defense. Instead God gives free will to creatures (such as humans and angels) who then cause evil by their free actions. But why would God give free will to other creatures, knowing the terrible consequences that might flow from it? The standard answer, given by Augustine, was that "free will is one of the good things." Without free will, he reasoned, there would be no *moral* good or evil among creatures, no genuine responsibility or blameworthiness, and creatures could not choose to love God of their own free wills (love being a greater good when it is *freely* given). God therefore allows evil for a greater good, but God is not the cause or source of evil.

But the Free Will Defense runs into trouble if predestination is true. As Rowe says: "How could I be responsible for a choice which, from eternity, God had ordained I would make at that particular moment of my life? How can it be that those who reject God's way do so of their own free will, if God, from eternity, destined them to reject his way?" If all acts are predested, the *ultimate* responsibility for good and evil acts would go back to God after all and the Free Will Defense would fail.

For this reason among others, *compatibilism* is more difficult to accept in a religious context if you are a theist who believes in an omnipotent, omniscient, and all-good God who created the universe. Compatibilists believe that freedom (in all the senses worth wanting) could exist in a *determined* world. But if we did live in a determined world and it was *also* true that *God had created that world,* then everything that happened in that world would have been predetermined, and hence predested, by God's act of creation. The ultimate responsibility for all that occurs would go back to God. That is one reason most (though not all) modern theists, as Rowe notes, believe that the free will God has given us could not exist in a determined world and therefore must be an *incompatibilist* or *libertarian* free will. The only way around this conclusion would *seem* to be accepting that, in creating the world, God predetermines every act, good and evil, that humans perform; and most theists are reluctant to concede that.

But suppose that someone who is a theist is reluctant to concede that God predetermines every act. Must he or she thereby deny that God is all-powerful and all-good? Not necessarily. For theists can say that God has the *power* to predestine all things but *chooses* not to exercise that power in order to give free will to humans. And if Augustine is right in saying that giving humans free will is a "good thing" (for without it there would be no genuine responsibility or blameworthiness), then theists can continue to hold that God is all-powerful and all-good, even though God chooses to limit God's own power by giving humans free will and not predestining everything they do.

3. Foreknowledge and Freedom

But if theists take this line, thus preserving God's power and goodness, another problem looms. For God is supposed to be not only all-powerful and all-good, according to the biblical traditions, but also *all-knowing* or *omniscient.* Though God might freely choose to restrain divine power over all events in order to give humans free will, it seems that God would nonetheless know everything that is going to happen. And there are reasons to believe that divine *foreknowledge* would be as much a threat to free will as divine *foreordination.* The problem posed by divine foreknowledge is clearly stated by a character named Evodius in Saint Augustine's classic dialogue *On the Free Choice of the Will.* Evodius says:

> I am deeply troubled by a certain question: How can it be that God has fore-knowledge of all future events, and yet we do not sin of necessity? Anyone who says that an event can happen otherwise than as God has foreknown it is making an insane and malicious attempt to destroy God's foreknowledge. If God therefore foreknew that a good man would sin . . . the sin was commit-ted of necessity, because God foreknew that it would happen. How then could there be free will when there is such inevitable necessity?[2]

In response to Evodius, Augustine makes a point that many other thinkers have since made on this topic. Augustine points out that merely foreknowing or foreseeing that something is going to happen is not the same thing as *causing* it to happen.

> Your foreknowledge that a man will sin does not of itself necessitate the sin. Your foreknowledge did not force him to sin. . . . In the same way, God's foreknowledge of future events does not compel them to take place. . . . God is not the evil cause of these acts though God justly avenges them. You may understand from this, therefore, how justly God punishes sins; for God does not do the things which he knows will happen.[3]

To illustrate Augustine's point, imagine scientists standing behind a screen observing everything we do, but not in any way interfering in our actions. They may know enough about us to predict everything we are going to do. But it does not follow that they cause what we do or are responsible for it, if they always remain behind the screen and never interfere. So it would be with God, Augustine is saying, if God merely foreknows what we will do. Although *foreordaining,* or predestining something makes it happen, merely *foreknowing* it does not make it happen. In short, foreknowledge is not the cause of what is foreknown.

4. Foreknowledge and the Consequence Argument

For many people, this distinction between *causing* or *predetermining* what will happen and merely *foreknowing* it solves the problem about divine foreknowledge and human freedom. Unfortunately, the problem is not so simply solved. For there are reasons to believe that foreknowledge itself might be incompatible with human freedom, even if foreknowledge is not the cause of what is foreknown. One way of seeing why this might be so is to consider the following argument, which has some interesting parallels to the Consequence Argument of chapter 3 for the incompatibility of free will and determinism. If God has foreknowledge of all events, including human actions, then the following conditions obtain.

1. God believed, at some time before we were born, that our present actions would occur.
2. God's beliefs cannot be mistaken.
3. It must be the case that <if God believed, at some time before we were born, that our present actions would occur and God's beliefs cannot be mistaken, then our present actions will occur>.
4. There is nothing we can now do to change the fact that God believed, at some time before we were born, that our present actions would occur.
5. There is nothing we can now do to change the fact that God's beliefs cannot be mistaken.
6. There is nothing we can now do to change the fact that <if God believed, at some time before we were born, that our present actions would occur and God's beliefs cannot be mistaken, then our present actions occur>.
7. Therefore there is nothing we can now do to change the fact that our present actions occur.

In short, if God has foreknown what we will do, we *cannot now do otherwise* than we actually do. Since this argument, like the Consequence

Argument, can be applied to any agents and actions at any times, we can infer from it that if God has foreknowledge of all events, no one can ever do otherwise; and if free will requires the power to do otherwise, then no one would have free will.

In assessing this argument, it is helpful to note the parallels between it and the Consequence Argument of chapter 3. Step 4 of this argument (There is nothing we can now to change the fact that God believed at a time before we were born that our present actions would occur) corresponds to premise 1 of the Consequence Argument (There is nothing we can now do to change the past). Step 5 of this argument (There is nothing we can now do to change the fact that God's beliefs cannot be mistaken) plays a similar role to premise 2 of the Consequence Argument (There is nothing we can now do to change the laws of nature). Just as the laws of nature make it necessary that, *given* the past, our present actions will occur (which is step 5 of the Consequence Argument), so the fact that God's beliefs cannot be mistaken makes it necessary that, *given* that God believed at a *past* time that our present actions would occur, our present actions will occur (step 3 of this argument). God's prior beliefs may not *cause* our present actions to occur, yet they make it *necessary* that our present actions will occur, *if* God's beliefs cannot be mistaken.

Consider, finally, premises 1 and 2 of this Foreknowledge Argument. It is hard for theists, if they believe God is infallible, to deny that God's beliefs cannot be mistaken (premise 2 of the argument). As for premise 1 of the argument (God believed, at a time before we were born, that our present actions would occur), it follows straightforwardly from the assumption that God has foreknowledge. Remember that the argument merely has to *assume* God has foreknowledge in order to show that *if* God has foreknowledge, then we would lack free will.

5. Eternalist Solutions to the Foreknowledge Problem: Boethius and Aquinas

This Foreknowledge Argument has provoked many responses through history. In the rest of this chapter, we will consider four of the most important attempts to respond to it and thereby to solve the problem of divine foreknowledge and human freedom. Three of these responses have their origins in medieval philosophy, but they have been refined in modern times. The first response was put forward by the philosopher Boethius (480–524 CE), who lived a century after Augustine, and was later defended by Saint Thomas Aquinas (1225–1274 CE), the most influential philosopher of the Middle Ages.

Boethius and Aquinas appeal to the *eternity* or *timelessness* of God to answer the foreknowledge problem. A perfect God would not be subject to time and change as we creatures are, they insist. But if God is eternal in the sense of being timeless, or outside time altogether, then we cannot say that God has *fore*knowledge of future events at all. For, foreknowledge implies that God is located at some point in time and knows at that time what is going to take place at future times; and this makes no sense if God is not in time. We must say that God knows everything that happens, to be sure. But if God is eternal in a timeless sense, then everything that happens must be known by God in an eternal present, as if God were directly seeing it happen at that particular moment. Thus, Boethius says of God's knowledge:

> It encompasses the infinite sweep of past and future, and regards all things in its simple comprehension as if they were now taking place. Thus, if you will think about foreknowledge by which God distinguishes all things, you will rightly consider it not to be a foreknowledge of future events, but knowledge of a never-changing present.[4]

Various images have been suggested to illustrate how God knows eternally a changing world. The simplest image is of a road we are walking on. Travelers on the road proceed one step at a time. But God sees their whole journey and the entire road all at once from above the road, so to speak, being outside of time.

If we accept this eternalist account of God's knowledge, it seems that premise 1 of the Foreknowledge Argument would be false: we could no longer say "God believed, *at a time before we were born,* that our present actions would occur." So our present actions would not be necessitated *by the past,* including by God's past beliefs. Thus, our actions could be free, even in a libertarian sense, since they might be undetermined by all past events in time, even though they were timelessly known by God. Divine *omniscience* could then be reconciled with human freedom, even if divine *foreknowledge* could not be; and the foreknowledge problem would be solved.

Or would it? There have been objections to this way of solving the foreknowledge problem. Many objections have to do with the idea of divine timelessness itself. How could a timeless being know a changing world? How can it be that events occurring in time are simultaneously present to God? If God is timeless, how can God interact with temporal creatures like us, reacting and responding to what we do, as God often does in the Bible? Defenders of divine timelessness have attempted to answer these objections to the idea that God is eternal in a timeless sense. But from our point of view, the more important question is whether ascribing timeless knowledge to God really does solve the problem of divine foreknowledge and human freedom. Some philosophers argue that it does not.

Some of these philosophers have questioned whether God's timeless knowledge of all that happens is not just as much a threat to our freedom as God's foreknowledge would be. They ask, in Rowe's words, how we could have done otherwise "if God knew *from eternity* what choice we would make at this particular time." Linda Zagzebski states this objection by saying that "we have no more reason to think that we can do anything about God's timeless knowledge than about God's past knowledge."[5] In support of this claim, Zagzebski suggests that an argument like that of section 4 could be reformulated so that it applies to God's eternal knowledge as well.

In place of premise 1 (God believed, at some time before we were born, that our present actions would occur), we would have premise 1*: God believes from eternity (timelessly) that our present actions occur. Since God's timeless beliefs also cannot be mistaken, it would be necessary that, if God believed from eternity that our present actions occur, then our present acts would occur. But there is nothing we can now do to change the fact that God believes from eternity that our present actions occur and nothing we can now do to change the fact that God's beliefs cannot be mistaken. So there is nothing we can now do to change the fact that our present actions occur. If this argument is correct, it would appear that God's timeless knowledge is just as much a threat to our freedom as God's foreknowledge would be. Zagzebski does not claim that this argument necessarily refutes the doctrine of divine timelessness. But she thinks it does show that appealing to God's timeless knowledge *alone* will not solve the problem of divine foreknowledge and human freedom without further arguments.

6. The Ockhamist Solution: William of Ockham

A different solution to the foreknowledge problem that has been much discussed by contemporary philosophers was suggested by the medieval philosopher William of Ockham (1285–1349 CE). Ockham argued that we can and should ascribe genuine *fore*knowledge of all future events to God. Thus he rejected the timeless solution of Boethius and Aquinas. To understand how God's foreknowledge can be reconciled with human freedom, Ockham appeals instead to a subtle distinction between two kinds of facts about the past, "hard facts" and "soft facts." To illustrate the difference, suppose

(H) Adam Jones was born at midnight at Mercy Hospital in Ames (Iowa) on May 1, 1950.

This is a *hard* fact about the past. It is a fact that is *simply* about the past in the sense that its being a fact about May 1, 1950, does not depend on any facts that might occur later in time. Nor is there anything anyone can do at a later time to change the past fact that Adam Jones was born at that place at that time.

But suppose now that Adam Jones had a son, John, born in 1975, and at midnight on June 1, 2000, John committed a murder. From then on, it became true that

> (S) The father of a murderer (namely, John's father, Adam Jones) was born at midnight at Mercy Hospital in Ames on May 1, 1950.

This is a *soft* fact about the past. It is *about* the past in the sense that it is about something that happened in 1950 (Adam Jones's birth). But it is *not simply* about the past because its truth also depends on something that happened at a later time in 2000. Unlike the hard fact H (Adam Jones was born . . . in Ames . . . in 1950), this soft fact S (the father of a murderer was born . . . in Ames . . . in 1950) was not a fact about the past at all at times *between* May 1, 1950 and June 1, 2000. (The soft fact became a fact about the past only after June 1, 2000.)

We may even suppose that John's murdering someone in 2000 was a *free* action that was undetermined and so John might have done otherwise. In that case, it would have been "up to John" *in 2000* whether the soft fact S would become a fact *about the past*. But this would not be so about the hard fact that Adam Jones was born in Ames on May 1, 1950. Nothing John or anyone else could do after May 1, 1950, could change the hard fact.

Now Ockham suggests that facts about God's foreknowledge, though they are about the past, are soft facts about the past rather than hard facts. They are not simply about the past because they refer to and require the truth of future events. Thus, God's knowing at earlier times that John will commit a murder in 2000 is a fact if and only if John does commit a murder in 2000. Ockham then argues that, while it is not in our power to affect hard facts about the past, it is in our power to affect soft facts about the past. If John's murder was a free action, then John could have done otherwise; he could have refrained from murdering. And if he had refrained from murdering, then God would have known *at earlier times* that John would refrain rather than knowing that John would commit murder.

We have to be cautious here. Ockham is not claiming that John's power to do otherwise in this sense is a power to *change* what God previously believed. We are not to imagine that God knew earlier that John would murder and that John changed what God had foreknown by refraining. That would be to assume that God's foreknowing was a *hard* fact about the past and we cannot change hard facts about the past. But if God's foreknowing was a soft fact, it does not have to be changed. For if John had refrained from murdering, the soft fact would simply have *been* different all along: God would have foreknown at all earlier times that John was going to refrain rather than having foreknown that John was going to murder.

This solution is certainly subtle. But it provokes more than a few questions. Can we believe that God's foreknowledge is really a soft fact about the past? If God had foreknowledge of a future event, it seems that God would have to believe at an earlier time that the event would occur. But a divine past belief seems to be as good a candidate for a hard fact about the past as anything else. If you or I believed today that a future event was going to occur tomorrow (say, an earthquake), the fact that we had this belief today would be a hard fact: whether the earthquake (or anything else) occurred tomorrow would not affect the fact that we *believed today* that it would occur. But Ockhamists would point out that God's beliefs are different from yours and mine. God's beliefs cannot be mistaken. So whether or not God *has* a certain belief today depends on what happens tomorrow. With you and me, by contrast, whether our belief was *true* would depend on the future, but our *having* the belief today would not depend on the future.

Yet this admitted difference in God's beliefs leads to further puzzles. If John's committing murder on June 1, 2000, was a *free* action, then John could have done otherwise—he could also have refrained; and whatever John did, God would have known that at all earlier times. So it seems that John has the power at this moment on June 1, 2000, to determine *what God has foreknown at all earlier times*. That would seem to preserve John's free will all right. For John's voluntary action would be *ultimately responsible* for what God had foreknown at earlier times rather than the other way around. But John's free will is thus preserved, it seems, by making God's foreknowledge quite mysterious. For God's foreknowledge at all earlier times—*even at times before John existed*—now seems to depend on what John does at this moment in time.

Another puzzling feature of divine foreknowledge on the Ockhamist view is this. Suppose it is now 1990. Can we truly say in 1990 that God *then* foreknew that John would commit murder in 2000? Apparently not, because what God believed at times before June 1, 2000, was not settled or determined *until* John acted one way or the other on June 1, 2000. If God's foreknowledge of a future free action is a soft fact about the past in this sense, then it seems that it would not *become* a fact about the past until after the time when the free action is performed. God's foreknowledge would be similar to the soft fact S—the fact that the father of a murderer was born in Ames on May 1, 1950—which did not become a fact about the past until after June 1, 2000, when John Jones committed murder.

Conceiving free actions in this way does preserve free will, as noted, since it seems to make God's foreknowledge depend on our free actions rather than the other way around. But it certainly makes God's foreknowledge difficult to understand. Ockham himself conceded this point. He said: "I maintain that it is impossible to express clearly the way in which God knows future [free actions]. Nevertheless, it must be held that He does so."

7. The Molinist Solution

The third solution to the foreknowledge problem originated with another late medieval thinker, the Spanish Jesuit philosopher and theologian Luis de Molina (1535–1600 CE). Like Ockham, Molina rejected the timeless solution to the foreknowledge problem of Boethius and Aquinas. But Molina sought a better answer than Ockham was able to give about *how* God can foreknow future free actions. To explain this, Molina introduced the notion of divine "middle knowledge."

Molina begins by distinguishing three types of knowledge that God would have. The first is God's knowledge of all that is *necessary* or *possible*. Being omniscient, God would know everything that *must* be and also every possibility—everything that *might* be. In addition, by a second kind of knowledge, God would know, among *contingent* things—those that might exist or might not exist—which of them *actually* existed because God had *willed* them to be so and not because they were necessary. But, between these two types of divine knowledge, according to Molina, there is another:

> The third type is *middle* knowledge, by which in virtue of the most profound and inscrutable comprehension of each free will, God saw in His own essence what each such will would do with its innate freedom were it to be placed in this, or in that or, indeed, in infinitely many orders of things—even though it would really be able, if it so willed, to do the opposite.[6]

Middle knowledge is thus the knowledge God has of how free creatures are going to exercise their freedom. By virtue of middle knowledge, according to Molina, God foreknows what each free creature *would* do, *if* placed in any possible situation, even though the creature is not determined to act as he or she does. So, for example, by middle knowledge,

God would know the following.

1. If the Apostle Peter were asked if he is a follower of Jesus (at a certain time and in certain circumstances), Peter would freely deny it.
2. If Molly were offered a job with the law firm in Dallas (at a certain time and in certain circumstances), she would freely choose it.

By middle knowledge, God would know these things even though both Peter and Molly were not determined to do what they did *and* both could have done otherwise.

Propositions like 1 and 2 are called *counterfactuals of freedom:* they describe what agents *would freely* do, *if* placed in various circumstances C (where it is assumed that the circumstances C do not determine how they will act). How can God know the truth of such counterfactuals of freedom *if* it is not necessitated or determined that the agents will do A in the circumstances C? God cannot foreknow the truth of such counterfactuals by the *first* kind of knowledge of what is necessary, Molina insists, because future free actions do not occur of necessity. God also cannot know in advance what free creatures, such as Peter and Molly, are going to freely do by knowing the laws of nature and the past because, by hypothesis, the past and laws of nature do not determine what they will do. God also cannot know what Peter and Molly are going to do by knowing everything about their characters, motives, and personalities, because their characters, motives, and personalities also do not determine which of several ways they might act.

Finally, God cannot know what Peter and Molly will *freely* do in the circumstances by virtue of Molina's *second* kind of knowledge either—by God's knowledge of what God has *willed* that they do. For free creatures do not always do what God wills (as in Peter's case); and if God's will *caused* creatures to do whatever they appear to freely do, then God would be ultimately responsible for the evil acts of creatures as well as for their good acts.

God therefore does not know the truth of counterfactuals of freedom by either the first or second kind of knowledge. Yet, Molina insists that there must be a truth to be known about what Peter is going to do in his circumstances and what Molly is going to do in hers, even if neither is determined to do what he or she does. And if there is a truth about what they are actually going to do, then God, being *omniscient,* would have to know that truth "in virtue of the most profound and inscrutable comprehension of each free will." God would not make them perform any given action, to be sure. The agents would act of their own free wills. But God would see "in His own essence what each such will would do with its innate freedom were it to be placed in this or in that circumstance."

If God did not have such middle knowledge, Molinists argue, Jesus would not have been able to know that Peter would freely deny that he was a follower of Jesus; nor would God have been able to foresee what various figures in the Bible were going to freely do. In the first book of Samuel, for example, God foresees and prophesies that Saul will freely choose to besiege the city of Keilah if David stays in the city. Without middle knowledge, Molinists insist, prophecy would not be possible where human free actions are concerned; and God's providence and ability to control all events in creation would be limited.

Nonetheless, it is difficult to understand how God can have middle knowledge of what free creatures will do. (Molina himself says that it involves an "inscrutable comprehension of each free will.") Critics of Molinism go further and say that middle knowledge is impossible. They focus on Molina's claim that *there must be a truth to be known* about what Peter will freely do if placed in certain circumstances and about what Molly will freely choose in certain circumstances, even if neither person is determined by those circumstances to do what he or she does. But *is* there a truth about what Peter and Molly will freely do *before* they actually do it? What would *make* counterfactuals of freedom of the form "If placed in circumstances C, the agent will freely do A" *true* before the agents themselves act? Such counterfactuals are not true of necessity, as we have seen. Nor are they true by virtue of the laws of nature. Nor are they true because God willed them to be true. (Otherwise God would be implicated in all human free actions, good and evil.)

Reflecting on all this, critics of Molinism, such as Robert Adams and William Hasker, have argued that there is nothing that makes counterfactuals of freedom true.[7] So there *is* no truth to be known, they say, by God or anyone else about what free agents *will* do before they act. There may be a truth, as Adams notes, about what free agents will *probably* do before they act; and God, being omniscient, would know such a truth. For example, it may be true that "If Molly were in circumstances C, she would *probably* choose to join the law firm in Dallas." For there may be facts about Molly's character, motives, and circumstances that make it probable (though not certain) that she will make this choice, if her choice is undetermined. Of course, there may also be other facts that make it probable she might choose the firm in Austin instead. (And there are no doubt other facts about Molly that make it highly *improbable* that she will choose neither firm, but decide instead to become a topless dancer in Seattle.)

In sum, there may be facts supporting statements about what free agents will *probably* do and *probably not* do; and God would know these facts. But there are no facts, according to critics of Molinism, that suffice to make it true that free agents, like Molly, would *definitely* make one choice rather than the other *before* they act. As you might guess, defenders of Molinism reject this criticism. They argue that, even though facts about the characters and circumstances of free agents and facts about the laws of nature do not suffice to make counterfactuals of freedom true, there must be some truths in the nature of things about what agents would do with their freedom in various circumstances. And if God were really omniscient, God would somehow know these truths.

8. The "Open Theism" View

The fourth and final solution to the foreknowledge problem is the "Open Theism" view. Defenders of this view do not think any of the previous solutions to the problem of foreknowledge are satisfactory. The only way out, they believe, is to deny that God *has* foreknowledge of future free actions. On this Open Theism view, the future is genuinely "open," and even God does not know what free agents are going to do before they act. Such a view was held by a few isolated figures in the history of religious thought. But it was usually regarded as unorthodox, if not scandalous, to deny that God had *complete* knowledge of the future. In the twentieth century, however, this "Open Theism" view was revived and defended by "process philosophers," such as Alfred North Whitehead and Charles Hartshorne, who argued that orthodox solutions to the problem of divine foreknowledge and human freedom were inadequate.[8] In recent decades, other philosophers and theologians have also defended Open Theism without necessarily accepting all the metaphysical presuppositions of process philosophers.[9]

Open Theists emphasize that denying God has foreknowledge of future free actions does not mean giving up the idea that God is *omniscient*. This sounds paradoxical but really is not, they insist: for they grant that God *does* know everything that happens and has happened. Nothing that occurs escapes God's knowledge. But the future *has not yet occurred* and is not yet real. So, when it comes to free actions, there is nothing real there to be known, at least not *yet*. God *can* know the events in the future that are necessary or determined by knowing what has already occurred and by knowing the laws of nature and the laws of logic. Thus God may know many things about the future, about the movements of stars and the falling of rocks and many other matters. But events such as human actions that are not necessary or determined are a different matter. They are not yet real and they may *or may not* occur at all. Not to know what *is not* (yet) or is not (yet) *real* and may never be is not to be lacking in omniscience. God will know all such future events when and if they become real, but not before.

The Open Theist view, according to its defenders, provides a more natural account of God's interactions with the created world and with humans, as described in the theistic scriptures. God gives free will to humans without knowing in advance what they will do with their free will. Humans then use this free will to do good or evil. God waits to see what they will do and reacts accordingly by rewarding or punishing them. In the Open Theist view, this is the simple, commonsense interpretation of the scriptures. Human free will is preserved and humans are ultimately responsible for their own free actions, not God. Moreover, God's goodness and justice are preserved because God justly punishes or rewards us for the actions for which we are ultimately responsible.

Given the simplicity of this solution to the foreknowledge problem, one may wonder why many theists regard the Open Theist view as unorthodox and why it is not more widely held. The answer is that it would require major changes in traditional theological views about the nature of God. On this Open Theist view, God can no longer be regarded as unchanging or immutable, another important attribute that has often been ascribed to God. For God comes to know many things that God did not know from eternity as the world unfolds; and thus God changes. God can also no longer be conceived of as timeless or beyond time. One could still say that God was eternal, but that would no longer mean beyond time, but rather that God exists at *all* times.

Traditionally, it was also held that God was the cause or creator of all things, but not the effect of anything. God was impassible and not affected by a changing world. On the Open Theist view, however, it seems that when God comes to know what we do, God is affected by us. In other words, God is no longer impassible. The Open Theist view also seems to require a different view of prophecy. God could prophesy earthquakes and other natural disasters with certainty, but where human free actions were concerned, such as Peter's denial or Saul's freely choosing to lay siege to the city of Keilah, God could know in advance only that these acts would probably occur, but would not know it with certainty. This is a limitation that is unacceptable to many theists.

Open Theists may respond (and many do respond) by arguing that the traditional understanding of the nature of God is in need of rethinking. The idea that a perfect Being would be entirely beyond time and change, impassible, or unaffected by changing things, and knowing everything about the future, is an idea of perfection that has its origins in Greek philosophy rather than in the biblical traditions. What is needed, they might argue, is a rethinking of the idea of perfection or what it means to say that God is perfect. By contrast, those who are reluctant to abandon traditional ways of thinking about God and cannot accept this Open Theist view must rely on one of the other solutions to the foreknowledge problem discussed in this chapter; or they must come up with a solution as yet unknown.

Suggested Reading

Augustine's classic work on foreknowledge and freedom is *On the Free Choice of the Will* (Bobbs-Merrill, 1964). A selection from this work can be found in my edited volume *Free Will* (Blackwell, 2002). Two fine general studies of the problem of divine foreknowledge and human freedom are William Hasker's *God, Time and Knowledge* (Cornell, 1989) and Linda T. Zagzebski's *The Dilemma of Freedom and Foreknowledge* (Oxford, 1991). Luis de Molina's view can be found in *On Divine Foreknowledge,* translated with a useful introduction by Alfredo Freddoso (Cornell, 1988). The most thorough modern defense of the Molinist view is Thomas Flint's *Divine Providence: The Molinist Account* (Cornell, 1998). Robert Merrihow Adams's critique of Molinism can be found in "Middle Knowledge and the Problem of Evil" (*American Philosophical Quarterly* 14, 1977). The Open Theist view is defended by Clark Pinnock, Richard Rice, John Sanders, William Hasker, and David Basinger in *The Openness of God* (InterVarsity, 1994). The Open Theist view of process philosophers such as Whitehead and Hartshorne is readably introduced in David Griffin and John B. Cobb, *Process Theology: An Introductory Exposition* (Westminster, 1976).

CHAPTER 14

Conclusion: Five Freedoms

1. Freedom of Self-realization

One reason the problem of free will is difficult is that "freedom" is a word with many meanings. At least five different notions of freedom have entered into the discussions of this book. Reflecting on these five notions is a useful way of reviewing the arguments of the book and of reviewing debates about free will in general. For all five of these notions of freedom play an important role in historical debates about free will.

The first of the five freedoms is the freedom emphasized by *classical compatibilists* of chapter 2. We may call it

> *The Freedom of Self-realization:* the *power* or *ability* to do what we want or will to do, which entails an absence of external *constraints* or *impediments* preventing us from realizing our wants and purposes in action.

Constraints that may undermine this freedom of self-realization are of many kinds, as we have seen—being in jail or tied up (physical restraint), coercion or force (someone's holding a gun to one's head), paralysis and other kinds of incapacity, threats or duress, lack of opportunity, political oppression, and the like. Such constraints are *external* in the sense that they are impediments outside our wills that prevent us from realizing our wills in action (hence the freedom of self-*realization*). Classical compatibilists tended to focus on such external constraints when talking about freedom. They had less to say about *internal* constraints within the will, such as compulsions, obsessions, neuroses, and addictions, that may also affect freedom. These internal constraints come into the picture with the second kind of freedom, to be considered in the next section.

Another way of describing this first freedom of self-realization is to say that it comprises all of what were called *surface* freedoms of action in chapter 1—freedoms to buy what we want, go where we please, live as we choose, without interference or harassment from others. Such surface freedoms were also the ones emphasized in the utopian community of Walden Two in which the citizens could do whatever they wanted (though they were conditioned since childhood to want only what they could have and do). There was no need for coercion or punishment in Walden Two to make citizens do what they did not want to do. So the surface freedom to act as one wanted was maximized—though at the expense of freedoms of other kinds.

This first freedom of self-realization is compatible with determinism, as argued by classical compatibilists such as Hobbes, Hume, and Mill. We might have the freedom to realize our wills in action without hindrances, even if our wills had been determined by circumstances over which we had no control. Thus, the freedom of self-realization is a compatibilist freedom. If it were the only kind of freedom worth wanting, then freedom would be compatible with determinism, as classical compatibilists argued.

But if there are different kinds of freedom at stake in free will debates, then the Compatibility Question—"Is freedom compatible with determinism?"—is too simple. The question should be "Is freedom *in every significant sense worth wanting* compatible with determinism?" Those who oppose classical compatibilism do not have to argue that the freedom of self-realization is not a legitimate kind of freedom worth wanting simply because it is compatible with determinism. Even if we lived in a determined world, we would prefer to be free of physical restraint, coercion, paralysis, threats, intimidation, oppression, and other such external constraints, rather than not to be free of these things. These compatibilist freedoms of self-realization would be preferable to their opposites even in a determined world. So we don't have to deny that they are valuable freedoms.

In addition, the freedom of self-realization includes all those *social* and *political* freedoms we so highly value—freedom to speak our minds without fear, to associate with whom we please; freedom from arbitrary search and seizure; freedom to vote and participate in the political process without intimidation, and so on. Such freedoms from external constraint are essential to our conception of *human rights* and to the very definition of free societies. So the issue is not whether the freedom of self-realization emphasized by classical compatibilists is an important freedom worth wanting. It is. The issue is whether the freedom of self-realization is the *only* kind of freedom worth wanting and whether at least some other freedoms worth wanting may not be compatible with determinism.

2. Freedom of (Reflective) Self-control

A second kind of freedom that entered our discussions was emphasized by "new" compatibilists of chapters 9 and 10, such as Frankfurt, Watson, Wallace, and Fischer, as well as by ancient thinkers, such as Plato, Aristotle, and the Stoics. We may call it

> *The Freedom of (Reflective or Rational) Self-control:* the power to *understand* and reflectively *evaluate* the reasons and motives one wants to act upon, or should act upon, and to *control* one's behavior in accordance with such reflectively considered reasons.

The best way to see how this freedom of reflective self-control goes beyond the freedom of self-realization is to consider Frankfurt's notion of a *wanton*. Wantons are persons who act impulsively on their desires without reflecting on what desires they should or should not have. Such beings, as Frankfurt notes, are not capable of having second-order desires about which first-order desires should move them to act, and they thus lack the conditions for full freedom of will. Wantons are simply pulled about by their first-order desires without reflecting on the desires they want to or should have.

Note that wantons in this sense may have a degree of freedom of *self-realization,* No external constraints may prevent them from doing whatever they desire. But they lack what Frankfurt calls the power of *reflective self-evaluation*—the power to reflect on what desires they want to move them to act. Lacking the power of reflective self-evaluation, wantons also lack the power to control their desires in terms of their reflections and reasoned judgments. So they also lack the power of *reflective self-control* even though they may have a measure of freedom to realize their desires in action and hence a measure of freedom of self-realization.

Another way to see how the freedom of reflective self-control goes beyond the freedom of self-realization is to consider Frankfurt's unwilling drug addict. Such a person, unlike the wanton, *is* capable of reflective self-evaluation. The unwilling addict does not want to act on his desire for the drug. But he cannot resist the desire anyway and so cannot control his behavior in the light of his reflections. So, while the addict has the power of reflective *self-evaluation,* he lacks the power of reflective *self-control.* To have reflective self-control, one must not only be capable of reflecting on what desires or other motives one wants to have or should have (as the wanton is not), but also capable of controlling one's behavior in the light of such reflections (as the unwilling addict cannot).

As Frankfurt notes, this second freedom of reflective self-control allows one to take account of *internal* constraints on the will, such as compulsions, obsessions, addictions, and neuroses, which were neglected by classical compatibilists. Such internal constraints can also undermine freedom; and they can do so even when no external constraints would prevent us from doing what we want. Nothing external prevents the addict from avoiding the drug. No one is forcing him to take it. But he cannot resist taking it anyway, and thus he is internally constrained *by his own will*. He has a measure of *external* freedom of action, or self-realization, but he lacks the *internal* freedom of reflective self-control.

As we have seen, Frankfurt interprets the freedom of reflective self-control in terms of *higher-order desires*. Other new compatibilists interpret it differently, but they are describing a similar notion. Watson, for example, describes reflective self-control in terms of *values* and *desires*. Values are what our practical reasoning tells us are the best things to do or what we ought to do; and values in this sense may conflict with desires. Our reason may tell us that we ought to exercise if we want to stay fit (staying fit is a value), but we desire to watch TV instead. When desires win out in such conflicts, we are guilty of *weakness of will*. By contrast, when we are able to make our desires conform to our values or our reasoned judgments about what we ought to do, we have *reflective self-control*. Watson's view is thus similar to Frankfurt's, though instead of talking about higher-order desires ruling over first-order desires, he talks about values or reasoned judgments ruling over desires or passions.

Watson also notes the connection between the idea of reflective self-control and Plato's distinction between Reason and Desire. Plato spoke of Reason and Desire as two parts of the soul that can be at war with one another, like two horses pulling a chariot in different directions. When this happens, we lack harmony in the soul and our desires are uncontrolled. Lacking control over our desires, we are unfree. By contrast, when the two horses pull together, the soul is in harmony. Our desires conform to our Reason and we have *rational self-control,* which is another name for *reflective self-control.*

Is such rational or reflective self-control really a kind of *freedom?* Plato thought so. To be constantly moved by unruly and uncontrolled desires is to be unfree. It is to be a "slave to one's passions" and to be a slave is to be unfree. By contrast, to be in control of one's desires and passions is to be free. Now this is admittedly a different kind of freedom from the freedom of self-realization, which is the freedom to realize one's desires in action, *whatever* one's desires may be (controlled or uncontrolled). But the freedom of reflective self-control is a kind of freedom nonetheless. In fact, Plato and many other ancient thinkers, such as the Stoics, thought that the freedom of reflective self-control was the "true" freedom, since it meant that the soul was in control of itself.

Other new compatibilists, such as Wallace and Fischer, relate the freedom of reflective self-control to *moral responsibility*. To be held morally responsible, Wallace argues, persons must have the "power to grasp and apply moral reasons and . . . to control . . . [their] behavior in the light of those reasons." In short, morally responsible agents must have the power of reflective self-control. Agents who lack this power, such as the insane and the severely retarded, are normally exempted from responsibility. To hold agents responsible in a courtroom, for example, we require that they "be able to understand the difference between right and wrong and to control their behavior in the light of that knowledge." Those who are judged insane or mentally incompetent or otherwise fail this condition are exempted from responsibility. They lack *normative competence,* the mental capacity to properly grasp moral norms or rules of behavior and to control their behavior in accordance with such norms.

It is significant that issues about *responsibility* enter the picture with this second kind of freedom of reflective self-control. The first freedom of self-realization, by contrast, is merely a matter of being able to do what you want, whatever it might be. Questions about responsibility need not enter into such a conception of freedom as the mere absence of external impediments. With self-realization, the question is, "Can I get what I want?" With reflective self-control, the further question is, "What should I want?" As a consequence, when one moves beyond the freedom of self-realization to reflective self-control, questions about freedom and responsibility become intertwined; and they remain intertwined when further freedoms are considered from this point onward.

Though freedom of reflective self-control goes beyond freedom of self-realization in these ways, it is nonetheless also a *compatibilist* freedom. As we saw in chapters 9 and 10, new compatibilists, such as Frankfurt, Watson, and Wallace, argue that having the power to reflectively evaluate one's reasons for acting and to control one's behavior in the light of these evaluations is a freedom consistent with determinism. Even in a determined world, we could distinguish persons whose Reason was in control of their Desires from persons who lacked such reflective self-control (like wantons or addicts or compulsive persons); and even if determinism was true, we could distinguish those who were "able to understand the difference between right and wrong and able to control their behavior in the light of this knowledge" from those who lacked this normative competence owing to insanity or mental incompetence.

In fact, we have seen that some new compatibilists, such as Frankfurt and Wallace, argue that reflective self-control does not even require *alternative possibilities* or the power *to do otherwise*. Persons whose desires are always controlled by their Reason, or reasoned judgments, do not have to be able to do otherwise. To do otherwise would be to give in to weakness of will or to be ruled by uncontrolled desires and thus to lack reflective self-control; and if the freedom of reflective self-control did not require the power to do otherwise or alternative possibilities, that would be a further reason for thinking it compatible with determinism.

3. Freedom of Self-perfection

The third freedom is exemplified by the view of Susan Wolf described in chapter 9. But it is also a kind of freedom that has roots in ancient and medieval philosophy. Recall that Wolf thought the capacity for reflective self-control described by Frankfurt and Watson was necessary for freedom and responsibility, but not sufficient. Something else had to be added. True freedom and responsibility, according to Wolf, requires more than reflective self-evaluation and control. What it also requires is that agents be able "to do the *right* thing for the *right* reasons" or "to act in accordance with the True and the Good." We may call this ability

> *The Freedom of Self-perfection:* the power to understand and appreciate the right reasons for action and to guide one's behavior in accordance with the right reasons.

One immediately wants to ask what the "right" reasons are and who decides what they are. These are important questions that naturally arise in connection with the freedom of self-perfection. Unfortunately a full discussion of these questions would take us beyond the scope of this volume into the areas of ethics and ethical philosophy. But we can at least begin to address these questions about the right reasons for action by asking why philosophers such as Wolf think the freedom of self-perfection is important and how it is supposed to go beyond the freedom of reflective self-control.

To explain why reflective self-control is not enough for true freedom and responsibility, Wolf introduces the example of a dictator's son:

> JoJo is the favorite son of Jo the First, an evil and sadistic dictator of a small undeveloped country. Because of his father's special feelings for the boy, JoJo is given a special education and is allowed to accompany his father and observe his daily routine. In the light of this treatment, it is not surprising that little JoJo takes his father as a role model and develops values very much like Dad's. As an adult he does many of the same sorts of things his father did, including sending people to prison or to death or to torture chambers on the basis of whim. He is not *coerced* to do these things, he acts according to his own desires. Moreover, these are desires he wholly *wants* to have. When he

steps back and asks, "Do I really want to be this sort of person?" His answer is resoundingly "Yes," for this way of life expresses a crazy sort of power that is part of his deepest ideal.[1]

Wolf is saying that JoJo has the capacities for reflective self-evaluation and control described by philosophers such as Frankfurt and Watson. JoJo is "wholeheartedly" committed to being a sadistic dictator, in Frankfurt's sense. He has "the will he wants to have": his first-order desires are in conformity with his second-order desires. In Watson's terms, JoJo's desires are in conformity with his deepest *values* or ideals. His Reason and his Desires are in synch. JoJo's sadistic desires—repugnant as they may be—nonetheless express the "Real" or "Deep Self" that he has chosen to be in emulation of his father. Yet, despite all this, Wolf argues that "in the light of JoJo's heritage and upbringing—both of which he was powerless to control—it is dubious at best that he should be regarded as responsible for what he does. It is unclear that anyone with a childhood such as his could have developed into anything but the twisted and perverse sort of person he has become."

So Wolf thinks JoJo is not responsible because of his upbringing, which he was powerless to control. Yet JoJo has the powers of reflective self-evaluation and control described by Frankfurt and Watson. So what else is missing that would make him not responsible?

Wolf rejects the answer that would be given to this question by incompatibilists and libertarians. Incompatibilists and libertarians who take the line developed in chapter 11 would say something like this: to know whether JoJo was responsible for being the way he is, we have to know more about his background. If indeed his father's influence on his upbringing was so dominant that JoJo was *determined* to become the person he was—if there was nothing JoJo could have ever done differently to escape that overwhelming influence—then he would not be ultimately responsible for being the way he is. But Wolf cannot accept this incompatibilist or libertarian answer because it would require that JoJo and the rest of us somehow be capable of ultimate creation of our own deepest selves in an undetermined way. And Wolf—like the free will skeptics discussed in chapter 7, such as Strawson and Nietzsche—does not think such ultimate self-creation is possible. "Whether we are determined or undetermined," she says, "we cannot have created our deepest selves. Literal self-creation is not just empirically, but logically, impossible."[2]

What then, according to Wolf, *is* missing that would show that JoJo is not responsible? Her answer is that JoJo, because of his corrupted upbringing, lacks "the ability to know the difference between right and wrong." "A person," she says, "who, *even on reflection,* cannot see that having someone tortured because he failed to salute you is wrong plainly lacks the requisite ability." In short, JoJo lacks *the freedom of self-perfection*. Because of his upbringing, he is *incapable* "of understanding and appreciating the right reasons for action and of guiding his behavior in accordance with the right reasons." In this respect, JoJo is not like most other people. While the rest of us may also have been determined by our upbringings, most of us have been brought up so that we can appreciate the difference between right and wrong. We may sometimes fail to do the right thing for the right reasons, but we are *capable* of doing so, because we can understand the difference between right or wrong and can guide our behavior accordingly. JoJo's upbringing was such that he is utterly incapable of this.

Wolf then adds that this freedom, which JoJo lacks—the power "to do the right thing for the right reasons" or "to act in accordance with the True and the Good"—is compatible with determinism. JoJo, she argues, is not the way he is *simply* because he was determined. We may all have been determined by our upbringings. But JoJo is the way he is because *his* particular upbringing was so perverted and corrupted that he is incapable of doing the right thing for the right reasons. In other words, when it comes to being responsible agents, determinism is not the deciding factor. What matters are the *sorts* of upbringings we had. If children do not get the right start in life, they will not become responsible agents. And not only is the freedom of self-perfection compatible with determinism, according to Wolf, it is even compatible with not having alternative possibilities or the power to do otherwise. One has the freedom of self-perfection, she argues, when one has the ability to act in accordance with the True and the Good. But one can have that ability even "if one is psychologically determined to do the right thing for the right reasons."

All this makes us wonder whether the freedom of self-perfection really is a kind of *freedom* at all. Well, it is not freedom in the popular modern sense. In modern times we have come to think of freedom as just the ability to do whatever we want—whether it be the right thing for the right reasons *or* the wrong thing for the wrong reasons. In short, the popular modern conception of freedom is very much like the first of our freedoms of self-realization. But it was not always so. In fact, the freedom of self-perfection, like the freedom of reflective self-control, has also played an important role in the history of ideas about freedom.

In medieval times, for example, the freedom of self-perfection was ascribed to the saints in heaven who were no longer capable of doing evil. Seeing God directly, the saints could not do otherwise than act in accord with the True and the Good. They had attained a perfect state of *freedom from sin* and *freedom from temptations* to do evil that plague us humans in our fallen state. This is not freedom in our popular modern sense, to be sure. Yet, in medieval times it was regarded not only as a kind of freedom but as an ideal kind of freedom because it was the freedom that God possessed, since God was also not capable of doing evil. There was always a puzzle in medieval philosophy about how God could have free will, since God was incapable of doing evil and could not do otherwise than act in accord with the True and Good. In a puzzling way, it might seem that we humans had *more* freedom than God because we were capable of doing good *or* evil, while God was not. A common answer to this puzzle in medieval times was to say that God's freedom was different from ours. It was a more perfect freedom, a freedom from sin and temptation, in other words, a freedom of *self-perfection*.

Wolf's modern conception of freedom of self-perfection is not exactly like the medieval one. She requires that we have the *capacity* to do the right thing for the right reasons or to act in accord with the True and the Good (as JoJo does not). But even those of us who have this capacity may often fall short and may fail to do the right thing for the right reasons (unlike the saints). Yet, since we have at least the capacity to act in accord with the True and Good, even when we fall short, we are capable of *self-correction:* we can make ourselves better and *strive* toward self-perfection (as JoJo cannot). Wolf insists, however, that this ability for self-correction is still compatible with determinism. We may revise and correct our given natures and upbringings, but we cannot create ourselves out of nothing. Thus the freedom of self-perfection is to be distinguished from the ultimate freedom of *self-creation* that libertarians insist upon for free will, which Wolf thinks is impossible.

4. Freedom of Self-determination and Freedom of Self-formation

The three freedoms discussed so far are compatibilist freedoms. According to their defenders, they are all compatibile with determinism. The final two freedoms, by contrast, are incompatibilist or libertarian freedoms. To introduce them, let us return briefly to JoJo. Wolf thinks JoJo is not responsible because he lacks the freedom of self-perfection. As noted, incompatibilists and libertarians see it differently. They would say that we cannot tell whether JoJo is ultimately responsible for being the way he is without knowing more about his background. If his father's influence on JoJo's upbringing was so dominant that JoJo was determined to become the person he was—if there was nothing JoJo could have done differently to escape that overwhelming influence—then JoJo would not be ultimately responsible for being the way he is. Incompatibilists therefore ask: Who and what determined that JoJo has the will (character and motives) he now has? Did JoJo have some ultimate say in it, or was it completely due to his father or his heredity or environment or some other factor over which JoJo had no control?

In other words, JoJo's responsibility depends, for incompatibilists, on his possessing a further freedom that may be called

> *The Freedom of Self-determination:* the power or ability to act *of your own free will* in the sense of a will (character, motives and purposes) of your own making—a will that you yourself, to some degree, were *ultimately responsible* for forming.

As we saw in the example of Luther in chapter 8, being self-determining in this sense—acting "of your own free will"—does not require that JoJo or other agents have the power to do otherwise here and now. JoJo's will may have become so corrupted that he can no longer do otherwise. But he still might be ultimately responsible for what he does if he himself was responsible to some degree for creating his corrupt will by virtue of earlier undetermined acts in his life history. The freedom of self-determination thus presupposes a further incompatibilist freedom that may be called

> *The Freedom of Self-formation:* the power to form one's own will in a manner that is undetermined by one's past by virtue of *will-setting* or *self-forming* actions (SFAs) over which one has plural voluntary control.

Incompatibilists need not deny that the first three compatibilist freedoms are valuable and important freedoms worth wanting. What incompatibilists do usually insist upon is that the first three compatibilist freedoms are not enough to account of genuine freedom of the will and true responsibility. Incompatibilists might even grant the importance of the freedom of self-perfection as a kind of ideal freedom. But they will insist that what we want to know when we think about free will and responsibility is not merely whether someone is a saint who always does the right thing or a monster like JoJo. We also want to know whether saintly or monstrous persons were ultimately responsible to some degree for making themselves into the saints or monsters they became by exercising the freedoms of self-determination and self-formation.[3]

Note also that, while the freedom of self-determination presupposes the freedom of self-formation, it is important to distinguish the two, as the discussion of chapter 11 made clear. Not all self-determining acts are self-forming (though all self-forming acts are self-determining). Often we act from a will *already formed,* and are thus *self-determining;* but it is our own free will by virtue of the fact that we formed it by earlier acts that were *will-setting* or *self-forming* (SFAs). Individual self-determining acts do not therefore have to be undetermined and such that the agent could have done otherwise.

One might then ask what makes the freedom of self-determination an *incompatibilist* freedom. The answer is that while individual exercises of the freedom of self-determination do not have to be undetermined and such that the agent could have done otherwise, the freedom of self-determination itself cannot exist *in a determined world*. For it cannot exist unless *some* acts in the life histories of agents were undetermined and such that the agents could have done otherwise, namely, self-forming acts.

In opposition to these claims, compatibilists typically argue that freedom of self-determination does not require such an undetermined freedom of self-formation or self-creation. Freedom of self-determination *is* important, compatibilists will argue, but it can be interpreted in terms of one or more of the first three compatibilist freedoms—most likely, for example, as a combination of self-realization and reflective self-control. To be *self-determining,* they may say, is to be able to determine one's actions in terms of the Real or Deep Self with which one *identifies* or to which one is *wholeheartedly* committed; or it is to be able to control one's desires in terms of one's Reason or *values*—as well as being able to do what one wants without hindrances or impediments.

Incompatibilists, by contrast, will insist that being truly *self*-determining requires in addition that your Real or Deep Self—or your Reason or your values—cannot in turn be wholly determined by something outside or beyond your own self. You yourself must be in part responsible for being the kind of person you are. And so the free will issue is joined. Both compatibilists and incompatibilists think that the further freedom of *self-determination* is important for free will. But compatibilists would like to reduce the freedom of self-determination to one or another of the first three (compatibilist) freedoms, while incompatibilists insist that the freedom of self-determination must be extended beyond the first three freedoms to the fifth freedom of self-formation to account for genuine free will and responsibility.

To determine which side is right in this complex debate, many other questions must be addressed, as we have seen in this book: Do free will and responsibility require the power to do otherwise or alternative possibilities (chapters 8, 9, 10)? Is determinism compatible with the power to do otherwise (chapters 2, 3)? Is determinism compatible with ultimate responsibility (chapter 11)? Can we make sense of a free will that is incompatible with determinism (chapters 4, 5, 6)? Does such a free will require mind–body dualism or special kinds of causation (chapters 5, 6)? Is such a free will consistent the modern scientific knowledge of the cosmos and of human beings (chapter 12)? What kind of free will is consistent with religious belief in an all-powerful, all-good, and all-knowing God (chapter 13)? If ultimate responsibility and free will require the power of self-formation or self-creation, as incompatibilists insist, is it really possible for creatures like us to have free will, or is free will "the best self-contradiction conceived so far," as Nietzsche claimed? And if free will in the sense required for ultimate responsibility is impossible, can we live without belief in free will (chapter 7)?

Answering these questions has much to do with how we view ourselves, our place in the universe, and the meaning of our lives. These are the issues that the free will problem—like all the great problems of philosophy—ultimately addresses.

Notes

Chapter 1

1. For discussion of various interpretations of quantum physics in relation to free will, see essays by Robert Bishop and David Hodgson in Robert Kane, ed., *The Oxford Handbook of Free Will* (Oxford: Oxford University Press, 2002).
2. For example, Ted Honderich, *How Free Are You?* (Oxford: Oxford University Press, Clarendon Press, 1993).

Chapter 2

1. Thomas Hobbes, *Leviathan* (Indianapolis: Bobbs-Merrill, 1958), p. 108.
2. David Hume, *A Treatise on Human Nature* (Oxford: Oxford University Press, Clarendon Press, 1960), p. 411. An excellent account of Hume's compatibilist view is Paul Russell's *Freedom and Moral Sentiment* (New York: Oxford University Press, 1995).
3. Daniel Dennett, *Elbow Room: The Varieties of Free Will Worth Wanting* (Cambridge, MA: MIT Press, 1984), p. 61.
4. John Stuart Mill, *A System of Logic* (New York: Harper & Row, 1874), p. 254.

Chapter 3

1. Peter van Inwagen, *An Essay on Free Will* (Oxford: Oxford University Press, Clarendon Press, 1983), p. 16. The fuller version of the argument presented in the remainder of this section is my own interpretation of van Inwagen's argument.
2. van Inwagen, 1983; Carl Ginet, *On Action* (Cambridge: Cambridge University Press, 1990). I have put their response in my own words.
3. Michael McKenna, "Compatibilism," in Edward N. Zalta, ed., *The Stanford Encyclopedia of Philosophy,* online edition: http://plato.Stanford.edu/archives/sum2004/entries/compatibilism/. An objection of this kind was originally made by Keith Lehrer.

Chapter 4

1. This designation is Gary Watson's, in the second edition of *Free Will* (Oxford: Oxford University Press, 1982), p. 10.
2. Arthur Schopenhauer, *Prize Essay on the Freedom of the Will,* ed. with an introductions by Gunter Zoller. Translated by E.J.F. Payne. (Cambridge: Cambridge University Press, 1960), p. 47.
3. G. W. F. Leibniz, *Selections* (New York: Scribner's, 1951), p. 435.
4. This objection has been made by Galen Strawson, Alfred Mele, Bernard Berofsky, Bruce Waller, Richard Double, Mark Bernstein, and Ishtiyaque Haji. Statements of it can be found in the suggested readings for chapter 1 and for this chapter.
5. Bruce Waller, "Free Will Gone Out of Control: A Critical Study of R. Kane's *Free Will and Values,*" *Behaviorism* 16 (1988): 149–67; quotation, p. 151.
6. Alfred Mele, "Review of Kane, *The Significance of Free Will,*" *Journal of Philosophy* 95 (1998): 581–4; quotation, pp. 582–83.

Chapter 5

1. Simon Blackburn, *Think* (Oxford: Oxford University Press, 1999), p. 89.
2. Immanuel Kant, *Critique of Pure Reason* (London: Macmillan, 1958), pp. 409–15.
3. Kant, *Foundations of the Metaphysics of Morals* (Indianapolis: Bobbs-Merrill, 1959), pp. 64–72.
4. R. M. Chisholm, "Human Freedom and the Self," in Gary Watson, ed., 2nd ed., *Free Will* (Oxford: Oxford University Press, 2003),

pp. 24–35. Also in Robert Kane, ed., *Free Will,* (Oxford: Blackwell Publishers, 2002), pp. 47–58, and in Laura Waddell Ekstrom, ed., *Agency and Responsibility: Essays on the Metaphysics of Freedom* (Boulder, Co: Westview Press, 2001), pp. 126–37.

5. Ibid., p. 30.
6. Ibid., p. 31.
7. Richard Taylor, *Metaphysics* (Englewood Cliffs: Prentice-Hall, 1974), p. 56.
8. Chisholm, op. cit., p. 34.
9. Taylor, op. cit., p. 57
10. Taylor, op. cit., p. 55.
11. *The Works of Thomas Reid,* ed. W. Hamilton (Hildeshein: George Ulm, 1983), p. 599.
12. Chisholm, op. cit., p. 31.
13. Gary Watson, ed. *Free Will* (Oxford: Oxford University Press, 1982), p. 10.

Chapter 6

1. Carl Ginet, *On Action* (Cambridge: Cambridge University Press, 1990), 11ff.
2. Alfred Mele, *Motivation and Agency* (Oxford: Oxford University Press, 2003), pp. 42–43.
3. R. E. Hobart, "Free Will as Involving Determinism and Inconceivable Without It," *Mind* 32 (1934): 1–27; quotation, p. 5.
4. Timothy O'Connor, ed., *Persons and Causes: The Metaphysics of Free Will* (New York: Oxford University Press, 2000). pp. 85–95.
5. Stewart C. Goetz, "Review of O'Connor, *Persons and Causes,*" *Faith and Philosophy* 19 (2002): 116–20; p. 118. Also see his "A Non-causal Theory of Agency," *Philosophy and Phenomenological Research* 49 (1988): 303–16.
6. O'Connor, op. cit., pp. 85–95.
7. O'Connor, in Gary Watson ed., 2nd ed., *Free Will* (Oxford: Oxford University Press, 2003), pp. 271–72.
8. Ibid., p. 271.
9. Causal theorists of action include Donald Davidson, *Essays on Actions and Events* (Oxford: Oxford University Press, 1980), Alfred Mele, *Autonomous Agents: From Self-Control to Autonomy* (New York: Oxford University Press, 1995), and many others.
10. Randolph Clarke, *Libertarian Accounts of Free Will* (Oxford: Oxford University Press, 2003).
11. Gary Watson, ed., *Free Will* (Oxford: Oxford University Press, 1982).

12. Ginet, in Robert Kane, ed., *The Oxford Handbook of Free Will* (Oxford: Oxford University Press, 2002), p. 398.
13. O'Connor, op. cit., p. 79.
14. O'Connor, 2000; William Hasker, *The Emergent Self,* (Ithaca, NY: Cornell University Press, 1999).
15. Jan Cover and John O'Leary-Hawthorne, "Free Agency and Materialism," in D. Howard-Snyder and J. Jordan, eds., *Faith, Freedom and Rationality* (Lanham, MD: Rowman & Littlefield, 1996) make interesting arguments suggesting that this might be so.
16. See the suggested readings at end of chapter.

Chapter 7

1. Derk Pereboom, *Living Without Free Will* (Cambridge: Cambridge University Press, 2001), chapter 1.
2. Galen Strawson, *Freedom and Belief* (Oxford: Oxford University Press, 1986).
3. G. Strawson, "The Bounds of Freedom," in Robert Kane, ed., *The Oxford Handbook of Free Will* (Oxford: Oxford University Press, 2002), pp. 441–60; quotation, p. 444.
4. F. W. Nietzsche, in ibid.
5. Ted Honderich, *How Free Are You?* (Oxford: Oxford University Press, 1993).
6. Pereboom, 2001, p. 174.
7. Pereboom, "Living Without Free Will: The Case for Hard Compatibilism," in Kane, ed., *The Oxford Handbook of Free Will*, pp. 477–88; quotation, p. 486.
8. Ibid., p. 487.
9. Ibid., p. 485.
10. Saul Smilansky, *Free Will and Illusion* (Oxford: Oxford University Press, Clarendon Press, 2000).
11. Smilansky, "Free Will, Fundamental Dualism and the Centrality of Illusion," in Kane, ed., *The Oxford Handbook of Free Will*, pp. 489–505; quotation, pp. 498–89.
12. Ibid., p. 482.

Chapter 8

1. Daniel Dennett, *Elbow Room: The Varieties of Free Will Worth Wanting* (Cambridge: MIT Press, 1984), p. 133.

2. The designation "character examples" comes from David Shatz, "Compatibilism, Values and 'Could Have Done Otherwise,'" *Philosophical Topics* 16 (1988): 151–200.
3. Harry Frankfurt, "Alternate Possibilities and Moral Responsibilities," in Gary Watson, ed., 2nd ed., *Free Will* (Oxford: Oxford University Press, 2003), p. 169.
4. John Martin Fischer, "Frankfurt-type Examples and Semi-Compatibilism," in Robert Kane, ed., *The Oxford Handbook of Free Will* (Oxford: Oxford University Press, 2002), pp. 288–89.
5. See Robert Kane, *Free Will and Values* (Albany, NY: SUNY Press, 1985) p. 51; David Widerker "Libertarianism and Frankfurt's Attack on the Principle of Alternative Possibilities," *Philosophical Review,* 104, 1995: 247–61; Carl Ginet "In Defense of the Principle of Alternative Possibilities: Why I Don't Find Frankfurt's Argument Convincing," *Philosophical Perspectives* 10, 1996: 403–17; Keith Wyma, "Moral Responsibility and the Leeway for Action," *American Philosophical Quarterly* 34 (1997): 57–70.
6. Kane, 1985, p. 51.
7. Widerker, 1995, 248ff.
8. David Hunt, "Moral Responsibility and Avoidable Action," *Philosophical Studies* 97 (2000): 195–227.
9. Alfred Mele and David Robb, "Rescuing Frankfurt-style Cases," *Philosophical Review* 107 (1998): 97–112.

Chapter 9

1. Harry Frankfurt, "Freedom of the Will and a Concept of a Person," in Gary Watson. ed., 2nd ed., *Free Will* (Oxford: Oxford University Press, 2003), pp. 322–36. Also in Robert Kane, ed., *Free Will* (Oxford: Blackwell Publishers, 2002), pp. 127–144) and Laura Waddell Ekstrom, ed., *Agency and Responsibility: Essays on the Metaphysics of Freedom* (Boulder, Co: Westview Press, 2001), pp. 77–91.
2. Ibid., p. 336
3. Richard Double, *The Non-Reality of Free Will* (Oxford: Oxford University Press, 1991), p. 35.
4. Gary Watson "Free Agency," in Watson, ed., *Free Will,* p. 349.
5. Watson, op. cit., 339ff.
6. Plato, *Phaedrus* in *The Dialogues of Plato,* vol. II, trans. B. Jowett (New York: Kandom House, 1937), 237e–238c.
7. Watson, op. cit., p.350.
8. Watson, op. cit., p. 351.

9. Susan Wolf, "Sanity and the Metaphysics of Responsibility," in Kane, ed., *Free Will,* 147 ff.
10. Susan Wolf, *Freedom Within Reason* (Oxford: Oxford University Press, 1990) p. 79.
11. Ibid.
12. Ibid.
13. Jonathan Jacobs, *Choosing Character* (Ithaca, NY: Cornell University Press, 2002).

Chapter 10

1. Peter F. Strawson, "Freedom and Resentment," *Proceedings of the British Academy* 48 (1962): 1–25; quotation, p. 9.
2. R. Jay Wallace, *Responsibility and the Moral Sentiments* (Cambridge, MA: Harvard University Press, 1994).
3. Ibid., p. 157.
4. R. Jay Wallace, "Precis of *Responsibility and the Moral Sentiments*" and "Replies," *Philosophy and Phenomenological Research* 64 (2002): 681–82; 709–29; quotation, p. 681.
5. Ishtiyaque Haji, "Compatibilist Views of Freedom and Responsibility," in Robert Kane, ed., *The Oxford Handbook of Free Will* (Oxford: Oxford University Press, 2002), pp. 207–10.
6. Gideon Rosen, "The Case for Incompatibilism," *Philosophy and Phenomenological Research* 64 (2002): p. 700–708; quotation, p. 703.
7. Wallace, "Precis," p. 725.
8. Ibid.
9. John Martin Fischer and Mark Ravizza, *Responsibility and Control* (Cambridge: Cambridge University Press, 1998).
10. Ibid., p. 229.

Chapter 11

1. Incompatibilists who take this line are called "source incompatibilists."
2. J. L. Austin, "If and Cans," in J. O. Urmson and G. Warnock, eds., *Philosophical Papers* (Oxford: Oxford University Press, Clarendon Press, 1961), pp. 153–80.
3. In "The Dual Regress of Free Will," (in *Philosophical Perspectives,* vol. 14 [Oxford: Blackwell Publishers, 2000]), I provide an argument to show that the two regresses must eventually converge on the *same* actions, which I call self-forming actions or SFAs and which must be both will-setting *and* undetermined.

Chapter 12

1. An introduction to chaos is G. L. Baker and J. P. Gollub, *Chaotic Dynamics: An Introduction* (Cambridge: Cambridge University Press, 1990).

2. C. Skarda and W. Freeman, "How Brains Make Chaos in Order to Make Sense of the World?" *Behavioral and Brain Sciences* 10 (1987): 161–95.

3. Readable introductions for the nonspecialist about the role of neural networks (including recurrent networks) in cognitive processing include Paul M. Churchland, *The Engine of Reason, the Seat of the Soul* (Cambridge, MA: MIT Press, 1996) and Manfred Spitzer, *The Mind Within the Net* (Cambridge, MA: MIT Press, 1999).

4. I show in greater detail that each of these conditions can be satisfied by SFAs in *The Significance of Free Will* (Oxford: Oxford University Press, 1996), chapter 8.

5. Is it irrational to make efforts to do incompatible things? In most ordinary situations it is. But I believe that in certain special circumstances it is not irrational to make competing efforts: (i) when we are deliberating between competing options (such as a moral choice and an ambitious choice); (ii) when we intend to choose one or the other but cannot choose both; (iii) when we have powerful motives for wanting to choose each of the options for different and incommensurable reasons, so that we are deeply conflicted; (iv) when there is thus resistance in our will to either choice so that (v) if either choice is to have a chance of being made, effort will be needed to overcome the temptation to make the other choice; and (vi) we want to give each choice a fighting chance of being made because the motives for each choice are important to us. The motives for each choice define in part what sort of person we are; and we would taking them lightly if we did not make an effort in their behalf. These conditions are, of course, the conditions of SFAs.

6. Critical discussion and further objections to the view presented in this chapter can be found in a number of publications, including Daniel Dennett, *Freedom Evolves* (New York: Vintage Books, 2003), Randolph Clarke, *Libertarian Accounts of Free Will* (Oxford: Oxford University Press, 2003), Ishtiyaque Haji, *Deontic Morality and Control* (Cambridge: Cambridge University Press, 2002), Derk Pereboom, *Living Without Free Will* (Cambridge: Cambridge University Press, 2001), Timothy O'Connor, *Persons and Causes: The Metaphysics of Free Will* (New York: Oxford University Press, 2000), Saul Smilansky, *Free Will and Illusion* (Oxford: Oxford

University Press, Clarendon Press, 2000), Alfred Mele, *Autonomous Agents: From Self-Control to Autonomy* (New York: Oxford University Press, 1995), Richard Double, *The Non-reality of Free Will* (Oxford: Oxford University Press, 1991), Bruce Waller, *Freedom Without Responsibility* (Philadelphia: Temple University Press, 1990), Galen Strawson, "The Impossibility of Moral Responsibility," in Gary Watson, ed., 2nd ed., *Free Will* (Oxford: Oxford University Press, 2003), and Michael Almeida and Mark Bernstein, "Lucky Libertarianism," *Philosophical Studies* 113 (2003): 93–119. Further critical discussion and my responses to critics appear in two symposia on *The Significance of Free Will*, one in *Philosophy and Phenomenological Research*, LX (2000): 129–67, and the other in *Philosophical Explorations* II (1999): 95–121.

Chapter 13

1. William Rowe, *Philosophy of Religion* (Belmont CA: Wadsworth Publishing, 1993), p. 141.
2. Augustine, *On the Free Choice of the Will* (Indianapolis: Bobbs-Merrill, 1964) p. 25.
3. Ibid.
4. Boethius, *The Consolation of Philosophy* (New York: Bobbs-Merrill, 1962), prose VI.
5. Linda T. Zagzebski, "Recent Work on Divine Foreknowledge and Free Will" in Robert Kane, ed., *The Oxford Handbook of Free Will* (Oxford: Oxford University Press, 2002), pp. 45–64; quotation, p. 52.
6. Luis de Molina, *On Divine Foreknowledge* (Ithaca, NY: Cornell University Press, 1988), Disputation 52, paragraph 9. Translated with an introduction by Alfredo Freddoso.
7. Robert Merrihew Adams, "Middle Knowledge and the Problem of Evil," *American Philosophical Quarterly* 14 (1977): 1–12; William Hasker, "Middle Knowledge: A Refutation Revisited," *Faith and Philosophy* 12 (1995): 223–36.
8. For a good introduction to the process theology of Whitehead and Hartshorne by two of its prominent defenders, see David Griffin and John B. Cobb, *Process Theology: An Introductory Exposition* (Philadelphia: Westminster Press, 1976).
9. Clark Pinnock, Richard Rice, John Sanders, William Hasker, and David Basinger, *The Openness of God* (Downers Grove IL:InterVarsity Press, 1994).

Chapter 14

1. Susan Wolf, "Sanity and the Metaphysics of Responsibility." In Robert Kane, ed., *Free Will* (Oxford: Blackwell Publishers, 2002), p. 153.
2. Ibid., p. 154.
3. Jonathan Jacobs, in *Choosing Character* (Ithaca, NY: Cornell University Press, 2002), makes a strong case for saying that moral monsters like JoJo can be responsible for the way they are and act, even if they are now so corrupt that they can no longer do otherwise.

Index

A

Accidents, 125–26
Actions
 causal theory of, 60–61
 causation vs. unconstraint
  in, 18–19
 events and, 59–60
 free, 53, 57, 60, 63, 155,
  156, 157
 freedom of, 14, 17, 93, 95, 97,
  122, 128, 130
 nature of, 53–54
 self-forming (*see* Self-
  forming actions)
 simple indeterminism on,
  53–57
 sources or origins of, 120–22,
  123, 131
 Ultimate Responsibility and,
  120–22, 123, 125–26, 131
 will-setting (*see* Will-setting)
 will-settled, 128
Actish phenomenal quality,
 54, 56
Acts of will. *See* Volitions
Adams, Robert, 159

Addictions, 94–95, 101, 117,
 163, 165–66, 167
Admiration, 76–77
Agency, 143–45
Agent-causation, 44–51, 53,
 57–60, 62–64, 133
 assessing, 47–48
 causal indeterminism vs., 64
 causal theory of action
  vs., 61
 immanent, 46–47, 48, 49,
  50–51, 57
 non-event type, 45–46, 57,
  60, 62–64, 132
 randomness and, 48–51
 revisited, 57–59
 transeunt, 46, 47, 48, 57
Aitiai, 123
Akrasia, 99
Alfred P. Murrah Building,
 bombing of, 67
Alternative possibilities (AP),
 6–7, 80–92, 173. *See also*
 Principle of Alternative
 Possibilities
 freedom of reflective self-
  control and, 167–68